Over the past ten years or so a debate h
Reformed community. That debate co1
according to the reformed orthodox. W
they determinists? Do they defy these cate gories. Paul Helm's new book
Reforming Free Will: A Conversation on the History of Reformed Views on Compatibilism (1500–1800) brings much needed clarity to these questions. In this work, he displays his characteristic skill in theology, philosophy and history to argue that the reformed orthodox are rightly thought of as compatibilists. Skillfully avoiding any hint of anachronism, Helm offers a powerful indirect argument for this conclusion. The reader will learn much about the nature of free will from this work. It is a significant contribution to the growing literature on this topic. I highly recommend this work to anyone interested in this issue or those that surround it.

MICHAEL PATRICK PRECIADO
Minister, philosopher and author of *A Reformed View of Freedom: The Compatibilism of Guidance Control and Reformed Theology*

Paul Helm offers in *Reforming Free Will: A Conversation on the History of Reformed Views on Compatibilism (1500–1800),* a scholarly yet readable discussion with interlocutors Richard A. Muller and Anthonie Vos on Reformed Orthodoxy anthropology, in particular human freedom, with attention to issues, such as (synchronic) contingency, compatibilism, and necessity. The thoughts of Luther, Calvin, Turretin, Edwards, and others are carefully appraised, and will benefit many. Highly recommended, and a must-read for any serious student and scholar of early modern studies.

ADRIAAN C. NEELE
Professor, Historical Theology and Director of the Doctoral Program, Puritan Reformed Theological Seminary, Grand Rapids, Michigan

How free is the human will? Is Jonathan Edwards a compatibilist? Is compatibilism out of step with Reformed Orthodox thought as represented by Francis Turretin? Paul Helm's thought-provoking answer is worthy of finer engagement and examination by historians and theologians alike. In this work on Reformed Orthodox approaches to free will, human agency, and human choice, this scholarly contribution furthers the conversation on a range of debates historical, theological, and intellectual among proponents of synchronic contingency, indeterminism, and compatibilism.

TODD RESTER
Associate Professor of Church History, Westminster Theological Seminary, Philadelphia

REFORMING
FREE WILL

R.E.D.S.

REFORMED,
EXEGETICAL
AND
DOCTRINAL
STUDIES

REFORMING
FREE WILL

A CONVERSATION ON THE HISTORY OF
REFORMED VIEWS ON COMPATIBILISM (1500–1800)

PAUL HELM

SERIES EDITORS J.V. FESKO & MATTHEW BARRETT

MENTOR
Encouraging Christians to Think

Copyright © Paul Helm 2020

paperback ISBN 978-1-5271-0606-2
epub ISBN 978-1-5271-0663-5
mobi ISBN 978-1-5271-0664-2

10 9 8 7 6 5 4 3 2 1

Published in 2020
in the
Mentor Imprint
by
Christian Focus Publications Ltd,
Geanies House, Fearn, Ross-shire,
IV20 1TW, Great Britain.

www.christianfocus.com

Cover design
by Pete Barnsley

Printed by
Bell & Bain, Glasgow

CONTENTS

To Jim and Jan Elkin

The term 'free-will' [*liberum arbitrium*] is not found in Holy Scripture so far as I know. Yet what it means should not be taken lightly, for it is widely debated; it provokes considerable controversy these days, and has always done so among scholars and theologians.

Peter Martyr Vermigli (1499–1562)

… I don't mean to call him [Isaac Watts] an Arminian; however in that doctrine he agrees with Arminians, and departs from the current and general opinion of Calvinists.

Jonathan Edwards (1703–58)

Series Preface

Reformed, Exegetical and Doctrinal Studies (R.E.D.S.) presents new studies informed by rigorous exegetical attention to the biblical text, engagement with the history of doctrine, with a goal of refined dogmatic formulation.

R.E.D.S. covers a spectrum of doctrinal topics, addresses contemporary challenges in theological studies, and is driven by the Word of God, seeking to draw theological conclusions based upon the authority and teaching of Scripture itself.

Each volume also explores pastoral implications so that they contribute to the church's theological and practical understanding of God's Word. One of the virtues that sets R.E.D.S. apart is its ability to apply dogmatics to the Christian life. In doing so, these volumes are characterized by the rare combination of theological weightiness and warm, pastoral application, much in the tradition of John Calvin's *Institutes of the Christian Religion*.

These volumes do not merely repeat material accessible in other books but retrieve and remind the church of forgotten truths to enrich contemporary discussion.

Matthew Barrett
J. V. Fesko

Preface

I owe a debt of gratitude to two scholars in particular. The first of these is Richard Muller, with whom I have had numerous conversations and e-mail exchanges on Reformed Orthodoxy, and who has helped me to cultivate an interest in their theology. We have each developed the skill of making criticisms that do not impair a friendship.

Reforming Free Will has been written with him perched on my shoulder, at least that is how it has seemed, when the question 'What would Richard have said?' has frequently occurred to me. Since we first debated the relation of Jonathan Edwards to the RO, I think we have come to understand each other better, and this would not have happened without his friendship and encouragement. My interest has resulted in an interest in Reformed anthropology, which led to *Human Nature from Calvin to Edwards*. Purposely, there is almost no reference to free will in that book. Because of its polemical nature, it would have been out of place in what is a purely didactic effort.

The other person is Mike Preciado, who has now published a version of his dissertation,[1] in which he expounds the defence of compatibilism offered by John Martin Fischer and Mark Ravizza SJ, in what they call 'Guidance Control'. He applies its results to elucidate the anthropology of seventeenth-century Reformed confessionalism and to the views of

---

1. *A Reformed View of Freedom* (Eugene, Or., Pickwick Publications, 2019).

Jonathan Edwards. His book should be read alongside this book. I've benefited from his advice in a number of places.

The views on free will that Richard Muller expressed in *Divine Will and Human Choice*,[2] (Grand Rapids, Michigan, 2017) which is in line with his paper 'Jonathan Edwards and the Absence of Free Choice: A Parting of Ways in the Reformed Tradition',[3] and which also partly connects with the work of Antonie Vos's interpretative key to Reformed Orthodoxy based on Duns Scotus's idea of 'synchronic contingency', which he has aired his doubts about in a number of publications. I have looked critically at Vos's work since interacting with it in the *Nederlands Theologisch Tijdschrift* of 2003, and it has received exposure in *Reformed Thought on Freedom*, in 2010. This is a work of some of Vos's 'Research Group' including William J. van Asselt, J. Martin Bac, and Roelf T. te Velde. It consists of translated sections of 17th century Reformed theologians on human freedom, and a commentary on each of them, revealing their allegedly Scotist character. The influence attached to Duns Scotus is examined by Muller in his *Divine Will and Human Choice*. The view of Reformed Orthodoxy on free will as a form of non-determinism is still held by Muller.

I am grateful for Matthew Barrett and John Fesko for inviting me to publish in their series, and for the help and encouragement they have given to me, and to Gerard O'Daly for a paper. Thanks to all who helped with the publication of the book, especially to Rosanna Burton. Most of all I am indebted to my steadfast wife, Angela.

Some material in what follows has been taken from earlier publications, as follows:

'Synchronic Contingency in Reformed Scholasticism: A Note of Caution', *Nederlands Theologisch Tijdschrift* (2003).

'*Reformed Thought on Freedom*: Some Further Thoughts', *Journal of Reformed Theology*, 4 (2010).

'Francis Turretin and Jonathan Edwards on Contingency and Necessity', *Learning from the Past*, edd. Jon Balserak and Richard Snoddy (London, Bloomsbury, 2015).

'Francis Turretin and Jonathan Edwards on Compatibilism,' (*Journal of Reformed Theology*, 2018)

PAUL HELM
Cold Aston, Gloucestershire

2. Grand Rapids, Michigan, Baker, 2017.

3. *Jonathan Edwards Studies*, 2011.

Introduction

In the course of the last twenty years, there has been an attempt to reconstruct Reformed Orthodox (RO) anthropology by the introduction of what is called 'synchronic contingency', a form of indeterminism. This has been motivated by the belief (on the part if not the whole), that traditional, confessional Reformed theology is necessitarian in character until the arrival of scholastically educated Reformed around the second half of the sixteenth century. This in turn is motivated by the thought that predestination and the bondage of the will to sin have necessitarian implications, as Antonie Vos (1944–) has tried to show. But that does not mean that predestination is the 'central dogma' of Calvinism as was once widely held among academic treatments of Calvin. Invoking synchronic contingency is thought to be the answer to these defects and, lo and behold, it is claimed that RO theology invoked it explicitly.

It is necessary to say something about the terms 'synchronic contingency' and 'compatibilism' that characterize the two views. In the age-old dispute about free will there are the two main positions which contradict each other, determinism of which the Reformed version is compatibilism, the view that determinism is compatible with human moral responsibility.[1] There are a number of varieties of determinism,

---

1. For the meaning of these and other unfamiliar terms that occur in this book, consult the Glossary.

and of compatibilism, as will become clear. The other position is human indeterministic freedom of which the appeal to synchronic contingency is a version. As we shall see, Richard Muller whose views I examine in what follows, holds that the RO maintained a form of indeterminism.

Nature and Grace

Much of this book has to do with the powers and the situations in the life of human beings. It's not exclusively, nor even, concerned with the bondage of the will to sin. So the question of the nature of free will is at the interface of nature and grace, using the resources of what people have learned about human nature in the course of human culture. In the Bible we are not presented with a doctrine of human nature, of its structure and workings. So an account of human nature is distinct from a topic in dogmatic theology, say of the person of Christ, or the work of the Holy Spirit in regeneration and sanctification, which attempt the systemization of the data of special revelation. Though these topics are debated, nevertheless for a Reformed mind the relevant data are wholly within the parameters of Scripture.

In the case of a theological study of human nature and its powers, things are different. There are anthropological data in Scripture, references to the mind, the will, the emotions and appetites, the memory and the conscience, the sense of deity; virtues and vices. But there is also (to us) the rather strange practice of Scripture using the language of the body to refer to the mind – the heart, bowels, the reins. In Scripture, the mind deceives, including self-deception, the memory fades, the emotions are raised, the conscience bears witness, in varying degrees. But there is no specially revealed account of the workings of the whole, no mention or use of the faculties or powers of the mind, much less of the place of each element in the working of the whole. This territory is sometimes referred to as the study of the 'civic' uses of human mental activity. At the same time, there is a recognition from special revelation of the unfathomable character of human thought and action, the depth of its wickedness, the development of virtues and vices, and the character of the regenerated human spirit as the renewed image of God in mankind.

Among these (and more) topics there has been considerable theological interest in the 'freedom of the will', as contrasted to compulsive action, fatalism, and so on, and how it relates to revealed truth about providence and predestination. Historically, the work on 'free will', a term widely used in human society, has come to be divided into various forms of compatibilism or incompatibilism, sometimes referred respectably to as libertarianism and compatibilism, and with how Reformed theology in the seventeenth and eighteenth centuries were influenced by these two tendencies. In addition, the tendency has been among theologians to characterize God in our image, not vice versa. So theologians anthropomorphise the mind of God, imputing to Him 'intellect, will and power',[2] all the while affirming His simplicity and eternality.

So the subject of free will, as we shall consider it, is an important aspect of human createdness even when fallen or regenerated, even when the operation of the saving grace of God is left to one side. What are a created person's powers? In the light of what powers and faculties are human beings responsible individuals in the everyday? But of course the grace of God and how it operates are in the wings. Our createdness is spoiled by the Fall, so that our free choices are not holy and pure, and we need the Redeemer. How does the possession of such powers mesh with the gracious, saving work of Christ, with divine providence and predestination, and with the activity of the Holy Spirit? These matters are central to Christian theology. The historic position of the Reformed faith is that theology takes in such createdness. Faith sits on nature. It also stretches our horizons, as when the Apostle Paul introduced the novel term 'spiritual body' (1 Cor. 15). This book is thus a contribution to anthropology, taking in its relations to factors that inform theological judgments.

The Christian faith is not gnostic, but it takes place within the natural arena, just as God's eternal Son was made flesh by being united to human nature at a certain time and place. Nature and grace are not a 'dichotomy', though they are radically different. They are not at odds, not necessarily so. A study of past efforts to understand how fallen human nature needs and receives the grace of God warrants such a book on an important aspect of human nature, in a series devoted to Christian dogmatic theology.

To illustrate how views of free will as a part of human nature mesh with the will in its emancipation from sin through divine grace, here

---

2. Francis Turretin, *Institutes Of Elenctic Theology*, trans G. M. Giger, ed. James T. Dennison Jr. 3 volumes (Phillipsburg, NJ. P & R Publishing, 1992-7), I. p. 206.

is part of the twentieth-century Reformed theologian Louis Berkhof's (1879–1939) summary discussion of the divine decree.

> Man is a free agent with the power of rational self-determination. He can reflect upon, and in an intelligent way choose, certain ends, and can also determine his action with respect to them. The decree of God however, carries with it necessity. God has decreed to effectuate all things or, if He has not decreed that, He has at least determined that they must come to pass ... The prophet Jeremiah predicted that the Chaldean would take Jerusalem. He knew the coming event as a certainty, and yet the Chaldeans freely followed their own desires in fulfilling the prediction. Such certainty is indeed inconsistent with the Pelagian liberty of indifference, according to which the will of man is not determined in any way, but is entirely indeterminate, so that in every volition it can decide in opposition, but is entirely indeterminate, not only to all outward inducements, but also to all inward considerations and inducements and judgments, inclinations and desires, and even to the whole character and inner state of man.[3]

And here is part of his account of effectual calling, writing of Augustine's view and that of Pelagius:

> Pelagius sought the explanation for this [the divine call] in the arbitrary will of man. Man has by nature a perfectly free will, so that he can accept or reject the gospel, as he sees fit, and thus either obtain or fail to obtain the blessings of salvation .... Semi-Pelagianism sought to mediate between the two and to avoid both the Augustinian denial of free will and the Pelagian depreciation of divine grace. It assumed the presence of the seeds of virtue in man, which of themselves tended to bear good fruit, but held that these needed the fructifying influence of divine grace for their development. The grace necessary for this is given to all men gratuitously, so that they are with the aid of it able to accept the gospel call unto salvation. The call will therefore be effective provided man, aided by divine grace, accepts it.[4]

So we see here one instance of how different kinds of choice cohere best with different theological positions. In his discussion Berkhof mentions the 'power of rational self-determination', the ability to

---

3. Louis Berkhof, *Systematic Theology*, 1941 (London, Banner of Truth Trust, 1959), p. 106.

4. ibid., p. 458.

reflect in an intelligent way, choose certain ends, and to act in their fulfillment. He contrasts such a view of free choice with Pelagian freedom as indifference according to which the will of man is not determined in any way, but it is entirely indeterminate, so that in every act of willing, it has the power to have decided its opposite. He distinguishes each of these different views from naturalistic, materialistic, pantheistic and rationalistic determinism in contrast to rational self-determination.[5]

The Synchronic Contingency Proposal

As already mentioned, what follows is an endeavour to show in the first place that the synchronic contingency view of Vos is not the view of the Reformed Confessionalism of the seventeenth century, labeled 'Reformed Orthodoxy', RO for short. Under its spell a group of scholars have claimed that central Reformed theologians of the seventeenth century were indeterminists, in their book *Reformed Thought on Freedom (RTF)*. We are indebted to Richard Muller (1948–) who in his book *Divine Will and Human Choice* (2017) has subjected the idea that the synchronic contingent view of freedom, and its alleged originator Duns Scotus (1266–1308), significantly affects (if it does not control) the Reformed theology of that period, to serious examination. He holds that the major theological influence was Thomas Aquinas.

However, Muller himself nonetheless takes the view, towards the end of his book, that the Reformed were to a degree under the influence of indeterminism. As a consequence he thinks that they advocated the possibility of the 'contingency' of human choice, understanding contingency as a variety of indeterminism. This is consistent with Muller's view on another question which will occupy us in the Second Part, whether Jonathan Edwards's compatibilism is in the Reformed tradition. In support of this, in his lecture 'Jonathan Edwards and the Absence of Free Choice: A Parting of Ways in the Reformed Tradition',[6] he argues that Edwards's compatibilistic view of the freedom of the will (a judgment with which this book concurs) marks a fork in the road of the Reformed confessional tradition. So this issue of human freedom,

---

5. ibid., pp. 106-7.
6. *Jonathan Edwards Studies*, I. 1. 2011.

besides having intrinsic importance, also raises questions about the identity and continuity of Reformed theology.[7]

My aims in what follows are not simply to endorse negative things about synchronic contingency, but to show that its implausibility has the cosequence of making Turretin and his fellow RO theologians into compatibilists, and to make clear that Edwards is in the same compatibilistic anthropological tradition.

Diachronic Contingency

Diachronic contingency is contingency within some temporal series of the changing creation, so it has no relevance to our God's timelessly eternal life. This can be underlined by the distinction in Muller's words:

> In brief, 'diachronic contingency,' as attributed by Vos and others to Aristotle, Aquinas and the pre-Scotus tradition generally, allows for contingency only over the course of time but assumes the determination of particular events or actions. Using the standard example of Socrates sitting, Socrates can either sit or run, sit at one time and run at another, but inasmuch as he cannot do both at the same time, his sitting at one moment and his running at the same moment are both understood to be impossible – as necessary in the sense that at neither moment could the case be otherwise.[8]

Such temporal sequences have an accidental or temporal necessity.

Part One of this study (Chaps. 1–3) is a discussion of synchronicity and an assessment of Vos's claims that Luther and Calvin were necessitarian. The Second Part (Chaps. 4–7) is mainly on Muller's half-way position, that according to the RO, freedom is a matter of indeterministic free choice of a diachronic variety. The consequence of this position has serious implications. Muller thinks that it is distinctive of RO theology, that human choice is an indeterministic matter; 'there is also a simultaneous presence of the unactualized potency to the opposite ...'.[9] Later we will look at Muller's view on Edwards, expressed chiefly in his 2011 article

---

7. For further discussion on the character of the Reformed tradition, see Matthew C. Bingham, Chris Caughey, R. Scott Clark, Crawford Gribben and D. G. Hart, *On Being Reformed, Debates over a Theological Identity* (London, Palgrave Macmillan, 2018).

8. Muller, *Divine Will and Human Choice* (Grand Rapids, Mich. Baker, 2017), pp. 47-8.

9. ibid.

'Jonathan Edwards and the Absence of Free Choice: A Parting of Ways in the Reformed Tradition?', and in the conclusion of his 2017 book *Divine Will and Human Choice*. As noted, I shall counter-argue that Turretin has a compatibilistic view of human nature and that Edwards is similarly compatibilistic. Muller's concentration on Turretin has meant that I have also concentrated on him. In the book he stands for RO as a movement, though we shall refer to others of them.

Like anyone who has read Muller's writings, I am indebted in many ways to his scholarly erudition in the history of the Reformed tradition. I align myself more with him than with Vos, because I endorse many of his qualifications of Vos. Nevertheless, I doubt that Jonathan Edwards represents a parting of ways from the RO, not at least on human free will. So we are not only concerned with issues of human freedom, but also on the wider debate about Reformed tradition and its identity.

The introduction of synchronic contingency would have had seismic consequences for Reformed theology in the seventeenth century, because of the way RO theologians such as Gisbertus Voetius (1589–1676) and Francis Turretin (1623–1687) and hosts of others defended it against Arminian and Jesuit Roman Catholic anthropology. These positions are significantly different from the RO, who each adopted a libertarian free position (which I shall refer to as 'Franciscan freedom'[10]) as we shall see in due course. This opens up the question of how Arminians and Jesuits differ in their anthropology from the Reformed. In the case of Edwards, things were interestingly different, in that Edwards was not a scholastic but had fallen under the influence of John Locke and (due to his scientific interests) of Sir Isaac Newton, and others, and that these influenced his arguments and their conceptualization in his *The Freedom of the Will*.

In Part Two (Chaps. 4–7) I offer three separate arguments for placing the RO among the compatibilists. These arguments are indirect, in order to respect Muller's claim that the term 'determinism' was never used in the seventeenth century, and that the question cannot be begged by nowadays imputing it to the RO.

---

10. I take this term from Eleonore Stump as it occurs in 'Aquinas's Account of Freedom; Intellect and Will', *The Monist*, 1997.

Discussing Edwards in contrast to his RO forbears provides an interesting test case for Muller's claim about reformed scholastic theology, that it was an eclectic conceptual scheme inherited in the main from Aristotle and Aquinas, and adapted further to take account of the distinctives of Reformed theology in the sixteenth and seventeenth centuries. Those unfamiliar with this territory will be helped by the fact that in the course of the book we plough the same field from a number of different angles.

This study is therefore in the history of the theology of the early modern period in the light of what I regard as these novel views regarding synchronic contingency, a libertarian proposal in theology, and less directly a contribution to Christian systematic theology. As was stated at the outset, the book lies in facts about human nature. There is no revealed doctrine of man as there is a doctrine of the Holy Trinity, say, or of justification. As a consequence, Christian theology is in places a partly revealed, partly natural discipline. There are instances of particular people exercising their wills in Scripture, but not a Christian doctrine of the human will as such, just as there is from the New Testament no revealed Greek language, nor geography of Palestine.

Historically, as already noted in Berkhof, there are mainly two ways of thinking of human free will. One thinks of the will as 'free' in that it is an independent or autonomous power. This is known as libertarianism or indeterminism. The other is that the will is the product of our reasons, desires for attaining a goal or goals, which are prior to actions, and bring them about. This is determinism or compatibilism. Compatibilism takes it that determinism can be consistent with human accountability. In the light of what was said earlier there is no definitive Christian theological resolution of this difference, since there are no data of revelation that would settle it decisively.[11]

Having said this, there are factors that are appealed to for one or other point of view, some of them theological. For example Vos's advocacy of Reformed indeterminism, of 'Franciscan liberty', Stump's term, to refer to the Scotian position. His argument is that God Himself is an indeterminist, and hence that it is a consequence of the human race, created in the image of God, that men and women are indeterminist

---

11. See the Glossary.

too. Determinists take their position as a consequence of philosophical argument as coherent with the sovereignty of God, or with the doctrine of grace or both. Augustine, who systematically developed the doctrine of saving grace, is said by many to have been a compatibilist.[12] This book is in this Augustinian tradition.

---

12. Gerard O'Daly, 'Predestination and Freedom in Augustine's Ethics', in *The Philosophy in Christianity* ed. G. Vesey (C.U.P. 1989) and Katherin Rogers, *Anselm on Freedom* (Oxford, Oxford University Press, 2008).

PART ONE

CHAPTER 1

Orientation

Some people understand compatibilism, the view that we possess free will in the sense that the will is caused by the mind, or the intellect, as being integral to the RO or to 'Calvinism', though we need to bear in mind that RO is a theological tradition that is the product of other minds than John Calvin's. By contrast there have been Calvinists who hold that Calvinism is consistent with indeterminism or libertarianism. A number of the Calvinists, students of Calvin and of Reformed theology, that we shall refer to, hold such a view. But we need to remember that even Calvinistic compatibilists will recognize that, if God works miracles, then these events have no creaturely cause.

Further, Calvinism is not only creaturely, it embraces divine freedom as well as human freedom, the Creator as well as the creature. God in the Westminster Confession is said to be 'most free'. I take it that this is a reference to God's sovereignty, and His aseity. God is differently situated from His creatures. He is not in any way the product of His circumstances, of causal factors that originate outside or earlier than Himself. He has aseity, independence and self-sufficiency. Hence the 'most' in 'most free'. There are questions that when asked of God make no sense of the creature, such as how old God is, or how many parts He is constructed out of. As the Apostle Paul said, 'From him and through him and to him are all things' (Rom. 11:36). So strictly speaking, one might think that the question of determinism and compatibilism should embrace every will, non-divine and divine, but it cannot do so.

'Rabbi' John Duncan

In his *Colloquia Peripatetica* Duncan asserts,

I dissent from Jonathan Edwards's doctrine, because he hazards a speculation, on will *qua* will, and therefore in reference to all will, divine and human. It is fatal to establish a necessary chain throughout every will in the universe. The divine acts are free. They are necessary, I maintain, *qua* moral, though free *qua* will. But I am a determinist as much as Edwards.[1]

I dare to say that 'Rabbi' Duncan has here not got things quite right on Edwards. Edwards was a classical theist, stressing divine fullness and perfection. He wrote in correspondence to a Scottish friend after his ejection from his Northampton pulpit that he could subscribe to the Westminster Confession. Although Jonathan Edwards (1703–1758) was a compatibilist regarding the changeable creation, he was in fact able to distinguish the conditions of the Creator from those of His creatures, and did so. In Part IV of his *Freedom of the Will* Edwards has a Section 7, entitled 'Concerning the Necessity of the Divine Will'. His point is that though God's perfections could not be other than they are, nevertheless God is worthy of our worship and admiration, of praise and thanksgiving. God cannot create or change or modify His perfections. The Supreme Being is the source of all other beings. He spoke and it was done. Those creatures that are external to Him do not determine God's actions; He acts according to His untold power and wisdom.

> As though there were some disadvantage, meanness, and subjection, in such a necessity; a thing by which will was confined, kept under, and held in servitude by something, which, as it were, maintained a strong and invincible power and dominion over it, by bonds that held him fast, and that he could by no means deliver himself from .... 'Tis no disadvantage or dishonor to a being, necessarily to act in the most excellent and happy manner, from the necessary perfection of his own nature. This argues no imperfection, inferiority or dependence, nor any want of dignity, privilege or ascendency.'[2]

The reason why it is not to have a diminished freedom, to be necessarily *most* holy, is because holiness in itself is an excellent and honor-

---

1. *Colloquia Peripatetica,* John Duncan, Collected by William Knight, Sixth Edition (Edinburgh, Oliphant, Anderson & Ferrier, 1907), p. 29.

2. Jonathan Edwards, *The Freedom of the Will* ed. Paul Ramsey. *The Works of Jonathan Edwards Volume I* (New Haven, Conn., Yale University Press, 1957), p. 377.

able state. For the same reason, it is no dishonor to be *most* wise, and in every case to act most wisely, or do the thing which is the wisest of all; for wisdom is also in itself excellent and honorable. And so on. God is most necessary and free by being Himself. What I venture to say is that what 'Rabbi' Duncan has missed is the conditions between Creator and the creature, in supposing the idea of determinism would have a parallel effect on both the Creator and the creature if determinism is granted on either. The human creature is a product of the creation, it depends on it and is constrained by it, and has freedom as the power and choice that he or she is gifted with. The Creator is by definition radically other than this. He is not created, but is possessed of aseity, *aseitas*, independence, (Not that He has created Himself! For He was not created, <u>full stop</u>.) When He acts directly, making a change in so doing, that change is determined, but God is never determined by a change.

The Creator cannot be determined. Hence He cannot have a determiner. Hence determinism cannot touch Him. His actions are expressions of power and wisdom of which the grandest of creatures have no real understanding, though we all have some. (Rom. 1:18-20). So if the creature is determined *ad extra* in everything he does, and so is determined, the Creator cannot be determined. So the question of whether God is acted upon does not arise.

But though Edwards holds that God had no reason to change whatever is in His plan, this emphasis on the nature of divine freedom does not mean for Edwards that God cannot be thought of making possible such a deviation from what He had done. For he says that God could do what He has not in fact done. The Bible refers to matters that could have happened but have not occurred nor never will occur. Christ refers to the stones that could have been turned into children of Abraham. 'And do not presume to say to yourselves, "We have Abraham as our father", for I tell you, God is able from these stones to raise up children for Abraham' (Matt. 3:9).

In Edwards's case there are instances of him thinking what God could have done, or that he thinks that God could do. These are some of what we can call his 'thought experiments'. These are experiments in language, part of the stock in trade of philosophers. They have a long history, but Locke gave them a new lease of life, and Edwards follows Locke. By such experiments we are intended to put pressure on our intellectual intuitions. In his book on the freedom of the will he uses thought experiments sparingly. For example, he writes in Part IV S. 8, 'Some Further Objections Against the Moral Necessity of God's Volitions Considered'[3] as follows – 'Let us for clearness' sake suppose, that God had at the beginning made two globes .... perfectly alike in every respect, and placed them near one to another ...'.[4]

The details do not concern us. The fact is, here is a valid *supposition* on Edwards's part which for all we know God never chose. The supposition is certainly not incoherent. The question is, given what Edwards allows regarding God's necessity, is such a supposition allowable consistently? Everything that happens is an expression of the wisdom and power (and other perfections) of almighty God. Here is something that God has not done. For him 'it is impossible but that God should be good'[5] and this impossibility reaches down to each expression of that goodness, no matter how seemingly trivial, as it contributes to the goodness of the whole.

The Bondage of the Will

The news that this book is about free will may arouse the belief that it is an account of the bondage of the will to sin, which both Calvin and Luther wrote books about. But in fact this important revealed truth is hardly mentioned in what is to follow. Rather we are to be concerned with human choice, human agency as such, including what in earlier times was called 'civic freedom', and not with the nature of such agency when fallen, or as enjoying the Spirit's work of regeneration. We shall pay most attention to human wills. The divine will is largely, but not wholly, excluded from our argument. What follows is therefore principally an exercise in anthropology, not in theology in the sense of the doctrine of God, but in human choice.

As we noted 'compatiblism' refers to a position that maintains the consistency or 'compatibility' with a determinism which, if it meets certain conditions, is in turn consistent or compatible with human responsibility, of blame for what a person ought not to have done, and

---

3. ibid., p. 364f.
4. ibid.
5. ibid., p. 480.

of praise for doing what he ought to have done. As we shall see, the RO and Edwards in their accounts of human freedom each had criteria for human responsibility, having to do with a person's moral ability or not, or of his being compelled to do what he does or not.

This Chapter's Purpose

This opening chapter is intended to familiarize the reader with the work of Antonie Vos and his group and their re-construction of the seventeenth century Reformed Orthodox theologians as emancipated from what Vos calls necessitarianism, which we shall say more about shortly. This is to be found in several papers of his, and in his books on the theology and philosophy of the scholastic Duns Scotus (1266–1308). These sources are chiefly concerned with human freedom, less so with historical theory, of how doctrine is constructed, or with the conditions in which Christian doctrine develops.

So we are concerned with a feature of human nature as such, not with soteriology.[6] The aim is to show that the view of Jonathan Edwards on the freedom of the human will known as compatibilism, was held by representative RO theologians in the seventeenth century, and is consistent with the Westminster Confession of Faith. Together they all held that our actions are brought about by the activity of the human understanding and the will, from factors that affect us in our understanding that produces our choices. There were differences between them, of course, due to Edwards's dislike of scholasticism, whereas the RO were mostly dedicated scholastics, while at the same time Edwards made public his abiding admiration for the theology, but not for the scholasticism, of the central RO figures of Francis Turretin (1623-1687), and Petrus Van Mastricht (1630–1706).[7] So the aim of the effect of arguments that follow is to narrow some of the differences between the RO and Edwards by showing that they were both compatibilists.

---

6. For background see Paul Helm, *Human Nature from Calvin to Edwards* (Grand Rapids, Reformed Heritage Books, 2018).

7. Paul Helm, 'A Different Kind of Calvinism? Edwardsianism Compared with Older Forms of Reformed Thought', *After Jonathan Edwards*, edd. Oliver D. Crisp and Douglas A. Sweeney (New York, Oxford University Press, 2012). The very positive references of Edwards to Francis Turretin and Petrus Van Mastricht, suggest that Edwards distinguished between scholasticism as a philosophical style, and its theological content.

The Vos Project

In the First Part of this chapter we shall set out and examine the claims of Antonie Vos and his group of Dutch colleagues. Vos holds that the tendency of Christian theology down the ages has been to succumb to necessitarianism which it has taken from surrounding philosophy.

Vos prefers to use the term 'necessitarianism' to 'determinism', but I have not come across a discussion of the term. But it is one that is intended to cover both divine and human action, and those of creatures and of changes in inanimate objects. It covers the character of alternativity of men and women and that of their Creator. To discuss the term 'necessitarianism' when it includes the action of God would take us into matters which are somewhat speculative.

Besides, Vos largely confines his view to the topics of the doctrine of God and of the human will. He and his group do not venture to the question of how such an approach can be consistent with the commitment to the sovereign grace of God in the Augustinianism of the Reformed tradition, or of effectual calling, say, or to the Reformed view of meticulous divine providence or to the fundamental place played by the divine decree (or decrees) in Reformed theology. Vos hardly ever refers to such features, and what follows is confined to his view of the freedom of God, and its consequences for mankind made in the image of God. However, later we shall address the claim (from Scotus) that God's action is synchronously contingent.

Not all that is not God has synchronous agency, even if God's freedom were synchronically contingent in this sense. The created world is in time and space. And while Vos thinks Anselm plays a key role in introducing a non-necessitarian Christian theology, others such as Katherin Rogers think Anselm's doctrine of God is necessitarian but that His human creatures are libertarian.[8] And Norman Kretzmann thinks similarly of Thomas Aquinas, that is, he offers a necessitarian account of what God creates but a non-necessitarian account of the human beings that He has created. God's nature is essentially diffusive, and so not-creating is not an option for Him. But God has options over what He does in fact create.[9]

---

8. Rogers, *Anselm on Freedom*, pp. 18-19.

9. Norman, Kretzmann, *The Metaphysics of Theism* (Oxford, Clarendon Press, 1997), Chs. 7, 8.

It is rather inaccurate for Vos to highlight the distinction between two kinds of necessity, the necessity of the consequence and the necessity of the consequent, to be a necessity in order to establish synchronic indeterminism only. The two kinds of necessity are a significant feature of what is to follow, and we shall explain as we proceed beginning here. Vos says,

> Therefore, a case *of necessitas consequens/consequentiae* is not an innocent purely logical tool, but it enjoys the crucial function to make possible that reality can be connected with contingency. The proper function of this elementary distinction is just to escape from necessitarianism and determinism.[10] That may be a motive for which the distinction has been invoked, but such motives do not exhaust the possibilities. And, for centuries and centuries, this distinction will be appealed to, if opponents charge the Christian position to support determinism or to deny the freedom of the will, including Reformed scholasticism which did so always.[11]

We shall have reason to qualify this claim of Vos's later.

The distinction between the two necessities is routinely illustrated by the prophecy that not a bone of Jesus' body would be broken, in John 19:36. This was said to be an effect of the circumstances of the Roman soldiers who had no need to break any of Jesus' bones, since by that time Jesus was already dead. The necessity of the consequence had the effect of them not breaking a bone, rendering the unbreakability of Jesus' bones 'necessary' in the hypothetical sense. It is called that this term is a case of 'hypothetical necessity', given that God's decree was that not a bone of His Incarnate Son was to be broken. His was not the only case in Scripture. The same is true of any event that is 'according to Scripture' or 'that the Scripture might be fulfilled'. These are each 'hypotheses' that generate necessities.

Yet the questions regarding compatibilism and libertarianism cannot be begged in this fashion, in which Vos seems to treat God's synchronic freedom as providing a sort of blanket of non-necessity over every thing that God brings to pass. Man was created in the image of God, his actions conditioned by his creatureliness. Besides such external causes, the creation of a man made in the image of God, man also has internal sources of change, as when I change my mind, or become worried about the time I

---

10. 'Antonie Vos, 'Paul Helm on Medieval Scholasticism', p. 269.
11. ibid., p. 271.

am taking to read the newspaper, or I decide to go outside for a walk. The semantics of the scholastic concepts involved in the discussion of human freedom are a bit confusing. There are various kinds of classification of the necessary kinds of thing, including rocks and sheep and vegetation, and mankind in his freedom has both physical changes, such as growing old, and freedom of will, at least according to Francis Turretin,[12] though he makes no appeal to synchronic contingency in affirming this.

So this Vosian revision of Reformed theology has centred on the influence of John Duns Scotus on Reformed theology, in particular the idea of synchronic contingency, to understand the theology (doctrine of God) and anthropology (doctrine of man) of the RO. For Vos, such synchronous freedom, divine or human, is a choice for A, which could under exactly the same conditions, both for the chooser and for temporal or other conditions in which the choice of A took place, have been equally a choice for not-A or for B. (A compatibilist argues that for a choice to be different, the cause or reason of the choice must be different.) For some years Vos and his group have championed in various writings this Scotian doctrine of synchronic contingency as an antidote to the necessitarianism (as Vos judges it) of Reformed theology (its doctrine of God), citing Martin Luther and John Calvin as among its chief exponents. We shall consider the accuracy of this charge in the case of the two Reformers in chapters 2 and 3.[13] We shall see that Calvin for all his alleged necessitarianism, respected the two necessities, and that Luther had the resources to do so.

Vos's research group published *Freedom in Reformed Thought: The Concept of Free Choice in Early Modern Reformed Theology* (*FRT*) in 2010.[14] This sets out the detail of the Vosian/Scotian interpretation of

---

12. Turretin, *Institutes*, I. p. 462f.

13. The writings of Antonie Vos's that I shall refer to are: 'Always on Time: The Immutability of God', in *Understanding the Attributes of God* (Peter Lang, Frankfurt 1999) eds., Gijsbert van den Brink and Marcel Sarot; 'Scholasticism and Reformation' in *Reformation and Scholasticism*, eds., Willem J. Van Asselt and Eef Dekker (Grand Rapids, MI: Baker, 2001); 'The Systematic Place of Reformed Scholasticism: Reflections Concerning the Reception of Calvin's Thought', *Church History and Religious Culture*, Vol. 91, Nos. 1- 2 (2011): pp. 29-41; 'Paul Helm on Medieval Scholasticism' (*Journal of Reformed Theology*, 2014, pp. 263-83).

14. *Reformed Thought on Freedom, The Concept of Free Choice In Early Modern Reformed Theology*, edited by Willem J. van Asselt, J. Martin Bac, and Roelf T. te Velde (Grand Rapids, Baker, 2010).

synchronic contingent freedom in the translation and commentary of a series of seventeenth-century Reformed theologians. Richard Muller in his book *Divine Will and Human Choice*,[15] has offered criticism of this on the way to upholding his own non-compatibilism. He has shown in detail that the main influence upon the RO was that of Aquinas rather than of Scotus, but generally holds that the philosophical influences on the RO were somewhat eclectic.

Well, if I were to qualify the above, unlike the writers in *RTF* who hold to full-blooded synchronic contingency, Muller has a different view, that of a non-deterministic one of free will that is not the full Franciscan liberty of the will, but is not compatibilism either, but a case of diachronic synchronicism nonetheless. As in this rather unfortunately-worded passage:

> In rejecting both a determinist or compatibilist and a libertarian reading of Reformed orthodox thought, the authors of *Reformed Thought on Freedom* and I have consistently indicated that the early modern Reformed understood divine determination to be compatible with human freedom and, accordingly, stand in a long line of thinkers reaching back to Augustine.[16]

This is rather baffling, in that Muller sees himself having the same outlook as Vos, but he ends with a position some distance from it. Not to a ringing incompatibilism, but this *via media* must be a diachronic libertarianism. So all is not plain sailing, however, since Muller himself has a positive regard for the place of indeterminacy in human action, he defends a non-compatibilist understanding of freedom to explain the RO position on free will. I shall argue in chapters 4 to 7 that it is very likely that Muller is mistaken.

Compatibilism embraces both a view of the causal sources of human agency, and also what makes such agency blameworthy and praiseworthy, a matter of human responsibility. Both agency and responsibility are usually treated together.[17]

---

15. Muller, *Divine Will and Human Choice* (Grand Rapids, Baker, 2017), Ch. 6. See also 'Not Scotist: understandings of being, univocity, and analogy in early-modern Reformed thought' (*Reformation and Renaissance Review*, 2012).

16. 'Neither Libertarian nor Compatibilist: A Reply to Paul Helm'. (*Journal of Reformed Theology*. 13 (2019), p. 269.

17. In his book *A Reformed View of Freedom: The Compatibility of Guidance Control and Reformed Theology* (Pickwick Publications, 2019), Michael Preciado examines

It is a somewhat tall order to expect that every reader will come to these issues being already versed in their historical background, or of other matters about scholasticism that are to follow. So the remainder of this chapter is largely a 'getting to know you' session, to introduce the reader to a number of different issues raised by Vos and his group, in the hope that with the help of this chapter he or she will get more out of what follows than might otherwise be the case. The first item considers the already-mentioned view of synchronic contingency and with it the study of the history of the idea, which is what we are engaged in.

Necessitarianism, which Vos views as a perennial danger, is at least the view that regards any change in the entire creation as causally necessitated by other changes. In the case of Christian theism, which holds that God is the creator and providential upholder of the universe, for such a necessitarian the Creator Himself may be necessitated to create such a universe. That would be a kind of fatalism. But it seems to Vos that the RO, Confessional Reformed theologians, held a different view, that the eternally synchronic will of God is the necessitator of every change involving human choices within His creation, but that God was himself of sufficient wisdom and freedom to have created an alternative universe than the one He did create, or may have not created any universe at all. More on this later.

Vos says, '[C]lassic Reformed scholasticism offers us a theology of contingency and individuality, of goodness and will, and of freedom and grace. Rediscovering this comforting historical reality is a gift and a joy'.[18] How does it come that Vos is so voluble in his praise of SC and the joyous effect that His rejection of determinism produces? It must be because he thinks that this distinction of the two necessities has a liberating effect, thinking that predestination is a feature of 'necessitarianism'. But Vos must surely recognize that just as gifts are various, so are joys. As we have noted, in his view it is true of both of the wills of God and of human beings that they possess such contingency, which free the universe from necessitarianism. So the distinctiveness of his position lies in combining the necessity of the consequence with

compatibilism in its latest phase, that of the work of John Mark Fischer and Mark Ravizza SJ, on 'Guidance Control', and interestingly and skillfully applies it to both the Westminster Confession of Faith, the RO and to Jonathan Edwards.

18. Vos, 'Paul Helm on Medieval Scholasticism', p. 263.

Scotian synchronic contingency as both being essential to divine and human freedom. But then we are faced with the question of how this is different from the Jesuit and Arminian positions, who also appealed to 'Franciscan freedom', which the RO routinely rejected as they differed their position from that of contemporary Jesuits. We shall consider this question, and the business of synchronic contingency, in more detail in due course.

Vos is a philosopher, not primarily a theologian, and he has little to say about the details of Reformed theology from which his own views were allegedly developed. He has little interest in this side of things. In one place he identifies Socinianism with nominalism and then Arminianism and Molinism as also being nominalistic. And what this shows is that he is chiefly interested in the philosophical influences on those who have held such positions.[19] He states that the Socinians, though nominalistic, also had a stance in favour of 'extreme' contingency, stressing the absolute freedom of God. They disconnected the will of God from His essential virtues. He says that Molinism, *scientia media*, 'eliminates the pivotal role' of the divine will. These verdicts are sketchy, with no attempt to argue them or to go into any detail.[20]

It might be said that in giving prominence to the two necessities Vos and his group[21] seem to pursue a project that appears to be a variant of the 'central dogma', an idea of historians of Christian dogma in the nineteenth and early twentieth centuries, scholars such as Alexander Schweizer (1808–88), Heinrich Heppe (1820–74), and Hans Emil Weber (1882–1950).[22] The significance of the idea of synchronic contingency for the RO, in the work of Vos, has acted rather like a new central dogma, the dislodging of predestination and the enthroning of synchronic contingency. The two necessities seem to have had a similar *a priori* character to that of 'predestination' as the character of the earlier 'central' dogma of Calvinism. We shall need to bear that in mind.

---

19. Vos, 'The Systematic Place of Reformed Scholasticism: Reflections Concerning the Reception of Calvin's Thought', p. 40.

20. ibid., p. 40.

21. The Vos group contributed in various ways to *Reformed Thought on Freedom*.

22. An informative account of this earlier scholarship can be found in Willem J. van Asselt *Introduction to Reformed Scholasticism*, trans. Albert Gootjes (Grand Rapids, Reformation Heritage Books, 2009). Chapter 2.

Synchronic Contingency

So what exactly is Synchronic Contingency (SC)? As noted, according to Vos, it refers to the innate power of the free wills of individuals who when faced with a choice between alternatives A and B, are able to choose one alternative A at a moment of time while at the very same moment, under identical conditions, have the power to will the other alternative B. According to Vos, this was the new insight of Duns Scotus, though as we shall see he notes it has a history going back to the Christian philosopher and theologian Boethius (477–524) and later to Anselm of Canterbury (1033–1109). As already noted, such creaturely synchronic contingency is sometimes known as 'Franciscan freedom' because of its popularity in the Franciscan Order in the Roman Church.[23]

Eleonore Stump (1974–) states, 'For some mediaeval libertarians (and for some contemporaries), an act of the will is free only in case the agent could have performed a different act of the will in exactly the set of beliefs and desires.'[24] This is what she refers to as 'Franciscan Freedom' and cites Scotus. We shall consider the importance of this for Vos. According to him and his research group it was an insight also possessed by the Reformed scholastics such as Gisbertius Voetius (1589–1676) and Francis Turretin (1623–1687) and other RO theologians who are cited and expounded in *RTF*. And synchronic contingency is contrasted with diachronic contingency, a way of understanding temporal change. Contingency is a kind of change.

The Two Necessities in More Detail

The 'two necessities' are of key importance for Vos's argument as was mentioned earlier. As they may be unfamiliar to most readers, there is need for time and care to understand this scholastic distinction.

> *Necessity of the consequent* i.e. the necessity of something that cannot be other than what it is, which is to say, a simple or absolute necessity. *Necessity of the consequence*, i.e. not an absolute necessity, but a necessity brought about or conditioned by a previous contingent act or event so that the necessity itself arises out of contingent circumstances and thus is conditional necessity. On this scheme, there is no necessity that God decree what He decrees, but, granting the divine decree, God is bound by His own plan and promises.

---

23. Eleonore Stump, 'Aquinas's Account of Freedom; Intellect and Will', 1997.

24. ibid., p. 593.

Therefore, the fulfillment of the divine plan and the divine promises is necessary, but by a necessity of the consequence.[25]

So says Muller in his *Dictionary*. This is then applied to God, who possesses absoluteness. These are formulae of modal logic, a type of logical reasoning. The use of the necessity operator is warranted in referring to God, who is not a proposition or a set of these, but the *ens realissimum*, the fullest being, whose power, will and wisdom express His *aseitas*.[26]

Suppose that in this case the absolute being, God, has what Aquinas refers to as diffusiveness, or generosity?[27] The divine will, eternal and unconditional, may nonetheless for all we know, be that of the creator of X. Suppose that God could by His power and wisdom have created another world rather than the actual world, some other alternative state of affairs. In our thinking of God we need something like this in order to distinguish theism from what is called panentheism.[28] Or think of the distinction from the other end: if the creation is contingent, then there could have been another world, one in which (in Calvin's phrase) God 'could have saved us by a word', say. So we might say God's goodness, wisdom and so could not be like a creaturely alternative.

For Vos the distinction between the necessity of the consequent and the necessity of the consequence is of central importance in the development/emergence of divine contingency, in his view emancipating Christian theology from the thralldom of pagan necessitarianism. The occurrence of necessity of the consequence is a *sign* of divine libertarian freedom. The use of the distinction is a sign of the contingency of divine action, and (more controversially) of human action too.

Vos gives a fuller, more formal, basis of the two necessities distinction as follows:

The distinction between the *necessity of the consequence* (*necessitas consequentiae*) and the *necessity of the consequent* (*necessitas*

---

25. Richard Muller, *Dictionary of Latin and Greek Theological Terms* (Grand Rapids, Baker, 1985), p. 200, adapted from the entry 'necessitatis consequentiae'.

26. Richard Muller, *Post-Reformation Reformed Dogmatics*, Second Edition (Grand Rapids, Mich, Baker, 2003), I. p. 463-4.

27. Norman Kretzmann *The Metaphysics of Theism* (Oxford, OUP 1997), Chs. 7 and 8.

28. Oliver Crisp, *Jonathan Edwards on God and Creation* (New York, OUP 2012), p. 146f.).

consequentis) plays a crucial role in medieval logic and philosophy, and in theology as well.

This distinction is still indispensable for our modern set of instruments. Let us introduce some technical terminology, for the *necessity of the consequence* is simply implicative necessity. We look at the basic form of an implication:

(1) $p \rightarrow q$.

(1) symbolizes a conditional assertion, or implication: if *p*, then *q*. *If p, then q* is the whole of the implication: *p* implies *q*. In (1) we call *p* the *antecedent* of the implication $p \rightarrow q$, and *q* the *consequent*. In Latin, the word for *implication* – or *consequence* – is 'consequentia.'

When we deal with a logical implication in which more necessity operators occur, this distinction is decisive. A necessity operator can refer *either* to the antecedent and/or the consequent of the implication, *or* to the implication itself. The structure of an implication in which the necessity of the consequent obtains, is symbolized as follows:

(2) $p \rightarrow Nq$.

In (2) the necessity operator *N* determines the consequent *q* so that *q* is necessary and then *p* has also to be necessary. The structure of an implication in which the necessity of the consequence obtains, is symbolized as follows:

(3) $N (p \rightarrow q)$.

In (3) the necessity operator N [outside the bracket] determines the whole of the implication $p \rightarrow q$. The implicative relation itself is necessary, whereas neither *p* nor *q* have to be necessary, for *p* and *q* can be contingent. This implicative connective $N (\rightarrow)$ expresses the necessary entailment of modal propositional logic. What matters, is the necessity of the implicative relation, and not the real or ontological necessity of the antecedent and the consequent themselves. If the *necessitas consequentis* and *necessitas consequentiae* distinction is ignored, then the truth values of *p* and *q* have the same truth value of

(N) If *p*, then *q*.

So, *p* and *q* themselves have to be necessarily true. This is just the position of necessitarianism.[29]

Luther and Calvin as Necessitarians

In Chapters 2 and 3 we shall consider Vos's claim that the Reformers' position according to those who adopted a 'central dogma' view of Protestant theology, was necessitarian. Vos sets out Calvin's and Luther's alleged necessitarianism in various places. He says that the two necessities, the *necessitatis consequentiae,* the necessity of the consequence, and *necessitatis consequentis,* the necessity of the consequent, distinction, became in the early Christian centuries the cornerstone of the new Christian way of thinking, permitting contingency, until Luther ridiculed it in his *De Servo Arbitrio* (1525).[30] Furthermore,

> Calvin is convinced that God necessarily wills everything that happens and is done. He rightly connects *will* and *necessity.* If God necessarily wills everything there is, then he necessarily knows everything too. His knowledge cannot be different from the reality that he wills. God is omniscient, but because he necessarily knows everything he knows, the epistemic object must also be necessary, just as his act of knowing is necessary. Therefore, everything is necessary. Because the whole of reality is necessary, God knows and acts necessarily, and because God knows and acts necessarily, everything is necessary too.[31]

Vos claims that such necessitarian thinking can be undermined only under the influence of the contingency of indeterminism,

> Within the pattern of early modern theological and philosophical movements, it is not difficult to identify the place of classic Reformed scholasticism: within the framework of seventeenth-century theoretical forces it represents balanced necessity – contingency thinking, based on an elaborate toolbox filled by the richness and rigor of centuries. Can Calvin be responsible for this distinctive characteristic? This cannot be the case, because we have seen that Calvin's conceptual structures are entirely

---

29. Vos, 'Paul Helm on Medieval Scholasticism', *Journal of Reformed Theology*, 2014, pp. 266-7.

30. ibid., p. 269.

31. Vos, 'The Systematic Place of Reformed Scholasticism: Reflections Concerning the Reception of Calvin's Thought', p. 41.

different, because he was convinced that God *acts* just as He *is* – in a necessary way.[32]

As we shall see, this verdict on Calvin was somewhat hasty.

As part of spelling out Vos's synchronic contingency, its character and effects, we presently take all this at face value.[33] But we shall have reason to qualify Vos's necessitarian verdict. What becomes clear at points such as these is that his method is largely that of a philosophical theologian, rather than that of attempting a fully-fledged theology of the Reformed theologians in that era, with a reliance on the careful exegesis of Scripture and of the making of historical judgments regarding the occurrence of theological claims. This is undoubtedly a weakness in Vos's method, as will become evident later on.

Vos moves in argument from divine synchronic contingency to the human cases. But they are unargued for, being introduced *a priori*. There is no evidence of a careful induction from the data of Scripture to ascertain their meaning and implications. There is no strong verdict that if God's activity is synchronic contingent, human behavior is too.

Though we have mentioned 'synchronic contingency' a number of times, we now need to examine it more closely. To do this, we need to move to other technicalities. 'Synchronic contingency' is contrasted with 'diachronic contingency'. (Note that these are more terms that are scarcely if ever to be found *verbatim* in the seventeenth century.) As we saw from Stump they refer to two ways of being contingent: one features the possibility of the occurrence of two choices simultaneously, that in exactly the same time, at a given moment, a decision that could be made synchronously for A or for B, but not for both. The other is diachronic contingency, choice in a temporal sequence, the choice of B being *after* the choice of A, say.

Given divine synchronic contingency, at an eternal 'moment', God was free to create the universe, but He could equally freely have chosen not to create it. However, on such a view it does not follow that everything that changes within the creation is done so in a synchronic contingent

---

32. Vos, 'The Systematic Place of Reformed Scholasticism'. In footnote 37, Vos rather belatedly refers to Calvin's acceptance of the two necessities, which negates his critique of Calvin's alleged 'necessitarianism'.

33. ibid., p. 40.

manner. Within the cosmos that God has created, many subordinate creatures are moved by necessity, causal necessity, or physical necessity as Turretin calls it, or by coercion, through blackmail, or torture, or tiredness, or temper, say.

The supposition that everything that does move in the creation is synchronically contingent, must be an exaggeration, for obviously an array of contingently chosen changes may have different modes of changing; changing themselves or being changed. But these mechanisms are efficiently causal, hence 'contingent' in an additional sense. These causally created machines do not operate by logical necessity, but by causal necessity. Nonetheless they are contingent in the sense that they might not have occurred. It is not by a logical necessity that planes fly. What is necessary, and what non-necessary, depends on the powers of the created entities and of their component parts and circumstances. An event that is necessitated may be caused to move by a natural event e.g. a rock that is necessitated to fall down a slope may be prevented from rolling further by an obstruction. And so on. Vos may allow this, but he rarely, if ever, gives this impression.

And as we shall argue, an action may occur as a result of being caused by a person's desires, motives and intentions, his intelligence and purposing. It is such causal occurrences that are at the heart of compatibilism, informing the will towards the desired goal. One question that we need to focus attention on, is what, according to RO, are the forces of human action. Unlike the contingent features of the world externally, occurring by brute force, human beings have minds and wills capable of choosing alternatives, through preferences and desires, or the power of refusing to choose. As the RO Peter Martyr Vermigli (1499–1562) put it, 'Thus our works, which proceed from our will are said to be free, and those things produced in nature which may or may not come to pass, are contingent.'[34]

Arising from this discussion there are two senses of 'contingency', contingent as directly dependent on God's action, and contingent as causally brought about by intermediaries, cases of secondary causes, being upheld in so doing by God's power. There is more discussion

---

34. Peter Martyr Vermigli, *Predestination and Justification*, The Peter Martyr Library, Vol. 8 (Kirksville, Miss. 2003), ed. Frank A. James III., p. 71.

of the senses of 'contingent' later on. So according to Vos synchronic contingency is Duns Scotus's gift to the church, but it is not without its own difficulties, as we can see. Muller cautions the question-begging character of the theology arising from the enthusiasm of Vos's and his colleagues' use of the two necessities as follows:

> There is a danger that critics of the argument in *Reformed Thought on Freedom* will understand it as a declaration that all events in the actual world are uniformly contingent on the ground of the radical contingency of the order as a whole—or that contingency be defined solely with regard to the freedom of divine willing and not register the equally important point that temporal contingencies are also identified as not to be known or foreknown in their temporal causes and, in the case of free choice, as rooted in the potencies of the human agent as well as in the freedom of God. Yet it is clear both from what we have seen in the discussion of medieval backgrounds and from the approaches to the issue that we find among the early modern Reformed that this is not the case. The contingency of the world order, however rooted in the freedom of the divine will, was never the full explanation of contingency, nor was it ever assumed to rule out causal necessities within the temporal order.[35]

This is well said.

Let us think further about the nature of divine synchronic contingency, the *fons et origo* of human contingency according to Vos and his group, the view of Duns Scotus, and that of other Franciscan libertarians. We are to understand synchronic contingency as occurring in a 'moment' a particular stage of a temporal series. Given the divine willing at a particular moment in the series, 'synchronicity' means that there could have been an alternative willing at that very moment under the very same conditions, that is, given that moment's position in the series. So that a divine synchronically contingent choice is absolutely 'indifferent' as between choices that can be made at that moment in a way that is analogous to God's freedom in *creatio ex nihilo*. But the problem with this view is that according to scholastic theology in general, God exists not in a temporal series, but exists timelessly eternally. So how, if eternal, can it be synchronously so?

Richard Cross has put the problem as follows:

---

35. Muller, *Divine Will and Human Choice*, p. 212.

For the synchronic power for opposites is about a *power*, a power at one and the same time to do *a* or not-*a*. But an agent who, for example, wills *a* at *t*, does not retain its *opportunity* at *t* to will not-*a*. So the notion of choice at an instant entails merely that an immutable God has the power to will all sorts of thing that he does not in fact will; it does not entail that he had ever had to will these things. As Scotus states the problem relative to divine action, 'both the will and the effect are invariable'.[36]

We shall note an amplification of this difficulty later on.

James Dolezal characterizes divine freedom as a freedom of independence,[37] as does Katherin Rogers.[38] And we have noted that the RO closely link divine freedom with divine aseity. Some theologians have used the term 'indifference' to characterize the necessary absence of external factors constraining or even inclining God to act in one way rather than in another. For the RO God is not at the mercy of such factors, events and circumstances external to Him, or to the constraints of time or space, or to the limited strength of a body, or the influence of His past on His present.

In '*Reformed Thought on Freedom:* Some Further Thoughts'[39] I argued that *RTF* is a revisionist work of Reformed theology.[40] It is indisputably a central part of its project to see the RO theologians as benefitting from the Scotian notion of synchronic contingency in their concept of free choice, unlike those who are earlier in the Reformed tradition, such as (the compilers of *RTF* judge) John Calvin and possibly Jerome Zanchius (1516–1590) to commend it. The contributors to the book believe that such contingency, as their appeal to the two necessities view validates, is evidence of 'true alternativity' in acting,[41] and the presence of a truly

---

36. Richard Cross, *Duns Scotus on God* (Aldershot, Ashgate, 2005), p. 120. See also pp. 55-7.

37. James Dolezal, *God Without Parts* (Eugene, Or., Pickwick Publications, 2011), p. 203.

38. Katherin Rogers, *Anselm on Freedom*, p. 7.

39. Paul Helm, '*Reformed Thought on Freedom*: Some Further Thoughts', *Journal of Reformed Theology,* p. 4 (2010).

40. For an earlier foray into this territory, see Paul Helm, 'Synchronic Contingency in Reformed Scholasticism. A Note of Caution' (*Nederlands Theologisch Tijdschrift*, p. 57. 3, July 2003, pp. 207-222). This issue of the journal also contains a response by A. J. Beck and A. Vos, 'Conceptual Patterns related to Reformed Scholasticism' (pp. 223-233), and my reply, 'Synchronic Contingency Again' (pp. 234-238).

41. '*Reformed Thought on Freedom*; Some Further Thoughts', p. 42.

modal as opposed to a merely causal approach to matters of contingency and necessity.[42] So, among RO theologians that are reviewed in the book, Junius (1545–1602) is said to display distinctions that suggest a model of synchronic contingency.[43] Voetius[44] along with Turretin[45] are both said to presuppose the framework of synchronic contingency and alternativity. Readers of the book may note that the commentators, all sympathetic to synchronic contingency, experience considerable difficulty in commenting on cases of the occurrence of synchronic contingent terms in their chosen texts from RO theologians, as they examine instances of its alleged influence in their writings. This is not surprising, given the rarity of the references to 'synchronic contingency' within the writings they examine, though they do not seem to notice that, or to dwell on its significance.

So by synchronic contingency is meant a contingency of logically simultaneous willings. Suppose a world and an agent. The agent is free in the synchronically contingent sense if at the moment the agent chooses A (when the external world and the state of a free agent's 'internal' world is in state S) it is possible that at that very moment (the world being in state S) the agent chooses not-A or B instead. The Jesuits invoked a version of such contingency when they defined human freedom as 'A free potency by which all things requisite for acting being posited, someone can act or not act',[46] a case of 'Franciscan freedom'.

Synchronic contingency, taken literally, means that for one moment of time there is a true alternative choice at that moment to what

---

42. ibid., p. 89.

43. ibid., pp. 125, 232.

44. ibid., p. 167.

45. ibid., pp. 193, 195.

46. ibid., p. 148. Luis de Molina SJ (1535–1600), who with others developed the idea of God's middle knowledge, held to the view of human free will as follows: 'But freedom can be understood in another sense, insofar as it is to *necessity*. In this sense that agent is called free which, with all the prerequisites for acting posited, is able to act and able not to act [freedom of contradiction], or is able to do one thing in such a way that it is also able to do some contrary thing [freedom of contrariety]. And by virtue of this sort of freedom of will the faculty by which such an agent is able so to act is called free .... Luis de Molina SJ, *On Divine Foreknowledge, Part IV of the Concordia*, trans. with an Introduction and Notes by Alfred J. Freddoso (Ithaca NY, Cornell University Press, 1988), pp. 24-5. Freddoso calls it 'strongly indeterministic' (24), and so it is. This account was adopted by the Arminians. See John Owen, *A Display of Arminianism* (1642) (*Works* ed. W. H. Goold), X, p. 117.

occurred: a choice and at the same moment an alternative choice. In the words of Vos: 'A state of affairs *p* is contingent if − *p* is possible for the same moment'. He amplifies this: 'At any moment factual reality can be different from what and how it is … as is shown by Scotus, real contingency implies that the opposite is possible for the *same* moment, we call this contingency *"synchronic"*'.[47] And in the words of Scotus himself, a free power 'is not determined of itself, but can cause this act or the opposite act, and act or not act'.[48] For Scotus a free power is one that has at one and the same time more than one outcome under its scope. Richard Cross points out that as a consequence the notion of contingency, and modality in general, is to be thought of not temporally or diachronically, but synchronically, in terms of conceivable states of affairs.[49]

What this means, I think, is that for Scotus freedom is not simply a matter of logical contingency together with a choice that can freely be brought about. Something can only be freely brought about if at the moment it is chosen, in just the same circumstances, an alternative could have been chosen. A similar question may be posed about Vos's reference to Scotus's understanding of divine knowledge, 'that divine knowledge of the contingent is in the synchronic sense contingent'.[50]

An oddity about divine synchronic contingency that one immediately notices is that Vos, following Scotus, is content to apply a temporal adjective, 'simultaneous', to the life of a timelessly eternal God, to the mental action of the mind of a non-temporal being: to impute *synchronic* contingency to that being. How is this to be understood, I wonder? How can a timelessly eternal God possess the power of synchronously acting: at one moment, an eternal moment, however this is understood, having the power to decide otherwise than what he in fact decides? One answer offered by those who favour such contingency is to encourage us to think in terms of logical (or structural) 'moments' in the eternal divine life,

---

47. John Duns Scotus's *Contingency and Freedom, Lectura* I.39, p. 25, a fuller account of Vos's understanding of what Scotus means by synchronic contingency, though the phrase is not Scotus's, can be found in his *The Theology of John Duns Scotus* (Edinburgh: Edinburgh University Press, 2006).

48. Richard Cross, *Duns Scotus on God* (Aldershot: Ashgate, 2005), p. 56.

49. *Duns Scotus on God*, p. 57.

50. Vos, 'Scholasticism and Reformation' pp. 113-4.

where a moment is understood as a distinction drawn by our reason, and not one that is present in fact in the divine life, and so a structural rather than a temporal moment. That is, these 'moments' impose *distinctions* rather than *divisions*, in the divine mind, and are structural in the sense that an eternal moment is a logical feature of any free divine action. The idea comes to be that it is a necessary feature of a timelessly eternal free action that in its being performed, an alternative action (or no action) could be performed at that very moment, in exactly the same situation. But how can there be moments in the life of a timelessly eternal being?

Those who are acquainted with Reformed theology are familiar with debates that have occurred about the ordering of the divine decrees, where that order is understood in terms of a logical or rational ordering of the decrees in the eternal divine mind, not as a temporal series of decrees. To think of the divine decree as having such a structural ordering is acceptable if the divine decree is thought of in terms of means and ends. But there is an oddity about applying the notion of synchronic contingency to God when understood as timelessly eternal. At other times Muller is a strong advocate of the RO's adherence to analogy, though there is hardly a mention of this in *Divine Will and Human Power*.[51]

Muller discusses divine simultaneity at various steps in his argument in *Divine Will and Human Choice*. He evades the problems of eternal moments by saying, with Scott Macdonald, that a simultaneous potency occurs in a purely *logical* 'moment'.[52] But the reader may wonder at this point if purely logical moments are not purely imaginary, 'logical and non-temporal but nonetheless corresponding with the temporal sequencies of the created order' as Muller expresses this.[53] That is, it is a case of a logical sequence mapping a temporal sequence. But how can it be that a logical sequence of a *temporal sequence* subsists in the timelessly eternal divine mind ascribed by RO theology, and by Christian theology more generally?

Not only is such a proposal speculative and therefore unprofitable, it appears to be incoherent. What are these alleged moments phases

51. But see Muller, *Divine Will and Human Choice*, p. 56.

52. ibid., p. 56.

53. ibid., p. 56.

of? Not of time, because then it would follow that God's eternal life has a temporal dimension, certain moments being later or earlier or simultaneous with other moments, since these moments do not simply mark boundaries, like midnight is a boundary between two days, say, but the 'moments' are units in the duration of time, consisting of seconds or nanoseconds, allegedly in the timelessly eternal life of God.

The point about the nature of these moments is that we are forced to treat them as far as the mind of God is concerned, as if they were distinctions of the reason, not moments in time. Without such an understanding the phrase 'structural moments' which is employed in *RTF* is a category mistake. If we do forget it, if we treat these moments as temporally serial, then we begin to treat God in anthropomorphic terms, to 'psychologize' the eternal mind of God along the pattern of those of us who make up their minds when in time. Distinctions of reason, when applied to a timelessly eternal God, might offer a logical partition, but it can't offer anything temporal. To what extent are these partitions simply nominal? How do they correspond to and provide intelligibility to what they are moments of?

Since eternity, unlike time, has no moments of its own, talking of *instantes* or *momenta* of eternity must be introduced as ways of articulating the divine eternal life so as to make it accommodated to those whose existence is temporal, but certainly not to clarify it. In Edwards's view divine tenseless eternity was an aspect of the divine perfection.

> But as God is immutable, and so it is utterly and infinitely impossible that his view should be changed; so 'tis, for the same reason, just as impossible that the foreknown event should not exist: and that is to be impossible in the highest degree: and therefore the contrary is necessary. Nothing is more impossible than that the immutable God should be changed, by the succession of time; who comprehends all things, from eternity to eternity, in one, most perfect and unalterable view; so that his eternal duration is *vitae interminabilis, tota, simul, and perfecta possessio.*[54]

The quotation on the divine decrees supplied by Muller from the Anglican theologian Matthew Scrivener (1674), that 'we all know that

---

54. Edwards, *The Freedom of the Will*, p. 268.

the distinction of Instants in Order and Nature, do not infer a necessary distinction in duration: but that both Nature and Decrees might be coequal in eternity', makes the same point.[55]

Bearing these caveats in mind, we might attempt to parse synchronic contingency as it applies to God's eternal will along the following lines: at the same eternal 'moment', and granted that that moment is 'located' at a given 'stage' of God's life, given that God eternally wills to bring about X at that 'stage' He could have eternally willed to bring about Y and not X at that 'stage', or to have brought about nothing at the same stage. But it is hard to consider this suggestion as satisfactory.

The third argument given in the opening page of *RTF* is that God is indeterministically free, therefore those created in His image are correspondingly indeterministically free. But this inference is far from convincing, since it warrants the obvious falsehood, God is independent, possessing *aseitas*, therefore humankind is independent. But humankind is creaturely, and so dependent on God. Mankind is affected, caused to be and to do, by what is not itself. The freedoms of human beings are correspondingly different; for Vos, human freedom being at best a kind of analogy of divine synchronic contingency, whatever exactly this is.

Vos and his group assume that the RO also understood the freedom of God in terms of Scotian Synchronic Contingency. In fact taking once again Turretin as an example, he seems to have two ways of thinking of God's freedom. The first occurs as a feature of the role of God in creation, which stresses the aseity of God, and the source of creation in His powers of knowledge and wisdom. So the view is that God is indifferent, that is, sovereign over all operations of His perfections. God wills Himself necessarily, 'But other things he wills freely because, since no created thing is necessary with respect to God but contingent (as he could do without them), so he wills all things as that he could not will them (i.e. by the liberty not only of spontaneity, but also of indifference).[56]

The second account is given as part of his argument that creaturely liberty does not consist in indifference. '[J]ust in proportion to God's

55. See the discussion in Muller, *Divine Choice and Human Will*, p. 293.

56. Turretin, *Institutes*, I. p. 219.

liberty being more perfect than ours, so ought it to be farther removed from indifference (which instead of being a virtue is a defect of liberty.)'[57] We have already noted the distinction between different necessities. Here is the place to consider another distinction, between powers, *potentiae*. These are more central to Muller's interests, but when RO theologians consider them, they give no evidence in them of synchronic contingency. More on powers later.

Yet of the distinctions used by Vos and his group in their account of divine and human indeterminate freedom, the most relevant seems to be that between the 'simultaneity of potencies' and a 'potency of simultaneities' as discussed by the commentators in *RTF.*[58] Here at least there is an introduction of simultaneity. We shall examine how this distinction is understood and applied by Francis Turretin and others.

Turretin has this to say in elucidation of indifference. When a person prepares to choose, the will (a potency or 'power' of the soul) is indifferent in the sense that if A is the end or fulfillment of a choice it chooses for A, or if B then it chooses for B. If the mind is not made up, the will is likewise hesitant. 'We also confess that the will is indifferent as long as the intellect remains doubtful and uncertain whither to turn itself'.[59] This Turretin calls the *'simultaneity of power'*, it is the will considered in the abstract. This appears to be a necessity of free will, but not sufficient, for the sufficiency of freedom required for Turretin is not only the will but 'the previous light of reason and the judgment of the practical intellect'.[60]

Incidentally, in what follows later we shall be referring to the relation between the intellect and the will a good deal. For the theologians to be studied, the intellect is not confined to such activities as making sense of one's experience, or reasoning and deciding that what you thought was one issue is in fact more than one issue. It might be said that it is used here in a wider sense, taking in whatever factors that may influence the operations of the intellect. Central to the operations of the practical reason are a person's having or setting of objectives or goals. A person

57. Turretin, *Institutes,* I. p. 666.
58. *Reformed Thought on Freedom,* pp. 47, 193.
59. Turretin, *Institutes,* I. pp. 665-6.
60. ibid., I. p. 667.

may behave differently when he or she is in a crowd, or listening to music, saying or doing things which they may never have done alone. And think of the effects that emotions, or education, or tiredness, or the onset of certain moods solely or in combination may influence a person's goals, his choices.

Now consider the other half of the earlier distinction, the *power of simultaneity*. Does the will also have the power of willing ends such as A and B simultaneously? Can it choose A and B by acting one or the other at exactly the same moment? In this situation, what Turretin calls indifference 'in the second act' is not in the abstract but an act considered to be fully charged, fully informed.

> [W]hether the will (all requisites to acting being posited for the decree of God and his concourse; the judgment of the practical intellect etc.) is always so indifferent and undetermined that it can act or not act. This our opponents pretend in order that its own liberty may be left to the will. We deny it.[61]

Turretin states that his opponents the Socinians and Remonstrants hold the view that the choice is a matter of pure indifference, and that in this case of the mind being made up, the will, if it is free, remains indifferent and undetermined. Determined and yet undetermined, made up and yet it still can will to act or not. Turretin says 'This our opponents pretend in order that its own liberty may be left to the will. We deny it.'[62] Why do they deny it? Because when the will is made up its choice has been made up, and it is no longer indifferent, until the occasion of the next choice. The will is subject to the judgment of the intellect.

So here again is a scholastic distinction involving simultaneity, but one which the RO regard as inoperable once the mind is made up. This is the similar reaction of Samuel Willard.

> How far there is an *Indifference* to be acknowledged in the Will, respecting *Voluntary* actions, needs not here to be curiously discussed; only we may observe, that though there may such things be allowed to the Will, *in actu primo*, which the Schools call *Simultas potentiae*, by vertue whereof the Will, according to its own nature, is capable of acting or not acting, or acting either thus or contrarily; and is capable of acting thus now, and

---

61. ibid., I. p. 666.
62. ibid., I. p. 666.

is afterwards capable of revoking that act: nay indeed, this is root of the liberty of the Will. Nevertheless, *in actu secundo*, which the Schools call *Potentia Simultatis*, which is the Wills applying it self to its act, it doth not then *act Indifferently*, but upon choice, by which it is Determined.[63]

Take the expression 'Fido can be inside his kennel and outside it'. This cannot mean that Fido has a potency for simultaneities, for he cannot be inside and outside his kennel at one and the same time. But Fido can, at one and the same time, possess the power to be in his kennel and the power to be outside it. He has the simultaneity of potencies. 'The camera can shoot in colour and in black and white'; this also has the simultaneity of potencies. And so on. So the distinction can be employed with respect to non-human animals, to artefacts, like a camera, and also to men and women. But the dog or the camera cannot act differently at the same time.

Next

In this chapter we have set out Vos's views, and some of the problems it generates. One of the theological positions he chiefly finds fault with are Luther's and Calvin's alleged necessitarianism. He only makes one, rather disparaging, comment on Luther, but gives more attention to Calvin, who in a way is his chief target. The next two chapters are concerned with each of these two Reformers.

---

63. Samuel Willard, *A Brief Reply to Mr George Kieth* (Boston, Samuel Phillips 1703), p. 15.

CHAPTER 2

Martin Luther and Necessity

The first chapter has acquainted the reader with the philosophical and theological background, the terminology and some of the arguments, of Vos's account of freedom as synchronic contingency. This is his allegedly liberating riposte to the traditional picture of magisterial Protestant necessitarianism derived from 19th century central dogma scholarship. We have penciled in the weaknesses in his argument. What follows are two chapters that are mainly historical, one on Luther's necessitarianism, and then one on Calvin's alleged necessitarianism.

There is much about Martin Luther's (1483–1546) views of God's necessity, and the necessity of men and women, in his *The Bondage of the Will*. In it he displays a certain roughness and exuberance, extending to a disparagement of the two necessities that we noted in the last chapter. His admirer John Calvin later referred to Luther's 'hardness' of expression. In what follows our intention is to try to make a consistent and sympathetic account of such references in Luther. Finally we briefly meet his more polished colleague, Philip Melanchthon (1497–1560), who recoiled at Luther's roughness. From him we encounter a positive appreciation of the two necessities once again.

Besides critically referring to Calvin's necessitarianism, which we shall consider in the next chapter, Antonie Vos also claims that Luther was tarred with the same brush. He notes that the scholastic distinction between the *necessitas consequentiae* and *necessitas consequentis*, which he, Vos, regards as the cornerstone of contingency in the history of Christian theology, was 'ridiculed' by Luther in his *De Servo Arbitrio* (1525).[1]

---

1. Vos, 'Paul Helm on Medieval Scholasticism', p. 269.

Necessity and Contingency

We shall begin by getting clear what Luther understands to be the scope of divine necessity. In his text, the strands of which I will attempt to disentangle, the necessities often appear closely together. To begin with, Luther ascribes necessity to God Himself. God's 'will is essential and changeless, because His nature is so'.[2] These are among his emphatic expressions: He refers to '[T]he necessary being', who has 'a necessity of his own essential nature', who possesses 'a divine and necessary nature', and he asserts that 'God exists necessarily'.[3] The being of God is necessary, so he underlines that the 'godhead'[4] has necessity. This is necessity in the absolute sense, necessity of the consequent, arising from God's own nature. From at least some of these statements it seems that the existence of God is necessary in this strongest sense, a case of absolute necessity, the denial of which would issue in a self-contradiction. Luther does not here at least use any contrasting language about God. God is absolutely necessary in His being.

God's Attributes

Luther also has a set of remarks in which he distinguishes between God's being and His nature. God, who has necessary existence, possesses 'a divine and necessarily existent nature'.[5] So, in the second place, not God's bare existence but His character, His attributes, also exist necessarily. Luther does not affirm the simplicity of God but nor does he deny it, and it is reasonable to suppose that simplicity is presupposed. The attributes of God he highlights include His knowledge, His omniscience. They are exercised in God's own Trinitarian being, *ad intra*, and also in His creation, *ad extra*.

'It is, then, fundamentally necessary and wholesome for Christians to know that God foreknows nothing contingently, but that He foresees, purposes, and does all things according to His own, immutable, eternal

---

2. Luther, *The Bondage of the Will*, trans. and ed. J. I. Packer and O. R. Johnston (London, James Clarke and Co., 1957), p. 80.

3. ibid., p. 82.

4. ibid., p. 83.

5. ibid., p. 82.

and infallible will.' This bombshell knocks 'free will' flat.[6] His nature remains unchanged to all eternity. Without the belief 'that God foreknows and wills all things, not contingently, but necessarily and immutably, how can you believe, trust and rely on His promises?'[7]

> And how can you be thus sure and certain, unless you know that certainly, infallibly, immutably and necessarily, He knows, wills and will perform, what He promises? .... Not only should we be sure that God wills, and will execute his will, necessarily and immutably .... If, then, we are taught and believe that we ought to be ignorant of the necessary foreknowledge of God and the necessity of events, Christian faith is utterly destroyed, and the promises of God and the whole gospel fall to the ground completely ...[8]

Luther refers also to the 'powers' of God, an alternative way of referring to God's attributes, which are God, and so are likewise necessary. So far, so straightforward.

The Creation

Further, necessity extends to the creation, to God's relation to what He has brought about *ad extra*.[9] These acts of creation are also necessary. Luther brackets together the necessity of men and of things. '[A]s His nature remains unchanged to all eternity, so do His justice and kindness. And what is said of His justice and kindness must be said also of His knowledge, His wisdom, His goodness, His will, and the other Divine attributes.'[10]

What God necessarily foreknows must come to pass. Could not God have willed other than He has, in which the 'contents' of His foreknowledge would have been very different? It is not clear that in his zeal to assert the utter reliability of God against Erasmus, his target in *The Bondage of the Will*, Luther has clearly distinguished between the necessity of God's attributes and the necessity of the exercise of His attributes or powers as such in His creation.

For the term 'the necessity of God's foreknowledge' can be taken to refer to more than one thing. In regard to His nature, as we have seen,

---

6. ibid., p. 80.
7. ibid., pp. 83-4.
8. ibid., p. 84.
9. ibid., p. 84.
10. ibid., p. 80.

Luther regards this as absolutely necessary as God Himself is. But the phrase can be taken to refer to the content of God's knowledge, His foreknowledge of His works *ad extra*, the creation and His redeeming purposes. God could not only not fail to be all-knowing. The content of His knowledge could not fail to be as it is. As we shall see, there is evidence that Luther does not clearly distinguish between these two cases. At such a point, God is uniformly, and perhaps excessively, necessary.

Besides, the idea of God necessitating everything by His fore-knowledge has a flattening effect, as if God's animate creation is treated by Him in the same way as His inanimate creation. Unless Luther holds that all that God wills He is necessitated to will, then he allows no place for the contingency of the objects of divine action *ad extra*. It may be this ill-considered language on absolute necessity is what worried later the likes of Calvin.

Contingency

However, besides saying quite a lot on necessity, rather surprisingly Luther has various remarks on contingency, though these are fewer.

Our existence, were it to be truly mutable, would by this be contingent.

> [A]ll we do, however it may appear to us to be done mutably and contingently, is in reality done necessarily and immutably in respect of God's will.[11]

> Lest we be deceived over our terms, let me explain that *being done contingently* does not, in Latin, signify that the thing done is itself contingent, but that it is being done by a contingent and mutable will – such as *is not* to be found in God! And a deed cannot be called *contingent* unless we do it 'contingently' i.e. by chance (as it were) and without premeditation; that is, when our will or hand fastens on something presented to us as if by chance, without our having previously thought or planned anything about it.[12]

> If I come to exist of necessity, it does not much worry me that my existence and being are in themselves mutable; contingent and mutable as I am (and I am not God, the necessary Being), yet I still come to exist![13]

---

11. ibid., p. 80.
12. ibid., p. 81.
13. ibid., p. 82.

This chimes with his earlier remarks, 'God foreknows and wills all things, not contingently, but necessarily and immutably ....'[14]

Here Luther seems to distinguish God's necessity, and the contingency of our mutable selves. If so, it is at odds with what we have already considered. There are places where Luther's thought seems to have a divergence. It seems from the quotation just given that Luther holds on the one hand that in virtue of God's foreknowledge, which occurs necessarily, what He foreknows is itself necessary. But then he seems also to say that we human beings can perform contingent actions which are contingent because they occur without forethought. Or even that we ourselves have a necessary existence, but we do things necessarily by chance (and so they are not necessary). But he may be going on to say that there are no such contingent states. We shall consider this later.

Besides this, there is evidence of another sort that may help us to understand Luther, for there are places in which he compares and contrasts this view of God's necessity with that of other views. There are two of these.

Stoicism

The first of his contrasts is where Luther compares his position on necessity with what he takes to be Stoicism, conflating his necessitarianism with being in the same stable as the Stoics' fate.

> And why should these matters be thought so recondite for us Christians that it is irreligious, idle, and vain to study and know them, when they are on the lips of heathen poets and ordinary people so frequently? How often does Vergil, for one, mention Fate. 'All things stand fixed by law immutable.' Again, 'Fixed is the day of every man.' Again, 'If the Fates summon you'. Again 'If thou shalt break the binding cord of Fate.'[15] The poet simply seeks to show that in the destruction of Troy and the beginnings of the Roman empire Fate did more than all the efforts of men. Indeed, he makes even his immortal gods subject to Fate. Jupiter and Juno themselves needs must yield to it.[16]

---

14. ibid., pp. 83-4.
15. Vergil. *Aeneid*, pp. 2.234, 6.883, 7.314, 10.465.
16. Luther, *The Bondage of the Will*, p. 83.

What he calls Stoic fate looks like universal fate ('All things are fixed by laws immutable') and while Luther does not say that his views equate with such fate, the fact is that he thinks that it was not uncommon to encounter such views in classical literature, and in everyday remarks, and that they are as strong as the necessitarian theological views he was defending. This also may have worried his friends. We shall see later that the RO had a rather ambivalent attitude to such fate, echoing Augustine's hesitation of using the word. Perhaps at this point Luther seems like this: If you can be serious about the fate of the Stoics, why can you not similarly be serious about God's necessity?

'Sophists'

The other view that Luther compared his own with are those he called 'Sophists'. Threaded through the various discussions of necessity in the book is Luther's discussion of the medieval distinction between what we earlier called the two necessities, *the necessity of the consequent* and *the necessity of the consequence* that we have seen Vos has such stock in. Luther's supportive attitude to the various applications of necessity that we have noted him use – the necessity of God's being, the necessity of the powers of His various attributes, and of His works of creation *ad extra* – are strengthened by his scornful treatment of this distinction, and are revealing of his position.

As we have already seen, in the first chapter, the distinction between the necessity of the consequent and the necessity of the consequence can be understood if we consider different ways in which necessity can be generated. If the necessity comes from conditions that are themselves necessary, this is a necessity of the consequent. (This is what Luther is favouring so far.) So if from God's necessary omniscience He knows the future then the future is a case of the necessity of the consequent, in this case divine omniscience, which is also necessary. If by contrast the necessity is the result of contingent circumstances, such as may not have been, such as a divine promise, or a prophecy, then what is promised, or prophesied, is a case of the necessity of the consequence.[17]

We will trace the importance of this distinction at the end of the next chapter. As we will see in the case of Calvin, the distinction is

---

17. Richard. A. Muller, *Dictionary of Latin and Greek Theological Terms*, pp. 1985, 200.

illustrated by the scriptural proof of Christ's bones being unbreakable, in John 19. Christ's bones were ordinary bones, not made of titanium or ceramic, say, but these ordinary bones were protected from being broken by a word from the Lord, by His 'singular providence' as Calvin puts it. They were not intrinsically unbreakable bones, a case of the necessity of the consequent, but by that word of prophecy from the Lord, they remained breakable to the end, yet none of the Messiah's bones could in fact be broken, which is a case of the necessity of the consequence. The prophetic word, being a divine word, was immutably sure, and thus its occurrence was immutable, ensuring that though the Messiah's bones were breakable they could in fact never be broken.

In his estimate of this distinction of the two necessities, Luther's reaction is to regard it as a 'sophistical' distinction, a scholastic distinction as he called it. Luther rather angrily reacts to it as follows:

> This is a point over which the Sophists have toiled for many years now (and have been defeated at last, and forced to give in): they maintained that *all things take place necessarily, but by necessity of consequence* (as they put it), *and not by necessity of the thing consequent* .... I shall not find it hard to show how unreal the distinction is. By *necessity of consequence,* they mean, roughly speaking, this: If God wills something, then it must needs be; but that which thus comes to be is something which of itself need not be; for only God exists necessarily, and everything else can cease to be, if God so wills. This is to say that God's action is necessary, if He wills it, but the thing done is not in itself necessary. But what do they establish by this play on words? This, I suppose – the thing done is not necessary; that is, it has no necessity in its own essential nature; which is just to say, that the thing done is not God Himself! Nonetheless, it remains true that each thing *does* happen necessarily, if God's action is necessary or there is a necessity of consequence, however true it may be that it does *not* happen necessarily, in the sense that it is not God and has no necessity of its own essential nature.[18]

This passage may be what Vos calls Luther's 'ridiculing' this distinction of the two necessities.[19] He appears to repudiate the idea of necessity arising from a state of affairs that has 'no necessity in its own essential

---

18. Luther, *The Bondage of the Will*, pp. 81-2.
19. 'Paul Helm on Medieval Scholasticism', p. 269.

nature'. That is, the distinction drawn by the 'Sophists' is one without a difference. What is Luther's argument for this conclusion?

Notice that Luther says, 'Nonetheless, it remains true that each thing does happen necessarily'. That is, that if the two necessities cover all the events in the creation, all these events occur necessarily. If everything is what Aristotle called hypothetically necessary, then it is necessary, and he added (unjustifiably), an absolute necessary.

This is perhaps the place to look a little further at the meaning of 'necessitarian'. Despite the fact Vos thinks that necessitarianism is of central importance, he nowhere, as far as I can see, says clearly what it means. With Luther's help we can say theistic necessitarianism is the view that everything that occurs is due to the outcome of God's absolute will. A weaker view would be that what are necessities are due to the action of God's free choice. A view that is not directly theistic is that of Stoic fate, that what God can bring about is due to factors external to Him that bring about His will. All these are kinds of 'necessitarian'.

The passage in Luther above continues,

> Nonetheless, it remains true that each thing *does* happen necessarily, if God's action is necessary or there is a necessity of consequence, however true it may be that it does *not* happen necessarily, in the sense that it is not God and has no necessity of its own essential nature. If I come to exist of necessity, it does not much worry me that my existence and being are in themselves mutable; contingent and mutable as I am (and I am not God, the necessary Being), yet I still come to exist![20]

So he holds that each alternative of the distinction is equally necessary in that it is equally the action of God, so he, Luther, comes to exist of necessity. But he is silent on the status of the actions of such a person. Are they necessary or not? So we see here that Luther is willing to concede the distinction, he is necessary in his existence if he exists by God's will, but not that all his actions are similarly necessary. So once again he seems to entertain the idea that someone can be necessary in accordance with God's will, and yet have contingent or mutable features. He does not reflect on the expression 'hypothetical necessity' but he, somewhat grudgingly, it must be said, makes place for contingent things made necessary by God's will.

---

20. Luther, *The Bondage of the Will*, p. 82.

Later in *The Bondage of the Will* he returns to the distinction between the necessary and the contingent. His forthrightness is further supported by his dislike of the Sophists. Luther himself is to reaffirm this conclusion later in the book.[21]

> The fancy about the necessity of *consequence* and of the thing *consequent* was refuted earlier. Let the Diatribe[22] invent and go on inventing, let it quibble and quibble again – If God foreknows that Judas would be a traitor, Judas became a traitor of necessity, and it was not in the power of Judas or of any creature to act differently, or to change his will, from that which God had foreseen. It is true that Judas acted willingly, and not under compulsion, but his willing was the work of God, brought into being by His omnipotence.[23]

Here, at the close of the quotation, he makes the distinction in human acts between acting willingly and acting under compulsion. Luther initially stated that God exists necessarily, that His attributes exist necessarily, and in creation and providence, necessity reigns. These statements are obviously necessitarian, in that he holds that the scholastic distinction between the necessity of the consequence and of the consequent yield necessitarian conclusions. Luther does not have any clear conception that God could have acted otherwise. But there are places where he wobbles in another direction.

There is an emerging pattern of forthrightness for necessitarianism, but alongside which are what we may call Luther's 'second thoughts', which are usually left undeveloped. One of these second thoughts is expressed in his dislike of the term 'necessity' as being harsh. For all his emphatic approval of the necessity of God's will he says he 'dislikes the word',[24] because it can be confused with compulsion. For this reason, and perhaps for other reasons, he toys with the expression 'necessity of infallibility',[25] but nevertheless discards it. Or perhaps does not develop it. The expression 'necessity of infallibility', another sophistical expression, is a reference to what God's foreknowledge renders the occurrence of future

---

21. ibid., e.g. pp. 213, 221-2.
22. The title of Erasmus's book that Luther was refuting.
23. Luther, *The Bondage of the Will*, p. 213.
24. ibid., e.g. pp. 81, 102, 212-3.
25. ibid., p. 220.

events certain, but it does not, unlike in divine predestination, necessitate the occurrence of them. Some of the RO come to make this distinction, too, as we shall see later, yet it was not, I think, universally held.

The distinction that Luther makes between voluntariness and compulsion at the level of human choice suggests that he favours overall a version of compatibilism, for the making of that distinction is characteristic of that outlook. He mentions during the earlier remarks on necessity: 'The will, whether it be God's or man's, does what it does, good or bad, under no compulsion, but just as it wants or pleases, as if totally free. Yet the will of God, which rules over our mutable will, is changeless and sure.'[26] These words bring together the tension for Luther we saw earlier, between the necessity of a man's existence and the contingency of his spontaneous, voluntary thoughts and actions.

Necessity and Compulsion

It remains significant, however, throughout his compressed (it must be said) impatient discussion in his *Bondage* of the sorts of necessity, or rather between their various applications, that Luther states that he dislikes the language of God *necessitating events in his creation*, because the word suggests compulsion. Here is his earlier statement in full:

> I could wish, indeed, that a better term was available for our discussion, than the accepted one, *necessity*, which cannot accurately be used of either man's will, or God's. Its meaning is too harsh, and foreign to the subject; for it suggests some sort of compulsion, and something that is against one's will, which is no part of the view under debate. The will, whether it be God's or man's, does what it does, good or bad, under no compulsion, but just as it wants or pleases, as if totally free. Yet the will of God, which rules over our mutable will, is changeless and sure – as Boetius sings, 'Immovable Thyself, Thou movement giv'st to all;' and our will, principally because of its corruption, can do no good of itself.[27]

It is the misleadingness of these expressions that worried him, not so much God's own necessity. Such unease is not by any means unique to Luther.

---

26. ibid., p. 81.

27. ibid., p. 81. This is a quotation from Boethius, *The Consolation of Philosophy*, trans. V. E. Watts (Harmondsworth, Middx, Penguin Books, 1969).

God's Liberty

Interestingly, later on, in his discussion of Erasmus's treatment of biblical texts, he says much the same about the necessity of God's power and foreknowledge except that he, surprisingly, after all he has said about God's necessity, ascribes God's exercise of power and knowledge to His liberty. Besides existing necessarily, '… if the foreknowledge and omnipotence of God are conceded, it naturally follows by irrefutable logic that we were not made by ourselves, nor live by ourselves, nor do anything by ourselves, but by His omnipotence'.[28] In what sense then does God have liberty, and we have contingency? He is 'the living and true God [who] must be One who by His own liberty imposes necessity on us.'[29] If Luther really means this, then he seems to have abandoned his dislike of the distinction between the two kinds of necessity. This looks like a kind of two stage view that we will say more about later: God exists, who may act necessarily, and yet who brings about His creatures freely. In this discussion Luther considers the will of God at length for what seems the first time.

At first glance it looks like Luther must hold that alternativity is at least a part of this divine liberty that he brings into play. But he does not say this. It could be that by God's liberty he simply has in mind only God's freedom from the influence of external factors or forces. But he does not say this either. God's liberty in the sense of His having the power of alternativity is one central place at which Luther's friends may later on seek to qualify his roughness of expression.

This is perhaps another of his 'second thoughts', like references to the necessity of immutability arising from God's foreknowledge, and the postulation of God's freedom, and necessity, and compulsion in contingent human choice. However, even in this later discussion there are expressions in which he reverts to his original 'refutation'.[30] It is difficult to thread them together to make a consistent position.

'… He [God] loves and hates according to His eternal and immutable nature. Thus it is that unexpected incidents and passions do not overtake God. And it is just this that compels the conclusion that there is no such

28. ibid., pp. 216-7.

29. ibid., p. 216.

30. ibid., pp. 213, 221, 226.

thing as 'free will': namely, the fact that the love and hate of God towards men is immutable and eternal, existing, not merely before there was any merit or work of "free-will", but before the world was made; and that all things take place in us of necessity, according as He has from eternity loved or not loved.'[31]

His denial of free will may be a reference to the indeterministic views of the 'sophists'.

In this response to Erasmus' *Diatribe*, Luther's method is to focus entirely upon the teaching of Scripture. For all his love of paradox, he devotes great attention to its detail.[32] In particular he pays attention to the grammatical mood of the expressions of Scripture, insisting that the passages that Erasmus cites which are imperatives to keep the law, 'prove and establish nothing about the ability of man, but only lay down what is and is not to be done'. Otherwise they would imply that mankind possessed full ability to observe what is commanded, which not even Erasmus thinks is the case. Later on he has a pretty full defense of the need to interpret Scripture *grammatically*, and not *figuratively*.[33]

Despite Luther's rather combative and crude discussions, and the unsatisfactoriness of his conclusions, trailing loose ends, he has enough distinctions, like ammunition in his arsenal, to lead to a more nuanced and definitive conclusion to divine and human necessity.

Luther, Melanchthon and Calvin

But it fell to Luther's friend Philip Melanchthon (1497–1560) to address the question of divine freedom and these other issues more satisfactorily. In the remainder of this chapter I shall consider Melanchthon's influence in his *Loci Communes*, and on Calvin's initial enthusiasm for Melanchthon, expressed for example in his Preface to his French translation of *Loci Communes* in 1546. Calvin's enthusiasm was later to be followed by his opposition to Melanchthon based on the Lutheran's weakening allegiance to the Augustinian conception of predestination.

What a survey of Luther's terminology used in *The Bondage of the Will* reveals is that while his language is rough in his treatment of necessity,

---

31. ibid., p. 226.
32. ibid., p. 101.
33. ibid., pp. 194-5.

he also recognized the validity of other terms, such as 'contingent'[34] and 'immutable', the contrast between 'caused' and 'compelled', and 'mutable'.[35] He uses 'necessitating' but he does not like it, as it seems when used of God to have the connotation of compulsion,[36] rather than of liberty.[37] So he has the tools to develop his account of God and His creatures, to put a brake on his own impulsiveness.

Melanchthon took little time in smoothing Luther's 'roughness'. His first edition of *Loci Communes* (1521), then in 1522 and subsequent editions, echo Luther's views and do not contain any direct criticism of him. But in later editions (1522 and subsequently) he modified a number of Luther's emphases, including those on freedom and necessity, and later, on predestination.[38] In later editions in 1544–5, and in 1555, he finesses Luther's views further. Here we shall be concerned with the locus 'Of God' and that on free will (Locus V) of the 1555 edition.[39]

Melanchthon's softening of Luther's thought in his *Loci Communes* shows in various ways. He revised the section on free will. In the chapter 'Of the Origin of Sin' he, without the qualifications that we have seen Luther make, distinguished between the necessity and contingency of human acts, and on good works which follow with the *necessitas consequentiae*, the necessity of the consequence.[40]

Initially Calvin admired Melanchthon as a fellow humanist, and a faithful evangelical. And as one who softened Luther's harsher expressions. It is only over Melanchthon's later disenchantment with predestination that he and Calvin fell out. As part of Calvin's controversy with Jerome Bolsec (d. 1585), a Carmelite monk who showed an interest

---

34. ibid., p. 80.
35. ibid., p. 82.
36. ibid., p. 81.
37. ibid., p. 206.
38. His rejection of predestination comes in a later phase of his thinking. Initially Calvin agreed with Melanchthon, and said so warmly, but could not abide his repudiation of predestination. He boiled over after Melanchthon's death in 1560. (See Gregory B. Graybill, *Evangelical Free Will, Philipp Melanchthon's Doctrinal Journey on the Origins of Faith*) (Oxford, Oxford University Press, 2010), pp. 310-11.
39. Philip Melanchthon, *Loci Communes* (first edition 1521), translated by Clyde Manschreck, with an Introduction by Hans Engelland (New York, Oxford University Press, 1965).
40. ibid., pp. 48f.

in Protestantism and visited Geneva in 1551, to whom as well as to Pighius, Calvin may have directed his *On the Eternal Predestination of God* (1552).[41] Melanchthon's moderating of Luther's harsh expressions was one thing; undertaking a radical theological revision was altogether another. We shall see the significance of Calvin's view in the next chapter, using it as a supplement to what we learn of Calvin's opinion of Luther's view of divine absolute necessity.

Melanchthon's *Loci Communes*, a compendium of Lutheran theology, echoes Luther's views and does not contain any direct criticism of him. But as we have already noted, in later editions Melanchthon modified a number of Luther's emphases, including those on freedom and necessity. In the editions in 1544–5 and in 1555, he finesses Luther's views further. Here we shall be concerned with the locus 'Of God' (Locus I) with locus IV, 'Of the Origin of Sin' and with that on 'Of Human Strength and Free Will' (Locus V) in the 1555 edition.

It is in Locus IV, 'Of the Origin of Sin, That Man Was Not and Furthermore Is Not Forced to Sin,' that he shows his greatest difference from Luther in his treatment of human nature, evil and especially free will (IV-V). He states that God is not the cause of evil, nor does He will it, nor does He compel or drive men to sin.[42] Man himself and the devils, and then men of their own free wills, unforced by God, departed from God and fell into sin. It is at this point that his modifying of Luther's assertions become evident.

The most obvious and striking feature of the chapter in the *Loci Communes* is that *the necessity of the consequent* and *the necessity of the consequence* are deployed without reserve. Generally, the result of their full deployment is clean contrary to what seems to be Luther's rather scornful skepticism of the distinction, and it enables Melanchthon, again generally, to give an account that does not have the flattening effect that was noted earlier of the rather indiscriminate character of Luther's necessitarianism.

Writing of what God does and permits (Luther rarely if ever has room for God's permission), Melanchthon says,

41. John Calvin, *On the Eternal Predestination of God* (1552), trans, J. K. S. Reid (London James Clarke and Co., 1961).

42. Melanchthon, *Loci Communes*, p. 45.

This raises complicated arguments about necessity and contingency, *de necessitate et contingentia*, that is, whether everything – the good and the evil, the holy and the sinful – must happen as it does, whether David *had* to commit adultery, and so on. And in particular to affirm that 'God does not desire sin, that he effects nothing pertaining to sin, and that sinful deeds *do not of necessity* happen.'[43]

We must note that 'to be necessary' or 'must be' have different meanings and usage, different 'degrees' as he puts it. The first applies to God: He is necessary in an absolute sense, necessary in Himself. God is necessarily eternal, omnipotent, living, wise, good and righteous. It cannot be otherwise. This is *necessitas absoluta,* absolute necessity.[44]

This material on Luther shows him somewhat confused but nevertheless aware of two things, God's necessity but also His freedom, as well as the contingency of certain states. But there are no definitions, and a general unsatisfactoriness of the discussion to which Calvin is sensitive. This is the moderating of Luther's deficiencies by Melanchthon, whom Calvin, as a fellow humanist, initially sides with. The idea that he took that distinction from Melanchthon is by no means certain given what Calvin said in his *Concerning the Eternal Predestination of God* about 'the schools'. We shall see these factors playing out in Calvin's thought in the next chapter.

Luther, Calvin and Pighius

In 1542 the Louvain theologian Albertus Pighius (1490–1542) published an extensive critique of, among other Reformation writings, the 1539 edition of Calvin's *Institutes*. Pighius's criticisms were entitled *Ten Books on Human Free Choice and Divine Grace*. The 'books' were in effect chapters. So concerned was Calvin to get out a reply, that he divided Pighius's book and produced his *Defence of the Sound and Orthodox Doctrine of the Bondage and Liberation of Human Choice against the misrepresentations of Albert Pighius of Kampen*[45] in time for display and sale at the 1543 Frankfurt book fair. He dedicated it to Melanchthon.

---

43. ibid., p. 48.

44. ibid., p. 49.

45. John Calvin, *The Bondage and Liberation of the Will: A Defence of the Orthodox Doctrine of Human Choice against Pighius.* (1543) Ed. A. N. S. Lane, trans, G. I. Davies (Grand Rapids, Baker, 1996).

Pighius had by this time died and Calvin dropped the idea of writing further 'in order not to insult a dead dog', as he delicately expressed it. But predestination had become a hot topic with the Bolsec affair in Geneva in 1551, so Calvin finished his critique of Pighius, in his *Concerning the Eternal Predestination of God*, in 1552.

Pighius's book was not only an attack on Calvin, but on Luther as well. As a consequence Calvin's *Bondage and Liberation of the Will*, dedicated to Melanchthon, contains a number of Calvin's comments on Luther's character and achievements, perhaps more than anywhere else. Writing of Luther's character and of Pighius' attack on it, among the things that Calvin says that Pighius alleges are that:

> [M]ost of [Luther's] doctrines are so absurd (and especially that one with which we are dealing), concerning the bondage of human choice, that if you want to persuade anyone of them, you have first to pluck out the "eyes" of his mind and take away all his rational sense. With what mean reproaches [Pighius] rails at that proposition, [to disown fleshly reason], which among those who bear the name of Christian ought no more to have to admit of debate than that God is one![46]

Calvin began with trying to understand Pighius's confused reaction to Luther:

> For since he could see that the statement of Luther's about absolute necessity which he quotes was less in agreement with the common understanding of mankind, he thought that this very point would be the most promising place for him to begin, so as to have the mind of the flesh agreeing with him but shuddering at the teaching of Luther.[47]

These are among others of Calvin's references to Luther in the book:

> He [Luther] was not seeking to deprive them [good works] of their praise and their reward before God .... It is certain that whatever good works can be cited do not please God by virtue of their own worth but by his gracious favour, because he wills to value them so much, even though they do not deserve it.[48]

Because of Luther's use of 'absolute necessity', Pighius emphasised it in his response and made it serve as a remark regarding the bondage of

---

46. ibid., pp. 24-5.
47. ibid., p. 36.
48. ibid., p. 26.

the will to sin, so misunderstanding this. Here are other comments of Calvin's concerning Luther's character and language.[49]

> Concerning Luther there is no reason to be in any doubt … that we consider him a distinguished apostle of Christ whose labour and ministry have done most in these times to bring back the purity of the gospel.[50]

> Again, it is not on his own authority that Luther condemns the whole of human nature as it is marred and corrupted after the fall, but he assents to the verdict of God, the most excellent and supreme Judge, against which no appeal is permitted.[51]

> It is also true that Philip Melanchthon, by careful and very adept softening of the outward form of some things which Luther had written in scholastic language, in a style alien to popular taste, accommodated them to the general mass of humanity and to common usage …[52]

And finally,

> But that teaching which is the chief issue in this controversy and the cause of everything else that is said we defend today just as it was put forward by Luther and others at the beginning. Even in those matters which I have declared to be not so necessary for faith there is no difference, apart from the softening of the form of expression so as to remove anything displeasing.[53]

It is part of our project to try to get a little closer to what concerned Calvin in what Luther said. What are these forms of expression and what was displeasing about them? Note what Calvin says of the need to soften Luther's form of expression. Each of them subscribed to God's sovereignty and to the bondage to sin of the wills of fallen humanity. But it is likely that Luther was in need of 'softening' because his account of these positions was disorderly by the abandon with which he ascribed

---

49. ibid., p. 36.

50. ibid., p. 28.

51. ibid., p. 49.

52. As we have seen, Philip Melanchthon took little time before he engaged in the softening of Luther's roughness. And as we have seen, his *Loci Communes* (first edition 1521) echoes Luther's views and does not contain any direct criticism of Luther. But in later editions he modified a number of Luther's emphases, including on freedom and necessity. In later editions in 1544–5 and in 1555, he finesses Luther's views further. See 'Of Human Strength and Free Will' (Locus V) in the 1555 edition.

53. Calvin, *The Bondage and Liberation of the Will*, p. 29.

'absolute necessity' of creaturely power. He showed that Pighius was himself confused between the providence of God, by which God rules over all, and the bondage of the human will to sin, a spiritual malady. Here is Calvin rather excitedly making this point against Pighius:

> I could wish that I had an opponent who would attack me from every side but not rush at me in a blind and confused combat as this man does, for, having resolved to discuss two different issues separately, he now mixes them up together. He says: If even to think anything good or evil is in nobody's power, but everything happens by 'absolute necessity' ... But he has undertaken to deal with the providence of God, on which this necessity depends, elsewhere, and this is just what he does in the last four books of his work. Why then does he now mix up this issue with the other one? Let him say whatever he has to say, even if it is weak, even if it is worthless; if only he will stay in one place, I will let him say it. But now that he has brought forward two issues for debate, and undertaken that he will speak about each one separately, why does he not fulfill in his actual discourse the promise which he made before? When he everywhere boasts that he is a good practitioner of orderly discourse, I dare not ascribe [his mixing issues together] to his inexperience; I know that it is done out of cunning and malice. For since he could see that the statement of Luther about absolute necessity which he quotes was less in agreement with the common understanding of mankind, he thought that this very point would be the most promising place for him to begin, so as to have the mind of the flesh agreeing with him but shuddering at the teaching of Luther.[54]

There are two sorts of necessity, one having to do with human sin and failure, the other to do with divine providence. But Pighius has mixed them up! And, Calvin implies, so had Luther's language a tendency to do so. Hence his expression requires 'softening'.[55]

Calvin asserted that Scripture teaches that fortuitous events are directed by the will of God. But to many this suggests Stoic fate. As we recall, Luther stressed the similarity between Stoicism, and God's necessitating of all things; in contrast Calvin makes a sharp distinction between the two in his second book on Pighius:

---

54. ibid., pp. 35-6

55. Paul Helm, 'Calvin, the "Two Issues", and the Structure of the *Institutes*.' *Calvin Theological Journal*, p. 42 (2007), pp. 341-348.

The nature of the Stoics' supposition is known. They weave their fate out of a Gordian complex of causes. In this they involve God Himself, making golden chains, as in the fable, with which to bind Him, so that He becomes subject to inferior causes. The astrologers of today imitate the Stoics, for they hold that an absolute necessity for all things originates from the position of the stars. Let the Stoics have their fate; for us, the free will of God disposes all things.[56]

In Stoicism God is subject to the course of nature, but for Calvin (and for Luther?) God is free, free from outside influences and most certainly from the necessitating forces of 'inferior causes'.[57] For Calvin, the necessity of events is the consequence of God's decree, while God's freedom is the source of contingency in the world. As Calvin goes on,

> Yet it seems absurd to remove contingency from the world. I omit to mention the distinctions employed in the schools. What I hold is, in my judgment, simple and needs no force to accommodate it usefully to life. What necessarily happens is what God decrees, and is therefore not exactly or of itself necessary by nature. I find a familiar example on the bones of Christ. Scripture testifies that Christ assumed a body quite like our own. That its bones were frangible no sane man doubts. But another and distinguishable question seems to arise here, whether any bone of His could be broken. For all things must necessarily remain intact and unimpaired because they are so determined by the fixed decree of God. And though I shrink from the received forms of speech, and the distinction between absolute and consequential necessity, I use them, but only lest any subtlety should prevent even the most simple of my readers from understanding what I say. Hence, considered naturally, the bones of Christ were frangible; but considered in the decree of God, which in His own time was manifested, they were no more liable to fracture than angels to the troubles of humanity. But though it is proper for us to regard the order of nature as divinely determined, I do not at all reject contingency in regard to human understanding.[58]

Given what he says about the divine decrees, and considering their importance in his theology, what he writes has considerable significance.

---

56. Calvin, *Concerning the Eternal Predestination of God*, p. 170..

57. ibid., p. 170.

58. ibid., p. 170.

This is a rather unpolished account of the two necessities, and maybe somewhat reluctantly delivered. But Calvin clearly sees the point. And in the definitive version of his *Institutes* several years later, in 1559, he gives a full and ungrudging version, as will be seen in the next chapter. Calvin seems to say that what is needed is a recognition of the contingency of God's action, though he does not mention Luther's stress on divine necessity in so many words. Significantly, he says not a word about synchronic contingency. He is a little more circumspect on necessity than Luther. He affirms that there are things that God might have done that He did not do,[59] the point that Luther seems to have been unclear about. God's will is not subject to what He has created, but rather He is the creation's Lord.

Also, Calvin offers something else that is mostly missing in Luther, the evidence provided by Augustine's writings against Pelagius. In his *Bondage* Luther, a member of the Augustinian Order, occasionally cites Augustine,[60] but first and foremost he is bent on tackling Erasmus' interpretation of Scripture. Calvin makes good use of Augustine not only to make clear the Bishop of Hippo's view of the bondage of the will, but to see, as Augustine did, the connectedness of the bondage of the will with other matters, and so to set them out more systematically than Luther what we may call the grammar of grace. Augustine features because Pighius had seriously misunderstood him, and Calvin wanted to put the record straight.

In this chapter we have seen Calvin edge towards acceptance of the two necessities, and thus of contingency. In the next chapter I try to answer the charge that Calvin is a necessitarian and show that he makes room for contingency via the room provided by the distinction of the two necessitates. There is an abundance of evidence that in very general terms, whether the result of struggle or of further reflection, God Himself is necessary, having *aseitas*, but that His actions, as His decrees, are contingent, though with necessitating effects, and that He created humankind as compatibilist. That Calvin's own views are compatibilist is shown in *Calvin at the Centre*.[61]

---

59. Where he mentions contingency, the French has 'as for what is called contingency, it means that things can happen in one way rather than another' (p. 170 fn. 1).

60. Luther, *The Bondage of the Will*, pp. 137-8, 142, 148.

61. Paul Helm, *Calvin at the Centre* (Oxford, Oxford University Press, 2010), Chapter 8, 'Calvin the Compatibilist.'

Melanchthon was held in high esteem by Luther, who died in 1546. The topical method of his *Loci Communes* was made for the making of careful distinctions, and it became the standard way among Protestants of organizing theologies thereafter. The theme of necessity was prominent in Locus I 'Of God', and in Locus V 'Of Human Strength and Free Will'.

The treatment is notably Lutheran with a focus on the need to know who God is in order that Christian prayers may be properly focused and addressed, and faith informed. He notes without criticism the knowledge of God among the heathen, implanted by God Himself. Yet this is only the knowledge of the law.[62] He stresses that this natural understanding must be surpassed by the knowledge of God's goodness and grace, the law supplanted by the gospel. He then turns to the nature of God, as He is in the 'many clear divine statements' in His word.

Calvin at first seems to go along with this, as seen in the Preface to the French translation of the *Loci Communes*, published in 1543, dedicated to Melanchthon, in which he refers to 'a most famous man, Philipp Melanchthon'. But later, perhaps he was irked by Melanchthon's remarks on what the Lutheran took to be Calvin's Stoic-like view of predestination, Melanchthon giving him the nickname 'Zeno', the name of an early Stoic, in 1552. Calvin evidently did not like nicknames, and drew a line at this, and persistently undermined Melanchthon thereafter. Nonetheless, I surmise that the one enduring thing he picked up from Melanchthon, if from no one else, was likely to have been the importance of the distinction between the two senses of necessity used in the later editions of the *Loci Communes*. These appeared to be more enduring and appeared in his second book on Pighius, that on predestination, published in 1552, as we have seen. And then more clearly in the 1559 *Institutes*, as we are about to see.

---

62. Melanchthon, *Loci Communes*, Loci V-VI.

CHAPTER 3

John Calvin, Necessity and Contingency

Earlier we distinguished between that kind of necessitarianism in which God, the creator of all, necessitates every change in His creation, and 'Stoic fate' in which God Himself is necessitated by influences external to Him, which are deplored as demeaning and belittling to the divine sufficiency and sovereignty. There are reasons from Calvin's writings to think that it is the first kind of necessitarianism that he favours, not the stronger, second version, in which God Himself is necessitated by factors outside Him. For him this second version would be indistinguishable from 'Stoic fate' which Calvin certainly does not favour.

In a number of places Antonie Vos has argued for the pivotal significance for Reformed Theology of Duns Scotus's concept of synchronic contingent freedom. He says that it frees Christian theology from necessitarianism, due especially to the influence of Aristotle. He has claimed that many (if not all) of the RO theologians adopted this Scotistic standpoint, both in their theological anthropology and in their doctrine of God. In so doing, he alleges, they successfully avoided the necessitarianism of Calvin's theology. Here, focusing exclusively on the doctrine of God, I aim to cast doubt on this necessitarian reading of Calvin. I also questioned the success of accounting for divine freedom in terms of synchronic contingency. The upshot of these two arguments, if successful, will be to show that *contra* Vos, the RO are in continuity with Calvin's doctrine of God rather than being a decisive modification of it along Scotistic lines.

This has the consequence that God may be an absolutely necessary Creator, while in respect of His creatures He gives them free choice, in the case of human beings the creaturely freedom of compatibilism. Vos seems to think that if God is an absolutely necessary Creator then everything He creates must possess a nature which necessitates its actions. This might reasonably be imputed to phrases of Luther's outlook, but this is obviously not Calvin's view.

Vos is unconvinced by the Renaissance historiography that sees a general breakdown of traditional medieval thought around 1600, with the birth of modern philosophy then filling the void left behind.[1] Rather, he says, the history of western universities shows strong continuity into the period of Reformed scholasticism. Within this trajectory Vos contends that Christian theology decisively broke free of Aristotelian influence employing the innovations of the Franciscan Duns Scotus in the thirteenth century, particularly his proposals regarding synchronic contingency.

> During the second half of the sixteenth century one went to great lengths in order to become familiar with the grand theology of the medieval past. The Iberian thinkers of Spain's and Portugal's Golden Age set an example. In the course of this reorientation Scotus' legacy became a major influence. Even the authoritative handbook of theology—Thomas Aquinas's *Summa Theologiae*—was read through Scotistically-tinted glasses. In this way the medieval heritage bore reformational fruit. The medieval point of view became a key in understanding reformed theology. In order to see the link between Augustinian theology and Scotus' innovations on the one hand and old reformed thought on the other hand, we need the historical background of medieval philosophical thought in contrast with ancient philosophy.[2]

So we are to see the newly-established Reformed universities – particularly such as Heidelberg and Leiden – as in continuity with the medieval university centres – such as Salamanca and Padua – and benefitting from the Scotistic innovations of the thirteenth century. These innovations are not to be underestimated:

> Duns Scotus reconstructed the doctrine of God at the end of the thirteenth century. One of the improvements he made was his answer to the question of what status had to be assigned to the divine knowledge of what is contingent. In the tradition of the theology of the church it was not disputed *that* God

---

1. Vos, 'Scholasticism and Reformation', p. 101.
2. ibid., p. 117.

knows the contingent, but could one call God's knowledge of the contingent itself contingent? Scotus' answer was affirmative: divine knowledge of the contingent is in the synchronic sense contingent. Herewith we have in fact met a quite important, non-deterministic conceptual infrastructure.[3]

It is claimed that this Scotian innovation was taken up by Reformed Orthodox theologians – Vos cites the work of Franciscus Gomarus (1563–1641) at Leiden, among others – in order to nullify the deterministic implications of Calvin's theology.[4] Those who interpret Gomarus and Dordt according to the harsh lines of this determinism in which 'God's fatherly face is hidden behind the concept of absolute power',[5] have failed to discern the influence of Scotus on post-Calvinian Reformed theology, both upon the doctrine of God and on anthropology. Vos thinks that these views are perhaps not surprising since Reformed Orthodoxy was a *terra incognita* until quite recently.[6]

For him, the sign of adherence to Scotist synchronic contingency is adherence to the two necessities distinction. But we have seen in the last chapter that Melanchthon observed it, with no sign of synchronic contingency. And Peter Martyr Vermigli (1498–1562) is another case in point: adherence to the two necessities formulae is a sign of a doctrine of God's freedom, and what seems to be a compatibilist view of free will.[7] This chapter will attempt to consolidate this conclusion by adding the case of Calvin.

Calvin's 'Necessitarianism'

In the previous chapter we have seen how Calvin came to utilize the two necessities, which I surmised may have come to Calvin via Melanchthon, but without any commitment to synchronic contingency. In 'The Systematic Place of Reformed Scholasticism: Reflections Concerning the Reception of Calvin's Thought,'[8] Vos has a discussion of Calvin's attitude

---

3. ibid., pp. 113-4.

4. ibid., p. 111. Another reference to Gomarus (on providence) can be found in Vos, 'The Systematic Place of Reformed Scholasticism', pp. 36-8.

5. ibid., p. 114.

6. ibid., p. 99.

7. On Vermigli's compatibilism, see Luca Baschera, 'Peter Martyr Vermigli on Free Will: The Aristotelian Heritage of Reformed Theology' (*Calvin Theological Journal* 2007).

8. Vos, *Church History and Religious Culture*, p. 2011.

towards necessity, and especially with respect to God's own relation to it. He claims that Calvin argued that necessity is consistent with the absence of coercion, and that God does what He does necessarily by nature. In Turretin too God's creating was in no way constrained, but rather He was in a state of indifference, a consequence of His aseity.[9] So for Calvin, God is not necessitated or compelled to be good by some force external to Him. He is good 'internally' and by virtue of His nature, essentially so. Similarly, by necessity God also acts voluntarily; if He is necessarily good, then He cannot want other than to be good.

Vos goes on to argue that for Calvin the primary essential meaning of necessity is that it is impossible for God to be different and alleges that 'a stronger meaning of "necessary" is impossible'. We have seen that according to Vos, Calvin expresses his own understanding of necessity in such passages as this, taken from his *The Bondage and Liberation of the Will*.

> But if his [God's] goodness is necessary, why am I not permitted to deduce from this that he wills the good as necessarily as he does it? Indeed since he continues unchanging in this respect, he is in a certain sense a necessity to himself, he is not coerced by another, nor however does he coerce himself, but of his own accord and voluntarily he tends to that which he does of necessity.[10]

Does this mean that everything that occurs, both in God and in His creation does so of absolute necessity? There is no need for speculation about the answer to this, for Calvin provides us with instances of why he thinks it does not. For example, in the *Institutes* Calvin writes about the spread of the gospel and about it being possible that God can will that the gospel be promoted in one country and not in another, or in both countries together.[11] More significantly, perhaps, is his treatment of the atonement, he claims that while in fact God has redeemed His church through the oblation of Christ, nevertheless 'God could have saved us by a word.'[12] So that 'saving us by a word' was a possibility, but

---

9. Turretin, *Institutes*, I. p. 219.

10. Calvin, *The Bondage and Liberation of the Will*, p. 149.

11. Calvin, *Institutes of the Christian Religion* (trams. William Beveridge, several editions), II.11.14.

12. For a discussion of this issue, see Paul Helm, *Calvin at the Centre*, Chapter 6.

one that God does not make actual, though which, according to Calvin, He could have actualized it. Nonetheless the word that He could have saved us by a word would be a state of affairs fully in accord with His infinitely good nature, and capable of being spontaneously and willingly brought about.

Besides providing such particular examples as these, Calvin also makes the point in general terms, as a matter of theological principle.

> The astrologers of today imitate the Stoics, for they hold that an absolute necessity for all things originates from the position of the stars. Let the Stoics have their fate; for us the free will of God disposes all things. Yet it seems absurd to remove contingency from the world …. What necessarily happens is what God decrees, and is therefore not exactly or of itself necessary by nature.[13]

What God decrees necessarily follows. What necessarily exists does so by God's will. But God's will is not absolutely necessary for Calvin, for otherwise God could not have saved us by a word, should He have willed it so. These words show Calvin's difference from some of Luther's expressions. God is free, free of compulsion or constraint from outside Himself, unlike the god of Stoic necessity. And what he concludes about natural necessity is true also about the will of God. What God decrees is necessary by a hypothetical or conditional necessity. So God is sovereign over His creation. It is because He has freely decreed W that W is necessary, not otherwise, with a necessity of the consequence, the consequence of His decree. (Vos seems to have said nothing about the place and character of God's decrees.) Consistently with this, as we saw in the last chapter, Calvin goes on to indicate that he is prepared to accept the 'received forms of speech', that is, the distinction between absolute and consequential (or hypothetical) necessity. Here is the similar, though more developed passage in the 1559 edition of the *Institutes*.

> We ought undoubtedly to hold that whatever changes are discerned in the world are produced from the secret stirring of God's hand. But what God has determined must necessarily so take place, even though it is neither unconditionally, nor of its own peculiar nature, necessary …. Whence again we see that distinctions concerning relative and absolute necessity,

---

13. *Concerning the Eternal Predestination of God*, p. 170.

likewise of consequent and consequence, were not recklessly invented in schools, when God subjected to fragility the bones of his Son which he had exempted from being broken, and thus restricted to the necessity of his own plan what could have happened naturally.[14]

Yet it seems absurd to remove contingency from the world. I omit to mention the distinctions employed in the schools. What I hold is, in my judgment, simple and needs no force to accommodate it usefully to life. What necessarily happens is what God decrees, and is therefore not exactly or of itself necessary by nature. I find a familiar example on the bones of Christ. Scripture testifies that Christ assumed a body quite like our own. That its bones were frangible no sane man doubts. But another and distinguishable question seems to arise here, whether any bone of His could be broken. For all things must necessarily remain intact and unimpaired because they are so determined by the fixed decree of God.[15]

Calvin seems to be saying that what is needed is a recognition of the metaphysical contingency of God's action, but he does not mention Luther's stress on divine necessity in so many words. There is alternativity in God's decree. So what He decreed is conditional upon God's wisdom, presumably. And the consequences of that decree, which is the gift of compatibilist freedom for those created in His image, is similarly conditional. So he is somewhat more circumspect and connected up on necessity than Luther. He affirms that there are things that God might have done that He did not do. God's will is not subject to what He has created, but rather He is the creation's Lord. Such passages find their way into the 1559 edition of his *Institutes*.

What seems to us contingence, faith will recognize as the secret impulse of God. The reason is not always equally apparent, but we ought undoubtedly to hold that all the changes which take place in the world are produced by the secret agency of the hand of God. At the same time, that which God has determined, though it must come to pass, is not, however, precisely or in its own nature, necessary.[16]

Once again, as in his book on predestination, he refers to the John 19 passage.

---

14. Calvin, *Institutes*, I.16.9.

15. Calvin, *Concerning the Eternal Predestination of God*, p. 170.

16. Calvin, *Institutes*, I.16.9.

We have a familiar example in the case of our Saviour's bones. As he assumed a body similar to ours, no sane man will deny that his bones were capable of being broken, and yet it was impossible that they should be broken (John 19:33, 36). Hence, again, we see that there was good ground for the distinction which the Schoolmen made between necessity, *secundem quid*, and necessity absolute, also between the necessity of consequent and of consequence. God made the bones of his Son frangible, though he exempted them from actual fracture; and thus, in reference to the necessity of his counsel, made that impossible which might have naturally taken place.[17]

And God's decree brings about the states of affairs that God in His wisdom causes to come to pass.

> As all future events are uncertain to us, so we hold them in suspense, as if they might incline to one side or the other. Yet in our hearts it nonetheless remains fixed that nothing will take place that the Lord has not previously foreseen.[18]

God foresees it by His will. Yet whatever God wills, He is not compelled to will. So it does not follow that the spread of the gospel in a particular way in one country, or in its denial to another, is necessitated other than by what God in His wisdom wills. Such a will is a choice, and a choice necessarily implies a course of action distinguished from a set of alternatives. Nothing is forced upon God, the sovereign Lord of creation. So Calvin invites us to think of alternative things that God could will, that He might perfectly consistently have willed, each alternative being in accordance with His necessarily good nature. This is not to say that God provides us with a transparent reason for what He does, only that His will is the uncaused cause of all things.

> For if his [God's] will has any cause, there must be something antecedent to it and to which it is annexed; this it were impious to imagine. The will of God is the supreme will of righteousness, so that everything which he wills must be held to be righteous by the mere fact of his willing it. Therefore when it is asked why the Lord did so, we must answer: because he pleased. But if you proceed further to ask why he pleased, you ask for something greater and more sublime than the will of God, and nothing such can be found.[19]

---

17. ibid., I.16.9.
18. ibid., I.16.9.
19. ibid., III.23.2.

Calvin is clearly thinking of the will of God as an aspect of His simple essence; it is essentially righteous, Calvin says. And God wills whatever He wills for a reason. Calvin sometimes uses the language of divine permission, though he follows Augustine's insistence that such permission is a willing permission.

> [B]ecause in a way unspeakably strange and wonderful, even what is done in opposition to His will does not defeat His will. For it would not be done did He not permit it (and of course His permission is not unwilling, but willing), nor would a Good Being permit evil to be done only that in His omnipotence He can turn evil into good.[20]

> But as the order, method, end, and necessity of events are, for the most part, hidden in the counsel of God, though it is certain that they are produced by the will of God, they have the appearance of being fortuitous, such be the form under which they present themselves to us, whether considered in their own nature, or estimated according to our knowledge and judgment.[21]

We do not know the order, reason, or end of what occurs, and to us often what occurs seems fortuitous. But we must recognize that it is divinely necessitated nonetheless. Presumably God's reason for willing as He does must be as specific as the character of what He wills. If what He wills has feature F, then God has a reason for what He wills having feature F. 'The will of God is the supreme rule of righteousness, so that everything which he wills must be held to be righteous by the mere fact of his willing it.'[22] God has the highest reason for willing as He does but He has no obligation to disclose to us what that reason is, and in any case, were He to do so, we would not be competent to pass judgment on it. So, that God has a reason does not amount to an explanation (in the epistemic sense) for us. God has a reason that is transparent to His own mind, but what that reason is may be shielded from us, part of the secret will of God.

It is fundamental to Calvin's view of divine action that God has a reason for whatever He wills. So His will is never capricious, a rootless volition, nor is God a tyrant; but His will is intrinsically and essentially

---

20. Augustine, *The Enchiridion on Faith, Hope and Love*, trans. J. F. Shaw. (Chicago, Henry Regnery, 1961.), Chapter C.

21. Calvin, *Institutes*, I. 6. 9.

22. ibid., III. 23. 2.

related to His character. For each of His willings, therefore, we are to reckon that God has a sufficient reason for doing what He does. But Calvin never speculates over whether the reason God has is 'the best of all possible reasons' or that He has an 'overriding reason' or somesuch.

So although Calvin does not employ the apparatus of alternative possible worlds, nor the 'foreknowledge of possibilities' in the manner of Gomarus,[23] say, it is clear that what he envisages the divine mind as having is consistent with various alternative possible outcomes, no doubt myriads of them. There are sets of alternative outcomes, consistent states of affairs any of which God could have chosen had He had a good reason to do so, for the making of any choice must be in accordance with His nature. No doubt there are also consistent states of affairs each of which God could not have chosen, sets of possibilities that are abhorrent to His nature. And any outcome which God might have chosen, if He had chosen it, that outcome would be necessary only because He chose it, spontaneously and willingly. So there is a distinction to be drawn between God willing certain outcomes according to His nature – wise, just, and so forth – and God willing a particular outcome necessarily. The latter does not follow from the former. The particular outcomes that He wills are thus hypothetically or conditionally necessary, and those He does not choose may be conditionally impossible.

Though Calvin does not write in terms of God's *possibilia* any more than he discusses Thomas Aquinas's position that, say, what God wills is constrained by the natures of what He has already created.[24]

So the necessity that God should act in accordance with His nature is a different sort of necessity than that possessed by states of affairs brought about by the divine will. God is necessarily wise, for example. Wisdom is a discriminable feature of His essence, such that any individual lacking such wisdom could not be God. Such wisdom is not given to Him, nor imposed on Him. God's wisdom is ontologically or essentially possessed by Him, in virtue of His aseity. In His wisdom God creates the heavens and the earth. These states of affairs are brought about, *causally* necessitated, by God's wisdom. He wills them, the products

---

23. Cited by Vos, 'The Systematic Place of Reformed Scholasticism: Reflections Concerning the Reception of Calvin's Thought', pp. 37-8.

24. For discussion of Thomas Aquinas's position on this, see Norman Kretzmann, *The Metaphysics of Creation* (Oxford, Clarendon Press, 1997), Ch.4.

of God's ontologically necessary wisdom, but they are not themselves metaphysically or ontologically necessary. 'I will not hesitate, therefore, simply to affirm with Augustine that "the will of God is the necessity of things" and that everything is necessary which he has willed, just as those things will certainly happen which he has foreseen.'[25] They are logically contingent, but causally necessary in virtue of His will, His choice of this and not of some other alternative. But because God wills them omnipotently and wisely and immutably they have the necessity of the consequence.

So there is an ambiguity over the expression, 'Whatever God wills, he wills necessarily'. Necessarily whatever God wills is wise, just, good, etc.: the action-*type* is necessitated by God's nature. But it does not follow that each action *token* is necessitated in the same way, or indeed that any action-token is necessitated in this way. Actions *ad extra* are causally necessitated by God's will. Such outcomes, if willed by God, must be in accordance with His nature and caused by Him. Jesus said that His Father could have stones raised up as children to Abraham (Matt. 3:9), and were He to have done so He would have brought about this state of affairs, causally necessitated it, a state of affairs that would have been a consistent expression of His nature. That is, there is a distinction between

> Necessarily, whatever God wills He wills wisely.
> And
> If God wills some particular wise act W, W is necessitated by
> God's will.
> And
> Whatever God wills *ad extra* has the necessity of the
> consequence.

In its first occurrence 'necessarily' denotes metaphysical or ontological necessity, while in its second occurrence 'necessitated', denotes causal necessity, and in its third occurrence 'necessity' draws attention to the immutability of whatever God wills. A particular caused action is willed by God in accordance with His nature, but Calvin does not say that its choice is simply logically entailed by that nature. But the choice having been made, it cannot fail.

---

25. Calvin, *Institutes*, III. 23.8.

In a number of places, Calvin himself respects the distinction between the manner in which God possesses powers, such as wisdom, and the manner in which creatures possess such powers, most notably in his Excursus 'Coercion versus Necessity' in *The Bondage and Liberation of the Will*. The question is that engendered by the compatibilistic concern of whether necessity excludes responsibility, praise and blame. And Calvin comments: 'We reply that God is good of necessity, but he obtains no less praise for his goodness because of the fact that he can only be good'.[26] Later on, we shall see such a position being echoed by both Turretin and Edwards.

> We do not argue that people are good or evil of necessity because God is good of necessity, but show by means of an example that it is not contrary to reason for a quality which exists of necessity nevertheless to be deemed worthy of praise or censure.[27]

Similarly with contingency. In discussing contingency in the *Institutes* in connection with divine providence, Calvin reserves the term 'contingent' for *causal* contingency, never denying that, should God have willed it, there would have been an alternative causal outcome from what in fact occurred. What he does deny is the presence of uncaused or self-caused events, of Fortune, or (it seems) of libertarianly-free human choices.

> What many talk of bare prescience is the merest trifling. Those do not err quite so grossly who attribute government to God, but still, as I have observed, a confused and promiscuous government which consists in giving an impulse and general movement to the machine of the globe and each of its parts, but does not specially direct the action of every creature[28]

One way of understanding his position is that he steers a mid-course between Epicurean Fortune and Stoic Fate. So the necessity that he ascribes to divine action is a conditional or hypothetical necessity, contrasting 'chance' or randomness (in a metaphysical sense) with divine contingency. It is impossible, however to tolerate this error.

> For, according to its abettors, there is nothing in this providence, which they call universal, to prevent all the creatures from being moved contingently, or

---

26. Calvin, *The Bondage and Liberation of the Will*, p. 147.

27. ibid., p. 147.

28. Calvin, *Institutes*, I.16.4.

to prevent man from turning himself in this direction or in that, according to the mere freedom of his own will. In this way, they make man a partner with God – God, by his energy, impressing man with the movement by which he can act, agreeably to the nature conferred upon him, while man voluntarily regulates his own actions. In short, their doctrine is, that the world, the affairs of men, and men themselves, are governed by the power, but not by the decree of God.[29]

Putting this in a rather different way, we can suppose that for Calvin, all the particular actions that God wills He does so as to necessitate their outcome, with a hypothetical necessity. It is because He chooses to bring about some action that it necessarily comes to pass, His choice being infallible and all-powerful and in accordance with His wise nature. 'What necessarily happens is what God decrees, and is therefore not exactly or of itself necessary by nature'.[30]

So, when Vos concludes that according to Calvin, 'therefore, everything is necessary. Because the whole of reality is necessary, God knows and acts necessarily, and because God knows and acts necessarily, everything is necessary too;'[31] these words are an exaggerated, inaccurate account of Calvin's view. This is due to Vos's failure to disambiguate what is ontologically necessary, a feature of God's essence, from what is causally necessary, a consequence of His will, and what is hypothetically necessary, necessary because what God wills is in accordance with His decree. Only in this way can Calvin's attitude towards God and necessity be made clear and its relation to those who followed him in Reformed Orthodoxy be properly assessed.

A sidelong glance at RO treatments of the divine decree does not give the impression that these theologians are engaging in a reconstruction of the doctrine of God along Scotist or any other lines. For example, take Turretin's short section on the divine will.[32] He makes the following points. A contrast needs to be drawn between absolute necessity and hypothetical necessity with respect to God. God wills Himself necessarily, but other things freely, because possible created things (with respect to

29. ibid., I.16.4.

30. Calvin, *Concerning the Eternal Predestination of God*, p. 170.

31. Vos, 'The Systematic Place of Reformed Scholasticism: Reflections Concerning the Reception of Calvin's Thought', p. 34.

32. Turretin, *Institutes*, I.218f.

God) are contingent. God's freedom consists in acts that are spontaneous and indifferent. Indifferent acts are those which God 'so wills that he could have willed them'. There is no suggestion that such indifference is a case of synchronic contingency; no reference to 'moments' or structures in the divine mind, for example, or references to time, but simply a reference to God's sovereign choice. Instead, indifference is linked to divine aseity. God cannot do without His wisdom, which is thus absolutely necessary, but He could do without the existence of planet Earth, which is thus only conditionally necessary. 'Contingent' is understood by reference to the divine essence. No created thing is necessary with respect to God, but contingent. Such things are contingent with respect to His own being. Interestingly, Turretin's emphasis is not on God's freedom to create A or B, but to create A or to refrain from creating it, the 'freedom of contradiction'. I suggest that all these points are consistent with Calvin's doctrine of God. The only difference between the two is stylistic, that whereas Calvin's views are scattered throughout his writings, Turretin gathers together his views in a formal and more self-aware manner, as we shall see.

How Can We Further Understand This?

The mainstream Christian view is both that God exists eternally, that He is not subject to time, and also that He is free. Free to create or not, or at least free to have created some alternative world to the actual world. Free to elect John or not, free to send more than twelve legions of angels to support the Mediator in His sufferings, or not, free to save us 'by a word' or through the self-offering of the God-man and our union with Him, and so on. As we have noted, for Calvin and Turretin there is a pattern of such possibilities discernible in Scripture.

The freedom that we have seen that Calvin refers to is in connection with the spread of the gospel, with whether or not God could have saved us by a word, and no doubt with much else besides. How might we express this notion of divine freedom, the freedom that (the mainstream Christian tradition claims) God possesses to create, or not, to elect, or not, and so forth? I shall consider two possible ways of doing this that have been proposed: *the logically contingent way*, and *the synchronically contingent way*. These may not be the only ways, but they are ways that are historically significant, and as we have seen in connection with what Antonie Vos argues, of interest still.

Divine Freedom

A paragraph in a recent doctoral dissertation captures rather well, I think, some of what this general Christian outlook, an outlook shared by Calvin, means by divine freedom.

> The freedom of God's will does not signal a second act of intention by which God's volition is further actualized, but rather is simply God willing. His volitional freedom lies in the fact that he does not will non-divine things with an absolute necessity, though he wills them immutably from eternity and never moves from a state of potential willing to actual willing.[33]

This passage may serve as a sort of text for some of what follows.[34] What I shall focus on, as you may imagine, is the thought that God's freedom means that He does not will the universe, or anything within it, with absolute necessity, with metaphysical necessity (as we noted earlier). He must therefore will the universe contingently. Nonetheless, He wills it, in James Dolezal's words, 'immutably from eternity'.

Dolezal's words invite us to distinguish, as we noted earlier, between the necessity or essentiality of God's essence, and the contingency of His actions, at least of His 'external' actions. God is good, necessarily, essentially good. He *is* love. He *is* light. Necessarily, in Him there is no darkness at all. All the long list of what we call the attributes of God, sometimes divided into the incommunicable and the communicable attributes, a division which becomes inoperable if God in His wisdom had seen fit not to create, are possessed essentially by God. They are of His essence.

---

33. James E. Dolezal, 'God Without Parts: Simplicity and the Metaphysics of Divine Absoluteness' (Ph.D thesis, Westminster Theological Seminary, 2011), p. 43. The thesis is published as *God without Parts: Divine Simplicity and the Metaphysics of God's Absoluteness* (Eugene, Or., Pickwick Publications, 2011), but without this passage.

34. Though I have stressed the problem that divine eternality poses for an understanding of divine freedom, the ultimate barrier to our understanding is divine simplicity, and with it the denial of change and of passive volitional potency in God. 'It is absolutely true that all movement is a changing of the state of a being. But when we hear of an act which is not a movement we are at a loss how to think about it. No matter how we try, we always imagine that creation [or any other free divine act] is a kind of change .... But in actual fact it is something quite different, something we are at a loss to put into words, so unfamiliar is it to the conditions of human experience' (Etienne Gilson, *The Christian Philosophy of St. Thomas Aquinas*, p. 122.). For Calvin's commitment to divine simplicity, see for example *Institutes*, I.13.2.

But what God does, or at least what He does *ad extra*, in connection with the existence and history of whatever is other than Himself in His triune glory, is not part of His essence. Whatever could exist and is not part of His essence must be contingent, for if it is willed, it is freely willed. Though, of course, *whatever* God thus creates must be, one may assume, in accordance with His essence, since one of His essential features or characteristics is immutability, and another is veracity. Nevertheless *what* He creates is up to Him. God in His wisdom may have seen fit to create some alternative universe. He would still be God in all His glory, independence and self-sufficiency, had there been no universe *ad extra*, or a universe distinct in character from the universe He in fact has created. God is necessarily good but only contingently the creator of the universe.

On this view it is not sufficient for God's freedom in creating, to say that He acts in accordance with His own nature, but that He wills contingently, to act or not to act. Or perhaps it is conceivable there are two versions of 'must act in accordance with His own nature': one in which that nature is utterly precise, containing a full description of the world God in fact wills, as well as innumerable equally full descriptions of the worlds that God does not will, and some of which He could not have willed; the other reading of God's nature is one in which that nature is invariant across various possible choices, as we argued at the beginning was Calvin's view. In each case God cannot but act in accordance with His own nature, but in the second of these cases God's will leaves Him free consistently to create one of a range of possibilities. So far, then, God acts freely when what He does is causally contingent and it is in accordance with God's nature, where there is at least one other outcome that is consistent with His nature, and He has a reason for creating this universe, a reason which He has kept to Himself.

Suppose we accept the idea that God's freedom may be expressed in this way. It seems to have been a widespread idea in medievalism. For example William Ockham, in arguing about the eternity of the world, and of creation, writes of God's power in terms of what can contingently be thought. Expressions such as 'It does not involve a contradiction; therefore, it could be brought about by God', and 'I maintain *probabiliter* that God could have made the world from eternity in virtue of the fact that no manifest contradiction appears [in that claim]' are typical.[35] So, for Ockham, if *p* is a possibility for God, or more guardedly, if it is possible God could bring about some state of affairs S, then God could have brought S about freely. That's what it means, or part of what it means, for God to be free. Although Ockham does not use the term 'freedom' here, he seems to have this in mind. But maybe not. Maybe Ockham is concerned simply with what an omnipotent being could bring about, were he sufficiently motivated to do so. Yet I don't think we can doubt that on the classical view, an appeal to contingency is how God's freedom is to be understood. Logical contingency can by definition only be a necessary condition of freedom; however, since though God could have made the world from eternity, Ockham thinks that He hasn't. This may be what John Calvin also has in mind, or part of it, though as far as I can see he nowhere tells us. A pity!

But we notice the presence of a potential friction between such logical contingency and what James Dolezal refers to as God's 'immutability from eternity'. There is no difficulty in asserting that things that God wills, He wills freely, but that they are nonetheless immutable by a conditional or hypothetical necessity. In such a sense, as we saw earlier, Calvin held the Johannine view that it was necessary that the bones of Jesus should not be broken, or impossible that death should hold the dead Messiah (John 19:36). But what we are really interested in is not the immutability that is a *consequence* of a free decision, but the immutability *of* a free decision. Not merely the immutability of the consequences of a decision, but of the decision itself. And here the question that gives rise to the friction is: How can an eternally immutable decision be a logically contingent decision, a logically possible decision for God?

Ockham (or an Ockhamist) might simply answer at this point, 'because an alternative eternally immutable decision regarding the creation can be thought, even though that decision, had it been taken,

---

35. These expressions are taken from Norman Kretzmann, 'Ockham and the Creation of the Beginningless World' (*Franciscan Studies,* Vol. 45, Annual XXIII, 1985). This outlook was shared by Duns Scotus who stated that omnipotence 'in its proper theological sense is He who is able to accomplish every effect and everything that is possible (that is, everything that is not by itself necessary nor includes contradiction)'.

would also have been eternally immutable'. So perhaps we might say that such a timeless God as that held by Calvin is free if: God chose A, and there exist in His mind alternative possibilities each of which is consistent to suppose God could have chosen but hasn't, to be distinguished from sets of possibilities none of which it is consistent to suppose God could have chosen.

It is clear from this discussion (I hope) that there are of course difficulties in understanding divine freedom given the general position regarding divine simplicity that Calvin adopts. As Brian Leftow has shown in his exposition of Aquinas's views on divine simplicity and divine freedom, if one thinks of divine freedom principally in terms of the opportunity to choose between alternatives, then it is impossible to fit this into Aquinas, not only because of his atemporalism but also because of the strength of his commitment to divine simplicity which seems to imply the necessity of the divine will, since for Aquinas the divine volition is an aspect of God's simple nature.[36]

I think it is fair to say that wherever Calvin dwells upon these features of God – His simplicity and atemporality – and the application of the difference between necessity and hypothetical necessity—his outlook is very similar to that of Aquinas, but he tends to cast a veil over the divine mind rather than attempt to work out a position in detail, as Aquinas does. For example, unlike Aquinas he says nothing about God's essential diffusiveness, His proneness to create. Rather than try to work out a version of divine simplicity that is more hospitable to divine freedom than Aquinas's (assuming Calvin was aware of the difficulties of Aquinas's view), Calvin takes the approach that the Creator-creature distinction sets up not only an intellectual barrier to understanding, but should also remind us of the moral and spiritual differences between ourselves and God.

> Therefore, when it is asked why the Lord did so, we must answer: Because he pleased. But if you proceed further to ask why he pleased, you ask for something greater and more sublime than God's will, and nothing such can be found.[37]

---

36. Brian Leftow 'Aquinas, Divine Simplicity and Divine Freedom' in *Metaphysics and God: Essays in Honor of Eleonore Stump*, ed. Kevin Timpe (New York and London: Routledge, 2009).

37. *Calvin, Institutes*, III. 23.2.

Calvin insists that it is impertinent, a loss of creaturely reserve, to try to span the ontological gap between the Creator and his creatures. Nevertheless he clearly holds that there are alternatives that God might have chosen. Maybe he holds a view like this: A situation in which God knows that there are other states of affairs He might have chosen is freer for God than one in which the states of affairs that He chose are the only ones that He might have chosen. For suppose that the one He chose had not been available, but the others had been. There is a sense in which God is freer in such a situation, than one in which there were no logically possible alternatives to the one He chose. In that situation there is little that is different between choosing freely, and being forced to choose. Here the 'might' in 'God might have chosen an alternative outcome' is not a statistical 'might' as in 'Brian might come sooner' referring to a possible or a likely choice that Brian might make, but the 'might' of availability, as 'You might find flowers at the supermarket'. So that while there are other decrees available to God, they are all only 'hypothetically actual'. Or maybe Calvin held that the issues so familiar to students of free will cannot apply to God, because all God's decrees are *ab initio* purposive. If God were not free it would not be because He was externally coerced. So there can be no causal contribution to any divine action that comes *to* God, that is in any sense prior to or anterior to God. The decrees are choices the reason(s) for which originate in God Himself.

If the idea of God's acting freely is to be informative, to have content, such logical contingency can only be a necessary condition of God's freedom. It is also necessary to be true that God has before His mind an array of alternatives one of which is available to Him. Peter Martyr Vermigli, but not Calvin, occasionally makes this point. 'God foreknew that many things were possible that never will be, the foreknowledge of God does not remove them from the possibility of existence.'[38] This might then delineate the logical character of God's freedom, or at least I am supposing that it is plausible that Ockham and many others, including Calvin, think that it might. Doubtless Vermigli has in mind the Apostle Paul's doxology in Romans 11.

> Oh, the depth of the riches, and wisdom and knowledge of God! How
> unsearchable are his judgements and how inscrutable his ways!

---

38. Vermigli, *Predestination and Justification*, p. 74.

For who has known the mind of the Lord

Or has been his counsellor?

Or who has given a gift to him that he might be repaid?

For from him and through him and to him are all things. To him be
glory for ever. Amen. (vv. 33-6)

The Atonement

Further supporting evidence of Calvin's view of divine freedom is
provided by statements that Calvin makes at several times and places,
though not in the *Institutes* (as far as I can tell), but in various of his
sermons and commentaries. Among these are the following:

> For if God had simply proclaimed our pardon by declaring that he had
> decided to receive us in mercy, despite our unworthiness, that would have
> been a great thing. Even then, we would never have been able to utter
> sufficient praise for such grace. But God has given us his own Son as a token
> of his love. Indeed, he has given us himself through his Son, and declared
> himself to be our Father. This so far outshines pardon alone that even if we
> employed all our faculties to worship and adore, we could never perfectly
> praise him for such mercy.[39]

> If God pardoned us without Jesus Christ interceding for us and being
> made our pledge, we should think nothing of it. We should all shrug our
> shoulders and make it an opportunity for giving ourselves greater license.
> But when we see that God did not spare His only Son, but treated Him with
> such an extreme severity that in His Body He underwent all the sorrows
> that it would be possible to suffer and then even in His soul He was afflicted
> to the limit, to the point of crying out 'My God, my God, why hast thou
> forsaken me?' – when we hear all this, it is impossible for us, unless we
> are harder than stone, not to shudder and be filled with such a fear and
> amazement as will utterly put us to confusion; impossible not to detest our
> offences and iniquities seeing that they provoke the anger of God against
> us in this way. This, then, is why it was necessary for all the correction of
> our peace to be laid upon Jesus Christ that we might find grace before God
> His Father ....[40]

39. Sermon on Gal. pp. 1.3-5, *John Calvin's Sermons on Galatians* (trans. Kathy Childress,
Edinburgh, Banner of Truth, 1997), p. 24.

40. *Sermons on Isaiah's Prophecy of the Death and Passion of Christ.* trans. and ed. T. H. L.
Parker (London, James Clarke and Co. 1956), p. 72.

Behind these sentiments of Calvin's is what he writes about the Incarnation in his *Institutes*:

> It deeply concerned us, that he who was to be our Mediator should be very God and very man. If the necessity be inquired into, it was not what is commonly termed simple or absolute, but flowed from the divine decree on which the salvation of man depended. What was best for us our most merciful Father determined.[41]

So the atonement was not absolute, but it was the result of a divine decree. Calvin's successor at Geneva, Francis Turretin, shares the same general outlook.

He adds, in his rather fuller account.

> It was not only suitable, but necessary (sin and the decree of God concerning the redemption of men concerning the redemption of men being supposed) that the Son of God should be incarnate in order to accomplish this work. (1) The question does not concern a simple and absolute necessity on the part of God for God could (if he had wished) leave man no less than the Devil in his destruction. Rather the question concerns a hypothesis—whether the will to save men being posited, the incarnation was necessary, or whether it could have been brought about by some other means. (2) Again, the question does not concern the necessity of the decree for no one denies that on the supposition of God's having decreed this, it ought necessarily to have been done. Rather the question concerns the necessity of nature—whether the decree being set aside and antecedently to it, it was necessary for the Son of God to become incarnate to redeem us. (3) The question does not concern the necessity of fitness because all confess that was in the highest decree fitting to the divine majesty—that his precepts might not be said to have been violated with impurity. Rather the question concerns the necessity of justice – that in no other way could the justice of God have been satisfied and our deliverance brought about (which we assert).[42]

'The question' which Turretin reflects on more than once is, I think, the question at the head of the section in which this passage occurs: *Was it necessary for the Son of God to be incarnate? We affirm.*[43] In this

---

41. Calvin, *Institutes,* II.12.1. For further discussion of Calvin on the necessity of the atonement, see Paul Helm, *Calvin at the Centre* (Oxford, Oxford University Press, 2010), Chapter 6.

42. Turretin, *Institutes,* 2.301.

43. ibid., 2.299.

passage, Turretin, like Calvin, maintained that the Incarnation was not necessary but free.

Summing Up

In this and the earlier chapter we have looked at how Martin Luther and John Calvin fared over the charge of 'necessitarianism'. We saw how Luther was somewhat heavy-handed in his treatment of God's absolute necessity, but that he has room for contingency, and that his distinction between compulsion and freedom suggests that he is sympathetic to a compatibilistic outlook. It has been argued that Calvin, due perhaps to the influence of Melanchthon, is in his *Concerning the Eternal Predestination of God* (1552) and in his definitive edition of the *Institutes* (1559) fully appraised of the distinction between the necessity of the consequent and the necessity of the consequence. But while this provides for contingency, he was not a necessitarian any more than was Francis Turretin. The history of Reformed theology is that the Reformed were not strongly necessitarian.

Conclusion of Part One

We have seen that Vos's and the *RTF*'s case for synchronic contingency is based on three logical/metaphysical premises. The first is the account of the two necessities. The second is acceptance of the truth of the Scotian position that God, who exists eternally, is free in the synchronic contingency sense. The third is the biblical claim that humankind is created in the *imago dei,* and as a consequence men and women also enjoy synchronic contingent freedom of the will.

We have also seen that Calvin subscribed to the two necessities distinction, both in the 1542 book on predestination, and also in the 1559 *Institutes.* So Vos's sharp criticism of Calvin as a necessitarian falls. Or else Turretin and other RO's are similarly afflicted, in holding that an alternative to the Incarnation can be envisaged.

The second argument is for the Vosian case for divine synchronic contingency as espoused by Richard Muller. For Richard Muller shares the Vosian outlook, referring to *RTF* as 'ground-breaking'.[1]

The opening page of *Reformed Thought on Freedom* states,

> The Reformed scholastics … certainly confessed a foundational involve-ment of God's will in creation and the history of salvation. Yet, for them this insistence on divine will precisely established a realm for human willing. Being constituted in freedom, reality is open for human freedom as well. God himself, acting freely, enables human beings—who are made in his image—to act freely alike.[2]

---

1. Muller, 'Neither Libertarian nor Compatibilist', 2019, p. 268.

2. *Reformed Thought on Freedom, The Concept of Free Choice in Early Modern Reformed Theology,* edd. Willem J. van Asselt, J.Martin Bac, and Roelf T. te Velde (Grand Rapids, Mich, Baker, 2010), p. 15. Hereafter as *RTF.*

However, we see from this that Vos's onslaught on 'necessitarianism' rests on an argument employing a couple of assumptions. He *assumes*, taking his lead from Scotus, that divine freedom is 'synchronously contingent' and that bearing in mind the nature of divine freedom, it follows that man's creation in the image of God entails that men and women, sharing that image, are also sources of synchronic libertarian freedom. These are highly questionable inferences, it seems to me.

The chief problem with this proposal is that it is odd that a theological argument is supported by a purely philosophical argument. Yet it seems to Vos and company that the presence of the two necessities that we have been distinguishing solves a range of theological issues. It permits God's own contingent choice; the creation is contingent, and likewise all things therein.

The theological method of Vos and his colleagues, largely drawn from philosophical sources, is emphatically *a priori*. The method of RO theologians was more complex and *a posteriori*, as can be seen from Chapter Two of the Westminster Confession, for example.

In regard to the two necessities distinction, I argue that its significance is exaggerated in *RTF*. Certainly it is not unique to Scotus. We have seen that Thomas employed it, and precedents are found in Boethius, as Vos recognizes, in Anselm as well. The RO use it routinely, but with no Scotist influence, or scarcely any. Readers of the *RTF* will look in vain for divine synchronic contingency in the RO texts examined in the book. It does not follow from mankind's creation in the *imago dei* that people share in God's eternal being; human powers are temporal and creaturely. None of them are timelessly eternal. Similarly, human beings do not possess God's *aseitas,* nor anything like it, in virtue of being created in God's image. Worst of all for Vos, Calvin endorses it.

In the case of Luther we saw that though he regarded the two necessities as a scholastic sophistry, he nonetheless has room for contingency, and distinguishes human from compulsion. So we may have all the tools for not maintaining that every thing that occurs does not occur by absolute necessity. Nevertheless there is a certain kind of roughness in his judgments of divine necessity that his colleague Philip Melanchthon took in hand. Nevertheless, given what Luther says about contingency he is not necessitarian in a strong sense since he tends to compatibilism.

Vos's argument thus has a number of flaws. It is interesting that the argument is wholly logical in character, apart from the assertion of the biblical doctrine that humankind is created in *imago dei*. It is a venture into philosophical theology, not derived from Scripture by careful exegesis.

Berkouwer and Pinnock embraced deterministic Calvinism when they were young theologians. However, later on they started to revolt against the 'Calvinism' of their youth and Dort. Paul Helm never joined or affirmed this uprising. It is not that I revolt against Dort, but I defend that Reformed scholasticism, including Dort, was never a kind of theological necessitarianism — this is in contrast with John Calvin's theology. Instead, classic Reformed scholasticism offers us a theology of contingency and individuality, of goodness and will, and of freedom and grace. Rediscovering this comforting historical reality is a gift and a joy.[3]

---

3. Vos, 'Paul Helm on Medieval Scholasticism', p. 263.

PART TWO

Part Two

CHAPTER 4

Some Context

Having spent some time on necessity and contingency in Luther and Calvin, and the weakness of Vos's arguments for Reformed indeterminism, we now approach the heart of this book. This is the question of whether Jonathan Edwards was an innovator in his compatibilistic account of human freedom, turning his back on the indeterminism of Reformed scholasticism, or whether they were compatibilists, and Edwards in his book on the freedom of the will was simply sharpening up that position. In this chapter I shall attempt to further explain some of the background of certain ideas in the debate between indeterminacy and compatibilism, in its application to the views of the RO. This has implications not only for Reformed theology, but also in philosophy and the ways that theology changes over time. The distinctiveness of Vos's view arises not in the importance of the two necessities alone, but also in the synchronic contingent view of freedom that the two necessities make room for. Vos's views have influenced the views of Richard Muller about compatibilism in his papers on Jonathan Edwards, in the closing pages of *Divine Will and Human Choice,* and a later paper in 2019. We shall consider his position in the later chapters.

In this chapter which gives readers what to expect in the chapters to come, we shall give readers a feel of Muller's attitude to Jonathan Edwards in his initial paper on the 'Parting of Ways' and then in his later work.

So far we have not been concerned with Edwards, except to uncontroversially call him a compatibilist, and therefore as one who is hostile to indeterminism. The developments or merely changes that we see in Edwards's anthropology as against that of the RO nevertheless seem to be consistent to what Muller regards as the eclectic character of Reformed scholasticism. Muller veers between thinking of scholasticism as an 'eclectic' bundle of ideas, while at other times of thinking of it as the indispensable means of understanding Reformed indeterminism. Of course not just any philosophical scheme can substitute for scholasticism in Reformed theology, but only one that covers the same ground. This feature of scholasticism is highlighted in a later chapter when we consider the place of causation in scholasticism. But Edwards himself was conscious of the difference between scholasticism and the language of John Locke.

The Modern Discussion of Compatibilism

The modern discussion of the compatibilism-indeterminism debate has claimed that there is no middle ground between an affirmation of determinism and its denial. There are two concepts, each of 'freedom', a kind of determinism, and a kind of libertarianism. Each is contradictory of the other, and each offers itself as an account of free action. Each position maintains that there is free will when there is alternativity in action. However, the two positions are crucially distinct between unconditional alternativity as seen in libertarianism, of which synchronic contingency is an example, and in diachronic simultaneity, Muller's view, and the conditional alternativity of compatibilism.

As we shall also see, Jonathan Edwards took some of the conceptuality of the new thinking of his time, that arose from the work of John Locke, and scholastic Reformed theologians such as Turretin and Van Mastricht. There are strands of novelty in his defence of the view he took from the RO. Edwards has a more unitary conception of the self, but this is a view that is not exceptional in RO, as we shall see in due course. He also uses mechanical analogies, while recognising in the next breath that human beings are not material machines, being not machines of any sort.[1] It is basic for him that every event has a cause. He also played the card of what the Reformed called the *sensus divinitatis*, corresponding to what Turretin called 'self-knowledge', in developing his account of personal responsibility, based on 'moral ability', a term which Turretin also used.[2]

---

1. Edwards, *Freedom of the Will*, p. 370. See also Paul Helm, '*Reformed Thought on Freedom*: Some Further Thoughts', *Journal of Reformed Theology*, 2010, pp. 201-2.

2. Michael Preciado connects up the 'mechanism ownership' with the theologians' *sensus divinitatis*, which together with the 'reasons responsiveness' element of Fischer

Placing reliance on unbiblical ideas, as Turretin on Aristotle, or Edwards on Locke the Arminian, is not an innovation. From the early centuries of the Christian era, Christian theologians have appropriated terms of their pagan contemporaries – Tertullian used Stoic thinking, Augustine used the neo-Platonists, while in the twelfth century Arab thinkers translated Aristotle's writings into Latin, when they were deemed useful they too were used by Catholic theologians beginning with Albert the Great. So Edwards affirming the language of some of his contemporaries such as John Locke and George Berkeley was not by itself a case of being captivated by secular unbelief. Both Locke and Berkeley were theists. It is one thing to *translate* Christian doctrine into secular concepts, another to *borrow* some secular concepts to expand an understanding of biblical ideas. God is three persons in one, but 'person' is given a new connotation in so claiming this, and 'trinity' was a wholly non-biblical construct, and so on. Aristotle was modified in being made useful. He had no term for 'conscience', and with Greek thinkers in general he held that matter is eternal.

On determinism Robert Kane states,

> An event (such as a choice or action) is *determined* when there are conditions obtaining earlier (such as the decrees of fate or the foreordaining acts of God or antecedent causes plus laws of nature) whose occurrence is a sufficient condition for the occurrence of the event. In other words, it *must* be the case that, *if* these earlier determining conditions obtain, then the determined event will occur.[3]

This reminds us that there are different sorts of determinism depending on the character of the factors that do the determining. To be sure 'compatibilism' was a new word for those who taught and thought about determinism in early modern Europe. *The Shorter Oxford English Dictionary* dates the currency of the suffix 'ism' used as 'Forming the name of a system of a theory, or practice' from the late seventeenth century.[4]

---

and Ravizza's 'guidance control', connected to Edwards's and the RO's 'moral ability', as a defence of compatibilism. See his *A Reformed View of Freedom,* Ch.4 'Rational Responsiveness and the Sensus Divinitatis'.

3. Robert Kane, *Contemporary Introduction to Free Will* (Oxford: Oxford University Press, 2005), pp. 5-6.

4. *The Shorter Oxford English Dictionary*, article 'ism' 2, forming the name of a system. Cited as first occurring in 1680, quoting 'He is nothing, no–ist, professing no 'ism', but superbism and irrationalism' (The poet Percy Bysshe Shelley (1792–1822)). The date for the first circulation of 'determinism' is given as 1846.

'Compatibilism' refers to the idea of a determinism that is compatible if a person is personally responsible for his actions, being praised or rewarded or being blamed or suffering loss for their actions. As regards the assessment of it for praise or blame, it is distinct from other sorts of determinism, such as fatalism, arising for example from astrology or logic or from some other source, or determinism arising from coercion, such as brainwashing or hypnotism, or materialist determinism or as Muller stated, 'mere automatons'.[5] Edwards and Turretin each refer to such cases.

So 'compatibilism' was a new word since early modernity. Neither Turretin nor Edwards use it. As noted, what is now recognized as 'compatibilism' was described as 'necessitarian' in the seventeenth century, even as 'fatalistic' by those who were opposed to it. But the point about determinism and later on about 'compatibilism' is that the terms were at home in a world of a Calvinist that had been influenced by John Locke (1632–1704) and the RO.

So it is distinctly unhelpful for Han Kwan Kim, for example, to say that Edwards derived his determinism from the materialist Thomas Hobbes, without even discussing materialism as an option for him, and so ignoring Edwards's assertion that he had not read Hobbes, and was not a materialist but an emphatic body-soul dualist.[6] A number of Reformed theologians were influenced by Descartes, and adopted his dualism. I am not aware that Muller criticises their 'Reformed' character for this.

Muller notes that there have been studies of nineteenth and early twentieth-century scholars which connected Edwards's theory of the freedom of the will with Hobbes, Locke and Collins, rather than with the older Reformed or Calvinistic tradition, notably an essay from 1879 by George Park Fisher and another from 1942 by Conrad Wright.[7] In fact, habitually to link Edwards with determinism, without distinguishing the different sorts of determinism that are available, as Hobbes and Locke

---

5. 'Neither Compatibilist Nor Libertarian', p. 267.

6. Hyun Kwan Kim, 'The Doctrine of Free Choice' in *A New Divinity*, edd. Mark Jones and Michael G. Haykin (Gottingen, Vandenhoeck & Ruprecht, 2018.) In the Section 'Concerning the Objection against the Doctrine Which Has Been Maintained, that It Agrees with the Stoical Doctrine of Fate, and the Opinion of Mr Hobbes'. (Pt III S.6) In it Edwards claimed 'I confess, it happens I never read Mr. Hobbes' (*Freedom of the Will*, p. 374).

7. Muller, 'Jonathan Edwards and the Absence of Free Choice', p. 4.

were different from each other, is unfortunate. Once a book was devoted to determinism, as Edwards did in his book on free will, then there was a good chance for some readers to be critical of it, and others supportive.

Having begun by refusing the term 'compatibilism' Muller later became willing to refer to it. So it is found in the conclusion of *Divine Will and Human Choice* published in 2017, and in his 'Jonathan Edwards and the Absence of Free Choice', in 2014, and in his discussion of Turretin and what allegedly distinguishes him from compatibilism. The issue of differences in terminology must not be exaggerated, however. In modern philosophy, the scholastic theory of synchronic contingency is sometimes referred to as the liberty of indifference, a liberty of which indifference is a sufficient condition, or contra-causal freedom. Richard Cross uses the term 'contra-causal' to characterize the sort of power that Scotus's power of contingency entails.[8] Weaving one's way through this varied terminology is a part of equipping oneself in this field.

Edwards did not shrink from all the various notions of Aristotelian causality in scholasticism—efficient, material, formal and final—for in his writing there are vestiges of most of these, as there are in our communicating in the twenty-first century. But there are differences. For the RO, the matter out of which I make a door is significant in making it, part of its 'form'. But in modernity, woodenness is not usually referred to as the *cause* of the door. Yet there are efficiencies, formalities and finalities in Edwards. Generally speaking Edwards is infrequent in his distinction between primary and secondary causes, as is found in the Westminster Confession, for instance. For Edwards's freedom is choice in the absence of coercion, and a choice that is not random, but is made for a reason or ground, hence the generous list of grounds that Edwards showers his reader with.[9] And for Edwards the metaphor of a chain does not fit the criss-crossing of causes and interruptions that make up the causes of our actions, and of which some critics of determinism make play. As he shows here:

> But the dependence and connection between acts of volition or choice, and their causes, according to established laws, is not so sensible and obvious. And we observe that choice is as it were a new principle of motion and

---

8. Richard Cross, *Duns Scotus on God* (Aldershot, Ashgate, 2005), p. 56.

9. Edwards, *Freedom of the Will*, pp. 180-1.

action, different from that established law and order in things which is most obvious, that is seen especially in both corporeal and sensible things; and also that choice often interposes, interrupts and alters the chain of events in these external objects, and causes 'em to proceed otherwise than they would do, if let alone, and left to go on according to the laws of motion among themselves.[10]

Nevertheless, he has no room for 'real contingency', the outcome of a perfect indifference in the will, that according to his contemporary libertarians such as Thomas Chubb (1679–1747) and Daniel Whitby (1658–1726) is of the essence of the freedom of the will. Such contingency is for Edwards either irrational or incoherent, flouting his core belief that all events, including human actions, necessarily have causes. Freedom is the effect of a properly-grounded or reasoned agency, and it is that view that is to be found in human freedom in both Edwards and the RO. This is the claim that this book is defending. 'Contingent' had come to have varied meanings by Edwards's time, so much so that he refused to use it.[11]

From the above we begin to get the mood of Muller's suspicion of determinism and compatibilism. He believes that RO scholasticism provides a view of human freedom that is neither compatibilist nor libertarian, as he puts it in the title of his 2019 paper, and from now on it is my purpose to show that this is inaccurate, even incoherent, and that the RO are determinists of a compatibilist kind, and so distinct from the position that the RO called 'chimerical',[12] or a 'pretence',[13] an action that is the product of pure indifference. Such an action is as follows:

> [I]f the will determines all its own free acts, the soul determines all the free acts of the will in the exercise of a power of willing and choosing; or, which is the same thing, it determines its own acts by choosing its own acts. If the will determines the will, then choice orders and determines the choice: and acts of choice are subject to the decision, and follows the conduct of other acts of choice,[14]

---

10. ibid., pp. 158-59. See also p. 382.

11. ibid., p. 155.

12. Voetius, cited in *Reformed Thought on Freedom*, p. 150.

13. Turretin, *Institutes*, I. p. 665.

14. Edwards, *Freedom of the Will*, p. 172.

So, the will begets another act of the will, and that act begets another act of the will, and so *ad infinitum*. So, there are no self-determining acts of the will alone, but it executes by which a person judges what is his end in some particular situation.

Faculty Psychology – The Powers of the Mind

Generalising, the RO held to 'faculty psychology' as part of their scholasticism. They held that the soul had essential faculties or powers: mainly intellect, will and affections or emotions, as well as the acts of conscience and of the memory. Actions are the outcome of the working of the faculties. So the issue of 'free will' has an anthropological aspect, as well as theological concerns about the doctrine of God. Later on, Chapter 7 develops the evidence of the roles of the faculties of the mind as an argument for the presumption of compatibilism. It has, I believe, to do with the concept of freedom which we get from Turretin's and the others' views of the relation between the reason or understanding and the will. RO faculty psychology, in fact, embraces a range of views, such as those exemplified by William Pemble, Samuel Willard and Bernardinus de Moor, for example, who we shall meet in due course.

There is plenty of evidence that RO scholasticism is not an ideology but a method, a help in expounding the Reformed faith, yet not a rigid framework. For the RO such as Pemble and Willard, with a rather different view of the faculties of the soul, as we have just mentioned, did not think they were veering in an unorthodox direction. The developments or changes that we find in Edwards's anthropology are within the spirit of what Muller regards as the character of Reformed scholasticism. It may well be that the language of John Bunyan, say, or that of the Puritan John Howe, are cases of non-scholastic or semi-scholastic. It is likely also, that some of those Reformed theologians who were influenced by covenant theology and their British disciples, the likes of Johannes Cocceius (1603–1669) and Herman Witsius (1636–1708), and Robert Rollock (1555–1599) or John Ball (1585-1640), held to a modified or reduced scholasticism. So there is a certain fluidity in their position, but all stressed the narrative of the divine revelation in a way that the scholastics intended.

There is another distinction of some importance in RO anthropology and to the resolution of the free will question. Following Aristotle, each

RO distinguishes human intellectual activities between the *theoretical* and the *practical*. In the operation of the theoretical reason the mind searches for truth, for information. For the practical reason the appetite is for the good state of affairs, for ends. And ends are achieved by identifying means. Suppose I want to know how many inhabitants live in Blackpool, then this is the business of the theoretical reason. But suppose I want to get to Blackpool, this is a matter of the practical reason, and is satisfied by following the directions there. These are the means to my end, how to get to Blackpool. The differences between determinism and indeterminism are a matter of the practical reason. Edwards would concur.

Muller on determinism

From the inception of his work on Edwards, in his article 'Jonathan Edwards and the Absence of Free Choice: A Parting of Ways in the Reformed Tradition', Muller has striven to tar Edwards with the determinist brush, in the expectation that this drives a wedge between him and the RO. There are such instances of this in nearly every page of the article. He has been convinced that Edwards is not fully 'Reformed'. We have already noted that there are numerous kinds of determinism, including materialist and physicalist versions like Hobbes and those who followed him. Hobbes was something of a bogeyman in the early modern period, because of his atheism. The Dissenter Joseph Priestley (1733–1804) was a determinist, and also a Socinian. Edwards rather hotly disavowed the slur (for him) that he was a fatalist, claiming that he had never read Thomas Hobbes (1588–1679).[15] So it is of little value to label a person as a determinist before his views are carefully examined. In the 2011 article, Muller does make some effort to address Edwards's views, but it is half-hearted. In Edwards's view, in the opening sentences of his work on the will, he says (in Part 1, Section 1),

> [T]he *Will* (without any metaphysical Refining) is, *That by which the Mind chuses any Thing*. The Faculty of the *Will*, is that Faculty or Power, or Principle of Mind, by which it is capable of *chusing*: an Act of *Will* is the same as an Act of *Chusing* or *Choice* ... it is that by which the Soul either *chuses* or *refuses* ... for every Act of Will whatsoever, the Mind chuses one

---

15. ibid., p. 374f.

Thing rather than another; it[chuses] something rather than the Contrary or rather than the Want or Non-Existence of that Thing.[16]

Muller takes from this that the will is the mind or soul in its act of choosing, which is markedly different from the traditional RO distinction between the operations of intellect and will. But if he had gone as far as Section 2 of Part 1 of Edwards's book on freedom Muller would have found that for Edwards the will is determined by the understanding. Each of which, will and understanding, Edwards refers to as 'faculties', making a kind of faculty psychology, like the RO. He infers that the will 'always follows the last dictate of the understanding', including its perceptions or apprehensions. This is remarkably similar to Turretin's remark, 'For since the will is a rational appetite, such is its nature that it must follow the judgment of the practical intellect'.[17] It seems rational to conclude that if Edwards's relation between the understanding and the will is deterministic, then so is Turretin's.

Synchronic Contingency

We have considered synchronic contingency already, in the various proposals of Antonie Vos and his group. But despite his criticism of Vos's reliance on Scotus, Muller has a positive use for diachronic contingency in his book *Divine Will and Human Choice*, and no doubt elsewhere. He thinks that there is a place for the working of diachronic contingency, using 'contingency' to mean 'pure alternativity', in a sense that approximates, and perhaps overlaps with, that of Vos.

Muller has forcefully argued that in investigating sources from which the Reformed developed their theology, it is more accurate to think of Reformed theologians of the late sixteenth and seventeenth centuries as being indebted to Thomas Aquinas rather than to Duns Scotus for their emphases and ways of working. This is in 'Not Scotist: understandings of being, univocity, and analogy in early-modern Reformed thought'.[18] At the end of *Divine Will and Human Choice*, however, Muller shows he still holds to a libertarian view of human freedom, it being situated in diachronic contingency in a root sense.

---

16. Cited in 'Jonathan Edwards and the Absence of Free Choice:', p. 13.

17. Turretin, *Institutes,* I. p. 663.

18. Muller, 'Not Scotist: understandings of being, univocity, and analogy in early-modern Reformed thought' (*Reformation and Renaissance Review*, 2012).

Among the Reformed writers of the era, as recognized by the authors of *Reformed Thought on Freedom,* the understanding of human freedom as a species of contingence draws on these distinctions [between the *sensus compositus* and *sensus divisus,* the *necessitatis consequentis* and *necessitas consequentiae,* and the *simultas potentiae* and the *potentia simultatis*][19] to argue a highly specified form of primary indifference to objects – a root, or in [Theophilus] Gale's language "habitual power" of negation or "radical indifference". Even so, Voetius and Turretin make the point against notions of indifference, that indifference, or *simultas potentiae,* exists only in a root sense, in the primary actuality of the will itself, prior to any operation.[20]

We have already seen that the two contingencies do not mark indeterminism, as Calvin (a compatibilist), respects them, in his writings against Pighius. But none of these distinctions entails indeterminism.

Turretin's View

For Turretin, human freedom is rational spontaneity consisting of two elements. 'There are two principal characteristics of free will in which its formal nature consists: (1) the choice, so that what is done is done by a previous judgment of reason; (2) the willingness, so that what is done is done voluntarily and without compulsion.'[21] Freedom is a product, then, of intellect and will, and 'the will can never oppose the decided and last judgment.' 'Hence it is evident that it is not here inquired concerning indifference in the first act or in the divided sense as to simultaneity of power which is called passive and objective (to wit, whether the will considered absolutely from its natural constitution, the requisites to action being withdrawn, is determinable to various objects and holds itself indifferently towards them.)'[22]

That is, what Turretin refers to as 'free will' denies 'Franciscan freedom'. The will has a natural equipoise, decided to one course of action or another by the operation of the intellect on it, or hesitating until the mind is made up.[23] There is no reference in all this to a root contingency,

---

19. *Divine Will and Human Choice,* p. 290. None of these distinctions entails indeterminism.

20. ibid., p. 290.

21. Turretin, *Institutes,* I. p. 664.

22. ibid., I. p. 665.

23. ibid., I. p. 665.

which remains a bit of a mystery. Later on, we shall consider this mystery further. Partly because of his fear of anachronism, Muller is reluctant to call such a view as 'compatibilist', but that is what it is. For Turretin the alternativity is that of the working of the will distinct from the working of the intellect, but as necessitated by the intellect; and this is compatibilistic.

Further, in his 'Parting of Ways' paper and his other paper of discussion in the reaction to it,[24] Muller has some revealing comments on his understanding of the RO view of the will that throw further light on his view of it, and by extension on contingency.

He questions Edwards's assertion that it is not the will that is free, but the man, and that by this he departed 'from the Reformed assumption of the freedom, in conjunction with the intellect, to choose freely according to its nature and arguing the determination of the will itself.' In pursuance of this latter claim Muller describes the relation of the will as an interrelation to the intellect. But we have seen that this is inaccurate. For Muller these alleged differences between Edwards and the RO found expression in his change from the RO's 'freedom of the will' to 'freedom of will'.[25] This is not quite accurate, however, for Edwards uses 'freedom of the will' and 'freedom of will' a number of times in his book without comment.

What Edwards was guarding against by his modification of faculty psychology is to avoid falling into what has come to be called the *homunculus* fallacy, the fallacy of the treating of the separate faculties of the soul as if the will, for example, had its own intellect, the intellect had a will, and so on. Edwards asserted,

> For the will itself is not an agent that has a will: the power of choosing, itself, has not a power of choosing. That which has the power of volition or choice is the man or the soul, and not the power of volition itself. And he that has the liberty of doing according to his will, is the agent or doer who is possessed the will; and not the will which he is possessed of.[26]

---

24. Muller, 'Jonathan Edwards and the Absence of Free Choice', and 'Jonathan Edwards, and Francis Turretin on Necessity, Contingency and Freedom of the Will'. (*Jonathan Edwards Studies* Vol. 4.).

25. Muller, 'Jonathan Edwards and the Absence of Free Choice', pp. 21-2.

26. Edwards, *Freedom of the Will*, p. 163. See also Helm, *Human Nature from Calvin to Edwards*, pp. 67, 257.

Here we must note Muller's words allegedly employed by the RO in characterizing the relation of intellect and will – 'interacting', and their 'conjoint act of choosing freely'. Later on he characterises that relationship as that of 'the interactive act of intellect and will'.[27] Here he claims, 'The older tradition understood that there had to be a root indifference prior to the engagement of will and intellect, defined by the potency of the will to multiple effects and characterized by freedom of contradiction and contrariety, in order for there to be freedom of choice'.[28] These views, in my view clearly mistaken, are repeated in the later article. When Muller writes 'Edwards presented the issue in terms of freedom of *will* and grounded the issue in the will itself without reference to the arbitrative function this is the intellect as being 'intrinsically free',[29] as intellect or understanding as having some of the features of the will. Edwards could not have been further from this.

The expression 'intertwining' is not found in Turretin, though. It suggests that the will has an intellect and also that there is a sort of parity or symmetry between the intellect and the will in their respective roles, calling for an intertwining. There is no avoiding the language of Turretin when he says that 'As it belongs to the intellect with regard to the decision of choice; so it belongs to the will with regard to the freedom. Hence you may rightly call it a mixed faculty, or a wedlock and meeting of both – the intellect as well as the will. Nevertheless you would not properly say that it consists rather in each faculty; for as the decision of the intellect is terminated in the will, so the liberty of the will has its roots in the intellect.'[30] A later 'compatibilist' would heartily concur!

The intellect and will are mutually connected by so strict a necessity that they can never be separated from each other. Their distinctions are to be sought in their different roles. 'Thus what is in the intellect affirmation and negation, that in the will is desire and avoidance.'[31]

---

27. Muller, 'Jonathan Edwards and the Absence of Free Choice', p. 20.

28. ibid., pp. 21-2.

29. 'Jonathan Edwards and the Absence of Free Choice', p. 20.

30. Turretin, *Institutes*, I. p. 660.

31. ibid., I. p. 660.

Turretin later calls their combination 'rational necessity'. 'For since the will is a rational appetite, such is its character that it must follow the last judgment of the practical intellect'.[32] Where Muller sees parity and conjoint activity, Turretin emphasizes the necessitating effect of the intellect on the will.

Turretin's contemporary Gisbertus Voetius (1589–1676) is very similar. 'The will is effectuated by the ultimate practical judgment of the intellect – not by a physical influx that would flow into it in a real way, but sweetly by an effective motion, as it is determined by that with which it agrees. The necessity that arises from this source does not destroy freedom but is even essential to determined freedom.'[33]

Note also,

> For if the will would not follow the lead of the intellect, then either the will would be directed to the unknown which is against its nature, because there is no such thing as desire for the unknown; or the will is directed to the bad as far as it is bad which is also against its nature, because by natural instinct everything loves itself.[34]

And in a parallel way Edwards has such things as this to say,

> On the whole, it is clearly manifest, that every effect has a necessary connection with its cause, or that which is the true ground and reason of its existence. And therefore if there be no event without a cause, as was proved before, then no event whatsoever is contingent in the manner that Arminians suppose the free acts of the will to be contingent.[35]

We noted earlier that neither the RO nor Edwards use the words 'compatibilism' or 'determinism', though Turretin, for example, uses the Latin verb *determinare* a number of times,[36] and Edwards refers to the determining of the will by the intellect.

---

32. ibid., I. p. 663.

33. Taken from *Reformed Thought on Freedom,* p. 152. 'A determined freedom' looks like determinism.

34. *Scholastic Discourse,* Johannes Maccovius (1588–1644). *On Theological and Philosophical Distinctions and Rules,* trans. Willem J. van Asselt, Michael D. Bell, Gert van den Brink, Rein Ferwerda (Apeldoorn, Holland, Instituut voor Reformatieonderzoek, Apeldoorn, Holland), 2009, p. 179.

35. Edwards, *The Freedom of the Will,* p. 216.

36. As we noted earlier RO discussion in the seventeenth century antedates the development of words with a suffix *ismus,* 'ism' in English.

He uses it not only in phrases such as 'determined by God'[37] which imply theological determinism, but also 'determined to it by a judgment of the intellect';[38] 'undetermined that it can act or not act';[39] 'although the will is free, this does not prevent its being determined by God and being always under subjection to him'.[40] This is so because liberty is not absolute, independent, and uncontrolled (the characteristics of God alone), but limited and dependent.[41]

Turretin's expressions are also similar to those of the other RO whom Edwards recommended, Petrus Van Mastricht (1630–1706), who taught at Utrecht during the second half of the seventeenth century. Writing of the will and the intellect, he says,

> Besides indifference, secondly for freedom is required counsel or choice, in which the will, by nature indifferent to both of two things, is determined to one or the other. And this determination, in the created will, at least concerning means, comes from the last judgment of the practical intellect, when it shows to the will that this or that thing either agrees or disagrees with its own particular propensity and inclination (with which willing has an inseparable connection).[42]

Note the alternativity here, 'to the will that this or that thing', that is central to compatibilism. Edwards holds that it is characteristic of Arminians and of those who take an Arminian view of the freedom of the will, to think of the will as free to choose autonomously, and unintelligibly. Edwards also contrasts this position to one that is grounded in, or determined by, what is its cause, which is the strongest motive the agent has to achieve an end in view on that occasion. The motive is what excites the will to volition, which may be a single consideration or several such.[43]

> Whatever is a motive, in this sense, must be something that is extant in the view of the understanding or perceiving faculty. Nothing can induce the

---

37. Turretin, *Institutes*, I. p. 664.

38. ibid., I. p. 668.

39. ibid., I. p. 666.

40. ibid., I. p. 668.

41. ibid., I. p. 664.

42. Petrus Van Mastricht, *Theoretical-Practical Theology*, trans. Todd M. Rester, ed. Joel R. Beeke (Grand Rapids, Mich., Reformation Heritage Books, 2018), pp. 2, 301.

43. Edwards, *Freedom of the Will*, p. 141.

mind to will or act anything, any further than it is perceived, or in some way or other in the mind's view; for what is wholly unperceived, and perfectly out of the mind's view, can't affect the mind at all.[44]

Edwards contrasts this account of the understanding and will, the will following what the mind's 'greatest apparent good' is, with the claim that the will is free, that is, arising from such strongest motives, the determiner of its own acts. Determinism depends on the idea of choice, and a choice is a preference and follows this pattern of choosing according to the strongest motive. The similarity with Turretin's view is striking, as I hope we shall see with increasing clarity in chapters 5 to 7.

Edwards did not invent this, of course, but writes in the tradition of determinists, his forbears who were RO, in a tradition going back to ancient times. Some of the Stoics were compatibilists. Compatibilism is consistent with human alternativity, the ability to choose. We are daily, perhaps constantly, faced by choices between A and B, or A and not-A. The compatibilist does not have any difficulty with such alternatives, provided that the choice of A or B or not-A is grounded, or 'for a reason'. For this reason the compatibilist is not compelled to do everything by hidden forces, nor does he think of his life as lying before him like a railway line. There is an openness during which a person makes up his mind to choose one alternative or another. The many psychological features that can occur in doing this – hesitating, experiencing the presence of tension in a state of indecision, reluctance, running over the pros and cons in his mind, compromising, and so on, the determinist understands. Sometimes there are times when a person does not know what to do, at other times he can be surprised and find himself making a choice.[45] All these features are capable of being accounted for in compatibilist fashion provided that these various choosings or hesitations are grounded in reasons or preferences, and are not whimsical or random.

A recurring puzzle is the way in which Muller misinterprets compatibilism as it is exhibited in the RO and Edwards. On the one hand he has a predisposition to characterize compatibilism as producing

---

44. ibid., p. 142.

45. For more on this, Paul Helm, 'The "Openness" in Compatibilism', in *Philosophical Essays Against Open Theism,* ed. Benjamin H. Arbour (London, Routledge, 2019).

human 'automata'.[46] On the other hand he provides explanations that are compatibilist in character, seemingly without realizing the fact, and in places he acknowledges that the older Reformed position is 'very close' to compatibilism.[47]

Muller's 2019 paper

To round out our characterisation of Muller's view that 'the older tradition understood that there had to be a root indifference prior to the engagement of will and intellect, defined by the potency of the will to multiple effects and characterized by freedom of contradiction and contrariety, in order for there to be freedom of choice'.[48] This is coupled with Muller's disinterest in Edwards position as in 'I leave aside the issue of the interpretation of Jonathan Edwards's approach to free will, as settled in an earlier essay.'[49] Muller says that Katherin Rogers's comments on anachronism are 'highly instructive' citing 4-8 of her book on Anselm.[50] It would have been helpful for Muller to elaborate on this. In this section of her book she very clearly distinguishes various types of compatibilism. Why did Muller not tell the reader, as he refers to Rogers's book, which he prefers?[51]

In the years in which I have been engaged with the new work on the RO, together with this issue of the compatibilism of the RO, and the thought of Jonathan Edwards, my chief discussant in this project, Richard Muller, has approached these issues from two fronts. One has been the exploration of the various faculties of the soul which we have just been referring to, and we shall examine later on. The other is to approach the issues in the sparer and more ambiguous language of the logic and metaphysics (as Muller sees it) of the soul and its powers. We have just seen this in his quotation about the understanding that there had to be a root indifference prior to the engagement of will and intellect, defined by the potency of the will to multiple effects and

---

46. Muller, 'Neither Libertarian nor Compatibilst', 2019, p. 267.

47. Muller, *Divine Will and Human Choice*, p. 295.

48. Muller 'Jonathan Edwards and the Absence of Free Choice', pp. 21-2.

49. Muller, 'Neither Libertarian nor Compatibilist' 2019, p. 270.

50. Katherin Rogers, *Anselm on Freedom*, pp. 4-8.

51. Muller, 'Neither Libertarian nor Compatibilst' 2019, p. 272.

characterized by freedom of contradiction and contrariety, in order for there to be freedom of choice.[52]

As far as I can see, no RO theologian posits the central role to the place of potencies in human action in constructions such as, 'multiple potencies' and 'root potencies'.[53]

> The place for synchronicity or simultaneity of potencies is precisely in the assumption of the older faculty psychology held by the Reformed, that the will simultaneously (or synchronously) has multiple capabilities or potencies—while the place for diachronicity is in the assumption also held by the reformed, as a simple matter of logic, that a person cannot do A and not-A at the same time, but both before and after doing A can choose to do not-A. That person, moreover, can choose wither A or not-A because he has potency or capacity for either and can be identified as free because the resident potency to choose not-A does not evaporate when a person chooses A: it just cannot be actualized in the same moment.[54]

Muller suggests,

> But isn't it the case that Edwards's voluntary determining is a matter of spontaneity (and not genuine alternativity), given that the will, with its predispositions, is only going to will one thing and that, given the denial of faculty psychology, there is no deliberation such that could bring about a different determination?

In this sense any system of human choice is going to end in one thing. Edwards certainly has a place for deliberation, as we have seen. He also has a place for alternativity in choice. Whether this is what Muller calls 'genuine alternativity' is what we are in the process of discussing. The expression 'genuine alternativity' is tantalizing until Muller demonstrates what is its contrast, what 'bogus alternativity' is. So, the use of scholastic terminology does not of itself entail a rejection of compatibilism. Even the materialist Thomas Hobbes occasionally uses scholastic terminology. What establishes non-compatibilism is not whether the contingency is 'genuine' or the use of the language of alternativity such that in doing

---

52. Muller 'Jonathan Edwards and the Absence of Free Choice', pp. 21-2.

53. Muller, *Divine will and Human Choice*. There are references to 'multiple potencies': pp. 151, 168, 169, 192, 235, 249, 299, 316; 'root potencies' and 'root': pp. 37, 41, 54, 74, 197, 212, 250, 251, 264, 266, 267, 271, 272, 273, 285, 287, 290, 304, 305, 315, 316.

54. Muller, 'Neither Libertarian nor Compatibilst', 2019, p. 274.

X a person 'could have done Y', but what particular senses attach to such expressions.

In other words, 'there are multiple potencies existing simultaneously, but there is (and can be) only a single contingency that is actualized.'[55] But this is precisely the point that a compatibilist such as Edwards makes.[56] At the same time there is the choice of alternative A or B, and the choice between them is made according to the preference of the intellect.

I should add that in his later paper Muller gets himself in something of a tangle in further discussion of potencies. Here Muller shows a preference to understanding the nature of free will in terms of potencies. It is not clear that transitioning to this language produces any gain. Muller also has a tendency to rapidly adopt one scholastic idiom in place of another. So here he rejects the understanding of synchronic contingency in terms of the will to an understanding in terms of potencies. In his book he had occasionally mentioned 'resident potencies'.[57] But in his later 2019 paper he recasts his understanding of scholastic free will, as he understands this, into potencies. I doubt a reader of this new discussion[58] will find in it fresh light on the libertarian position he defends.

One of the features that the latest paper shows is the complexity of his views. The words of Bishop Berkeley come to mind:

> Upon the whole, I am inclined to think that the far greater part, if not all, of those difficulties which have hitherto amused philosophers, and blocked up the way to knowledge, are entirely owing to ourselves. That we have first raised a dust and then complain we cannot see.[59]

So Turretin's being a compatibilist makes the best sense. The overall arguments of the next three chapters are indirect and cumulative, given the assumption that Turretin nowhere says 'I'm a compatibilist'. For the most part, understanding Turretin as a compatibilist in this indirect way will rest on several different considerations. We have provided a range of circumstantial evidence from Edwards to the RO. In the next chapter we find that like Turretin, Edwards thinks of choice as either a choice

55. Muller, 'Neither Libertarian nor Compatibilst', 2019, p. 285.
56. I am grateful to Michael Preciado at this point.
57. Muller, *Divine Will and Human Choice,* p. 323.
58. Muller, 'Neither Libertarian nor Compatibilist', pp. 274-5.
59. George Berkeley, *Principles of Human Knowledge,* Paragraph III.

between A and B, or as A and not-B. He employs efficient, formal and final causes in explaining it, though he does not use this language. He is, like Turretin of course, an opponent of Arminian indeterminacy. Like Turretin he held that God, the human nature of Christ, and the redeemed in heaven, act necessarily. And then, in the final section, where Muller allows that Turretin is close to being a compatibilist, I have tried to assess the strength of Muller's appeal to 'multiple potencies' as a defence of Turretin's incompatibilism.

This chapter ends by a consideration of the defence that Richard Muller has made in *Divine Will and Human Choice* in his discussion of Turretin as having a non-compatibilist view of freedom, and in his 2019 article.[60] In these he for a moment comes close to compatibilism, but then disappointingly falls short. This section offers an explanation of why this is so. Here is Muller:

> The compatibilist can allow for choice, indeed, for a version of alternativity, on the assumption that the will can, and in fact will choose a different end or object if something, whether in the background or in the circumstances surrounding the choice, is different. All things being equal, however, both the past and the present situation being identical, the choice will be the same. The older Reformed view and the modern compatibilist view are, admittedly, very close at this point. There is, however, a difference that can be identified in the retention of the fourfold causality in the older Reformed view, and its loss, specifically, the loss of an inwardly final causality in the classical compatibilist view.[61]

This is promising. But such a choice is subordinate to the intellect. But in his later article, Muller seems to renege on this: Compatibilists recognise the presence of human choices through the working of the human reason to formulate alternative ways of satisfying needs. But, disastrously, it finds the idea that these mechanisms are taken as 'Better to identify synchronic contingency as "the idea that the operation of intellect and will is such that the *requisites for choice* being present, an agent *simultaneously (or synchronically) has the potencies to choose* A; *to refuse it, choosing not-A*; *or to choose B*, hence 'synchronic.'[62] Here

60. 'Neither Libertarian nor Compatibilist', *Journal of Reformed Theology*.

61. *Divine Will and Human Choice*, p. 295.

62. 'Neither Libertarian nor Compatibilist', *Journal of Reformed Theology*, 2019, p. 273.

synchronicity seems to encompass both intellect and will. Muller's acceptance of this possibility entails his libertarianism. And there is no doubt that compatibilists recognize that at the same time the creaturely intellect may have before it various goals. The question is, what makes for the choice between them? The answer is in general terms: 'the satisfaction of some specific end'. Muller does not recognize this factor, as we shall see.

But if human choices are diachronic, as they must be, since we are necessarily creatures in time, then when a choice is made between alternatives, then as soon as it is completed, it is impossible for the completed choice to be renewed, for the choice once made is necessitated, by a historical or accidental necessity, the sense in which yesterday cannot be revisited. The existence of the capacity that was expressed the choice is a historical fact now, like the outcome of the Battle of Waterloo now.

Muller comes near to compatibilism when he states that it advocates 'a different end or object if something, whether in the background or in the circumstances surrounding the choice is different.' For the compatibilist, free actions are caused by reasons or motives, not simply by the background or circumstances of the choice, though a change in these might affect the agent's reason or appetite. So this is nearly but not quite, and Muller proceeds down the incompatibilist path.

Despite suggestions that his account of action is 'mechanical' Edwards's compatibilism is consistently teleological, and he certainly does not envisage any moment of genuine indifference, of pure alternativity, as necessary for freedom, nor does Turretin's account of the working of the intellect and the will guarantee a moment of pure alternativity either, at least I have been unable to detect one. Muller goes on to say, 'The older faculty psychology recognised habits that define capabilities, but not predispositions that rule intellect and will.' No not intellect and will together, but the intellect necessitates the will.

There is nothing in Turretin that indicates that if the past had been identical, the intellect could have judged differently, and the will likewise. For Edwards such a state of affairs would have been irrational or incoherent; not a strength of freedom, but a fatal weakness.

Another puzzling reaction is Muller's assertion that Turretin and the RO generally are committed to human choices that are to be understood in terms of 'multiple potencies', 'resident potencies to do things that they are not doing'. 'Potency' is a general term for the powers of the soul. It muffles the particularities of the various powers of the mind even if it does not intend to. This claim persists in registering an allegiance to synchronicity, albeit of a diachronic kind, in a seemingly non-deterministic interpretation of Turretin and other RO. In the pages of *Divine Choice and Human Will*, Muller appeals to the significance of unactualized multiple potencies in a number of places, as here:

> What Helm's counter-argument fails to appreciate, however, is that even as there is a diachronic movement of one of the will's potencies into actuality, there is also the simultaneous presence of the unactualized potency to the opposite (which of course cannot be actualized simultaneously). What Turretin and Voetius indicate—and the authors of *Reformed Thought on Freedom* identify—is that at *t1* the will has two unactualized potencies, one actualized to *p* and the other at *not-p,* just as in the realm of pure possibility, there remain two possibilities *p* and *not-p*, one to be actualized at t2 as a contingent, and the other not to be actualized, remaining a pure possible.[63]

This complex style invoking *potentiae* has largely taken over the style of Muller's 'Parting of Ways' paper and the one that followed.[64] It is not Turretin's language. In these writings Muller uses the difference between the phrases 'the freedom of the will' as standing for Turretin's indeterminism and 'freedom of will' as standing for Edwards's determinism. But on inspection these phrases are not used consistently in the literature in this way. The preferred way of expressing the point is subject to the difficulty with the old way, that Turretin does not write in terms of the will having a mind of its own, but of executing the last judgment of the intellect. As was routine with the RO, the will is said to be 'blind'.[65] Turretin's doctrine is that the will cannot self-trigger, and can trigger only at the behest of the intellect in an act of free will or free choice. This generates hypothetical necessities.

---

63. Muller, *Divine Will and Human Choice*, pp. 298-9. References to potencies, usually as 'unactualized' are found for example on pp. 294, 297, 298, and 299.

64. 'Jonathan Edwards and the Absence of Free Choice', and 'Jonathan Edwards and Francis Turretin on Necessity, Contingency, and Freedom of Will.'

65. See Helm, *Human Nature from Calvin to Edwards*, pp. 87, 152, 153-4.

This is the compatibilistic understanding of diachronic contingency, then, the agent having exercised his freedom of choice and determined its object, the will still having the unused potency. One actual, the chosen, the other remaining unchosen, a pure possibility. This seems to be Muller's way of characterising the moment of pure indifference, pure contingency, and its consequences.

This diachronic state of things is made clear, and this supports a compatibilistic outlook. But Muller's idea is that in the will there exists a residual potency that is present after the will has made a choice, and that this is relevant to the choice having been indeterministic. He understands a use of contingency not as an element in synchronic contingency but in diachronic contingency, as providing a vital element in Turretin's and others' understanding of contingency. But what is non-deterministically free about a diachronic free choice? It seems, only if the will is inherently two-fold, even after the choice is made. This is what Miller may call a 'root indifference'. But Turretin disavows this: 'For since the will is a rational appetite, such is its nature that it *must* follow the last judgment of the practical intellect.'[66]

A further critical question here is, is this interpretation of Turretin textually warranted? Muller says that,

> Turretin, arguably, assumed that the underlying requirement for freedom of choice, was a fundamental spontaneity of the will resting on this essential or root indifference in primary actuality – with the indifference defined in terms of a simultaneity of potencies, but rather than rest his understanding of freedom radically in this indifference, as did the Molinists, he rested it in the uncoerced or spontaneous passage, on the basis of an uncoerced judgment, from the indifferent *actus primus* to the determinate *actus secundus*.[67]

This is hard to follow, but here Muller's 'arguables', twice on the same page,[68] look tentative and speculative. There is nothing in Turretin that corresponds to these phrases, nor in any other ways of denoting resident, root potencies in Muller's sense. Turretin's view seems to be that this is not a case of the potency of simultaneity, but rather he is asserting that the potency of simultaneity has no application

---

in the *actus secundus* except on pain of committing the person to the unacceptable Jesuit view of synchronic simultaneity, what we have referred to as 'Franciscan freedom'. Turretin says that this is the view that the will is 'always so indifferent and undetermined that it can act or not act. This our opponents pretend in order that its own liberty may be left to the will. We deny it'.[69] Isn't Muller here running headlong into the Jesuit view of freedom, despite his protestations to the contrary?

On page 297 of his book, towards the end of the page, Muller states this,

> The freedom of choice is not constituted by the root indifference of the will, although clearly it could not exist without this indifference; one might say that, for Turretin, this root indifference which he views as a result of human mutability, is a necessary but not sufficient condition for human freedom. Freedom is constituted formally—its *ratio formalis*— by the willing response to a rational judgment made by the intellect. Arguably, Turretin grounds alternatively in the intellect, given that he does not assume that freedom resides in the ability of the will as it engages an object *in actu secundo* to refuse the judgment of the practical intellect.

This is close if not equivalent to determinism. A philosopher once said of the question of whether he should possibly publish his essays, 'I have tossed a coin, and it came down as I thought it would. It stood on its edge. And I knocked it down'.

Second, had he asserted it, what would possessing a non-actualised potency amount to? Such a potency is one of two potencies, one of which has been exercised, and so is spent, in a choice. And so is not the remaining potency now unrealizable, because it is already in the past? The remaining non-actualized potency is presumably a vestigial power that it is impossible at this stage to realize, because the other potency has been actualized in the choice, whatever it was. What does this trace of the past contribute to indeterminism in the present? Possessing an unrealized potency appears to be a 'scholastic' expression in the worst sense, like possessing a potency to eat the ice cream when I have chosen and eaten the trifle!

This leads to another epistemological difficulty. According to Muller, for Turretin the will is a multiple-way power (perhaps two ways, perhaps

---

69. Turretin, *Institutes*, I. p. 666.

many ways), freely intertwining with the intellect in pursuit of the end or ends of the practical reason. Suppose this is true. How different is this state of affairs from the will possessing synchronic contingency, Franciscan freedom? How is this to be established? Apart from Muller's general view of freedom as diachronic, how can one be sure that for the RO the will behaves as Muller claims? Is this proposal the fruit of introspection, or is this yet another instance of how *a priori* theory masks awareness of the causal powers of the soul, the will and the appetites? What is the evidence for such a vestigial, un-realizable potency? I suggest that the only evidence tolerable is the *a priori* requirements of Muller's understanding of a scholastic theory of indeterminate choice. There is no empirical evidence, only what we might call the requirement of the demands of the purely theoretical evidence.

Where is the textual evidence that Turretin argues for *interaction* between the understanding and will, not only of the influence of the intellect on the will, but of the will on the intellect? I have not been able to detect it. As we have seen, Turretin is emphatic that the intellect and the will are two faculties in which the intellect dominates, that it identifies an end or ends, and the means to achieve or obtain the end or ends lie in the exercise of the will. What Muller says on the same page is nearer to Turretin's position. 'For intellective judgment to be completed in a choice or election, it must be engaged by the will—and for the will to act on its freedom it must receive a judgment of the intellect.'[70] The idea that the will acts freely in the sense of purely indifferently on receiving the judgment of the intellect goes considerably beyond what Turretin states. This is closer to what Muller asserts by maintaining: 'He [Turretin] in no way implies the possibility of the will rejecting the intellectual judgment.'[71]

In his work over the years Muller has stressed the point that scholasticism is not an ideology, but that it is a 'rather eclectic Christian Aristotelianism' a mix of several philosophical sources.

Thus, the rather eclectic Christian Aristotelianism of the Protestant orthodox drew on rules of logic and devices like the fourfold causality in order to explain and develop their doctrinal formulae – and only seldom, if ever, to import a full-scale rational metaphysics or physics

---

70. Muller, *Divine Will and Human Choice*, p. 252.

71. ibid., p. 253.

into theology. Contrary to what is sometimes claimed, the four-fold causality (i.e. efficient, formal, material, and final causes), does not imply a particular metaphysic. Specifically it is not by nature 'deterministic'. One can use the model to delineate the soteriological patterns of the eternal decree of God and its execution in time; one also can use the model to describe the sources and effects of human sinfulness and human moral conduct: or one can use the model to explain how a carpenter makes a table.[72]

Well said in 1999, but by 2011 poor Edwards was criticized for being intellectually constrained by not having room for the four-fold causality of Aristotle. I hope that later on Muller will find room in the canvas for the philosophical influences of Locke.

---

72. Richard A. Muller, '*Ad fontes Argumentorum:* The Sources of Reformed Theology in the 17th Century', Inaugural Lecture, University of Utrecht, 1999. Reprinted in *After Calvin*, New York Oxford University Press, 2003, p. 55.

CHAPTER 5

Francis Turretin and Jonathan Edwards: Theologians of the Same Niche

In this and the next two chapters we shall be concerned with three arguments for the conclusion that Turretin (and the RO more generally) were compatibilists. I here try to understand more features of Richard Muller's lecture 'Jonathan Edwards and the Absence of Free Choice: A Parting of Ways in the Reformed Tradition' (2011), and his account of the RO position on human free will in *Divine Will and Human Choice* (2017), and in his latest article.[1] In the book he overcomes his reluctance to refer to 'compatibilism' while endeavouring to defend a RO middle way between compatibilism on the one hand and 'Franciscan freedom', on the other. We shall also refer to relevant passages of *RTF*.

This chapter will identify the very similar theological niche that both Turretin and Edwards occupied, which provides good presumptive evidence that it is reasonable to conclude that they were both compatibilists. They were both classical theists, Augustinians, confessing both predestination and meticulous divine providence, the divine decrees, and so on, and a Chalcedonian Christology, and both were explicitly opposed to the position of the Jesuits and Arminians on grace and free will. These common positions can be understood as the boundaries of what I call their common theological niche. What I aim to show is that the varied evidence we shall consider, evidence both

---

1. 'Neither Libertarian nor Compatibilist', *Journal of Reformed Theology*, 2019.

from Turretin and Edwards together, shows more and more clearly the compatibilism of Turretin and the RO.

Determinare and Determinism

To begin with a comment on Turretin's determinism. As we have learned, the language of *determinare*, 'to determine', is on the surface of his treatment of freedom in the Tenth Topic of his *Institutes*, 'The Free Will of Man in a State of Sin'. In his view, free will is a coming together of the faculties of the human intellect and will, it is what he calls the 'marriage' of these faculties. This is his view of any case of practical reason, where the mind is involved in determining what the agent should do. In contrast to the Pelagians, the opponents of Augustine, he argues that free will as he understands it is not 'repugnant' from every necessity. He identifies six necessities. Two of these, physical necessity (which is inconsistent with choice), and compulsion, are inconsistent with liberty, because they eliminate the operation of willingness.[2] The person who has lost a leg cannot run, however much he wills to, nor can a person who is blackmailed, or with a pistol to his head, do what he wills. The remaining four necessities that Turretin identifies are: the necessity of dependence on God, 'the highest ruler and free cause',[3] his foreknowledge and the decree; the 'rational necessity of determination', the last judgment of the intellect informing the agent of his true (or apparent) good, what he calls 'rational necessity'; the moral necessity of habits, good or bad; and finally the 'necessity of the event', the fact that if Socrates sits, necessarily he sits, a case of what is currently called accidental or historical necessity.[4]

> XI. Although the will is free, this does not prevent its being determined by God and hence being always under subjection to him. This is because liberty is not absolute, independent and uncontrolled (the characteristics of God alone), but limited and dependent. Otherwise if no faculty is free, except it is in subjection to no one, either a free will does not exist in creatures or every second cause will be the first [cause].[5]

---

2. Turretin, *Institutes*, I. p. 662.
3. ibid., I. p. 663.
4. ibid., I. p. 667-9.
5. ibid., I. p. 664.

Here is a formulation that looks pretty close to determinism, does it not? A free will of the creature is determined by God. Turretin does not regard this as a case of determinism, but this is only because he does not possess the word '*determinismus*'. In *RTF* the authors make valiant efforts to give an alternative understanding of *determinare* to eliminate its causal force. Such as:

> The distinction between natural and free cause is given with the way they 'determine' their act. This technical term 'determination' should not be associated with the *modern* term 'determinism' because that term did not exist yet, the concept of determinism was denoted by other terms like 'Stoic fate'. Rather, determination means that a cause gets directed to one effect. A natural cause is determined by its *nature* to the act; a free cause determines itself by freedom to one of possible acts. Hence, determination refers to the state of a cause: being undetermined means that the (free) cause has not yet directed itself to a certain effect. A determined cause will produce its determined effect, but still the effect can be either contingent (determined by a free act) or necessary (determined by a natural act).[6]

This is not very clear, and some of it could be made consistent with compatibilism, which is straightforwardly deterministic. In other places in the book, *determinare* is said by them to do with the assigning of a truth value to an expression.[7]

Further, the distinction is made between a natural and a free cause. A natural cause is one that results from an animal instinct, such as a sheep's desire for grass. And a free cause is one confronted with possible (more than one) outcomes, involving choice. The compatibilist can concur with this. So a determined act is the outcome of such an act. The authors of *RTF* do not consider a free act as one that is an action for a reason. In fact, the authors are not clear about acting for a reason, giving rise to conditioned alternativity. Their idea of alternativity is of a choice without a cause, which Vos and company impute to the RO. But Turretin's is another kind of choice, that of a reasoned or grounded alternativity. Bearing this in mind is vital in what is to follow.

---

6. *Reformed Thought on Freedom*, p. 31.

7. ibid., p. 189. 'Determinate' is from 'to determine', but it does not refer to some state that has been caused to be, but to be defined, to be definite, settled, or fixed. Turretin rarely if ever uses the term in this sense.

This points to the feature of 'creatureliness'. The will can be viewed in relation to the creation and decree of God, and as such it is ultimately determined by God, but it is also a human act, brought about by the combined powers of the reason and the will, to determine itself. So in this second sense 'it [the will] cannot be said to determine itself (because it is determined by the intellect whose last judgment it must follow.)'[8] Note the strong expression 'must follow'. At points like these Turretin, using *determinare*, may be said to convey a double determinism, working at different levels, that of the divine decree and of the human soul. He is quite ready to use expressions such as 'determine' and 'determinate' to characterize these, though not to use 'determinism' because apparently there was then no such word.

God's determining of the will, mentioned by Turretin above, generates a case of hypothetical necessity since the condition of the will is the outcome of God's decree. He has decreed a state of affairs in which the operation of the human intelligence and will combine to choose so and so. A hypothetical necessity is precisely what Reformed compatibilism is a case of, for it holds that the freedom of the will is an act of the will subordinate to the reason or understanding. The conclusion that this appears to be an avowal of determinism is unavoidable. And the grounded choices at the level of human creatureliness is another case of hypothetical necessity, since had there been a preponderating reason the person could have chosen what he wanted to accomplish. His action would be spontaneously free.

Conditions for Responsibility

Compatibilism is the view of determinism that is consistent with human responsibility for good or evil. Like later compatibilists, Turretin touches on the conditions of responsibility of human actions as follows:

> To be free, election ought to enjoy an immunity from coaction [i.e. from force] and physical necessity, but not from the extrinsic necessity of dependence upon God and the intrinsic determination by the intellect. And so far is the determination to one thing (made by the reason) from taking away free election, that it rather makes it perfect. It therefore elects this or that because it is determined to it by the judgment of the intellect.[9]

---

8. Turretin, *Institutes*, I. p. 664.
9. ibid., I. p. 668.

Brutes are without self-knowledge and so have no discernment between vicious or virtuous actions. And in a case of human responsibility, it is not due to indifference, choice, alone, but by the ability to obey or disobey freely, that is, without compulsion, from the previous operation of the intellect. And exhortations and commands are not removed by this state of affairs, but are rather established. For persuasion involves the provision of reasons and exhortations, costs and benefits, which may decisively affect the will. Finally, rewards or punishments are not due to the presence of indifference, but from spontaneity arising from a judgment of the intellect.[10]

Muller says,

> Among the differences between Edwards' view on freedom and those of the earlier Reformed tradition, perhaps the primary point concerns the basic language of freedom itself. Whereas the older tradition consistently presented the problem in terms of free *choice* or *liberum arbitrium*, understood as the interactive act of intellect and will, Edwards presented the issue in terms of freedom of *will* and grounded the issue in the will itself without reference to the arbitrative function of intellect.[11]

This is rather concerning. For one thing, Edwards had a unified account of the person, rather than one consisting of discrete faculties, in which it is not the will that is free but the man. He took this language from John Locke *verbatim*. But more appropriately, Edwards took that view in his book on the 'freedom of the will' (an expression which Turretin also uses).[12] The operation of free will is not arbitrary, but for Edwards it follows the last dictate of the understanding.[13]

By contrast, Muller has consistently held the view that the RO were indeterminists in their view of human free will, and that in any case determinism and compatibilism are essentially modern concepts, with a different pedigree from scholasticism. They are secular ideas developed in the early modern world by the impetus of the concept of mechanism

---

10. ibid., I. p. 668.

11. Muller, 'Jonathan Edwards and the Absence of Free Choice', p. 20.

12. For examples of Turretin using this expression, his Tenth Topic of the *Institutes* is entitled 'The Free Will of Man in a State of Sin'. The first Question discussed the term 'free will'.

13. Part I Section 2 of Edwards's book on free will is entitled 'Concerning the Determination of the Will', *Institutes,* I. p. 659f.

and the materialism of Thomas Hobbes. By contrast he holds that the RO had hylomorphic assumptions, sharing the teleological outlook of Thomas Aquinas, and which observed the scholastics' distinction between the theoretical and the practical reason, and their view that what is chosen was articulated in terms of the four-fold causality of Aristotle, and with a multiplicity of scholastic distinctions, some of which we shall meet later. John Locke, who Muller says was in turn influenced by Thomas Hobbes, influenced others among whom was the Calvinist Jonathan Edwards. The implication is that Locke is in this materialist determinist-compatibilist line of Hobbes, and that the RO, represented by Turretin, adopted the contingency of indeterminist free choice.[14] This is a misunderstanding.

Here is a little more evidence of the use of *determinare*, from another New Englander (besides Samuel Willard, who we shall consider in due course), John Norton (1606–63):

> The Will cannot be compelled: to say, That which is done willingly, is done constrainedly, is to affirm a contradiction; namely, that which is willing, is unwilling.[15]

God can determine the Will, and not prejudice the Nature of the Will, because He is an infinite Cause.

> God determineth the Will suitably and agreeably to it's own Nature; i.e., freely. He so determineth the Will as the Will determineth it self. God so determineth the Will, as a first free Agent, as that the Will determineth it self as a second free Agent. The Efficiency of God offereth no violence, nor changeth the nature of things, but governeth them according to their own natures; it reacheth from one end to the other mightily, and sweetly ordereth all things. The external, transient, efficacious Motion of God upon the Will, determineth the will with a real determination; the Will so moved, moveth it self with a real, and formal determination.[16]

---

14. Richard Muller, 'Jonathan Edwards and the Absence of Free Choice', Muller supposes that Hobbes and Locke were linked, and hence that Edwards's views, in which Edwards was influenced by Locke, were also influenced by Hobbes. But on Locke's ignorance of Hobbes, see for example Quentin Skinner. 'Meaning and Understanding in the History of Ideas' (*History and Theory*, 1969), pp. 25-6.

15. John Norton, *The Orthodox Evangelist* (London, John Macok, for Ludwick Lloyd, 1657), p. 114.

16. ibid., pp. 114-115. Norton cites Augustine, *The City of God*, Bk. VII, Ch. 30, trans. John Healey, edited R. V. G. Tasker, Two volumes (London, J. M. Dent & Sons, 1945),

God determines the will with a real determination, such that the will moves itself.

Self-knowledge and Conscience

Both Turretin and Edwards stress that human responsibility is distinct from that of non-human animals, and root it in conscience, part of the *sensus divinitate*, the sense of deity, or the *semen religionis,* the seed of religion. Turretin holds that animals act from the 'blind impulse of nature or a brute instinct and innate appetite, without, however, any light of reason (as the necessity in fire to burn, a combustible object being supplied; the necessity in a horse to eat the straw or grass put before him) and without any choice'.[17] And 'The natural brute, not knowing itself, does not have a relation of vice or virtue, but only the natural rational'.[18]

> [T]his power and stimulus of conscience (the inseparable attendant of crime either begun or finished) whose sense can neither be blunted, nor accusation escaped, nor testimony corrupted, nor can it fail to appear on the appointed day, nor its tribunal be shunned. For how comes it that the conscience is tormented after a crime committed (even in secret and with remote judges), where no danger threatened from men (even in those who held supreme power) unless because it is affected by a most intimate sense of deity ...?[19]

Edwards, far from being a mere mechanist when he discusses the origins of human action, and human possession of a sense of responsibility, alludes to the *sensus divinitatis* as Turretin did.

> The Apostle says, *Romans* 2:14–15, that 'the Gentiles, which have not the law, do by nature the things contained in the law; these, having not the law, are a law unto themselves: which show the work of the law written in their hearts, their conscience also bearing witness.' In order to men's having the law of God made known to them by the light of nature, two things are necessary. The light of nature must not [only] discover to them that these

---

'So does He [God] dispose of all the works of creation, that each one has the peculiar motion permitted it. For though it can do nothing without Him, yet is not anything that which He is' (I. p. 221).

17. Turretin, *Institutes*, I. p. 662.

18. ibid., I. p. 668.

19. ibid., I. p. 173.

and those things are their duty, i.e. that they are right, that there is a justice and equality in them, and the contrary unjust; but it must discover to 'em also, that 'tis the will of God that they should be done, and that they shall incur his displeasure by the contrary. For a law is a signification of the will of a lawgiver, with the danger of the effects of his displeasure, in case of the breach of that law.

The Gentiles had both these. Their natural consciences testified to the latter after this manner: natural conscience suggests to every man the relation and agreement there is, between that which is wrong or unjust, and punishment; this naturally disposes men to expect it. To think of wrong and injustice, especially such as often is seen without any punishment to balance it, is shocking to men's minds. Men therefore are naturally averse to thinking that there will be no punishment, especially when they themselves are great sufferers by injustice, and have it not in their power to avenge themselves; and the same sense made guilty persons jealous lest they should meet with their deserved punishment. And this kept up in the world, among all nations, the doctrine of a superior power, that would revenge iniquity; this sense of men's consciences kept alive that tradition, and made it easily and naturally received. The light of nature discovered the being of a deity otherwise; but this sense of conscience upheld this notion of him, that he was the revenger of evil, and it also made them the more easily believe the being of a deity itself. God also gave many evidences of it in his providence amongst the heathen, that he was the revenger of iniquity. When the light of nature discovered to 'em that there was a God that governed the world, they the more easily believed him to be a just being, and so that he hated injustice, because it appeared horrid to think of a supreme Judge of the universe, that was unjust. *Genesis* 18:25, 'Shall not the Judge of all the earth do right?'[20]

He develops this point in *The Freedom of the Will*,

The common people don't ascend up in their reflections and abstractions, to the metaphysical sources, relations and dependences of things, in order to form their notion of faultiness or blameworthiness. They don't wait till they have decided by their refinings, what first determines the will; whether it be determined by something extrinsic, or intrinsic; whether volition determines volition, or whether the understanding determines the will; whether there be any such thing as metaphysicians mean by

---

20. Edwards *Miscellany* p. 528, *WJE* online, Vol. 18.

contingence (if they have any meaning); whether there be a sort of a strange unaccountable sovereignty in the will, in the exercise of which, by its own sovereign acts, it brings to pass all its own sovereign acts. They don't take any part of their notion of fault or blame from the resolution of any such questions. If this were the case, there are multitudes, yea, the far greater part of mankind, nine hundred and ninety-nine out of a thousand would live and die without having any such notion as that of fault ever entering into their heads, or without so much as once having any conception that anybody was to be either blamed or commended for anything. To be sure, it would be a long time before men came to have such notions. Whereas 'tis manifest, they are some of the first notions that appear in children; who discover as soon as they can think, or speak, or act at all as rational creatures, a sense of desert. And certainly, in forming their notion of it, they make no use of metaphysics. All the ground they go upon consists in these two things; *experience*, and a *natural sensation* of a certain fitness or agreeableness which there is in uniting such moral evil as is above described, viz. *a being or doing wrong with the will*, and resentment in others, and pain inflicted on the person in whom this moral evil is. Which *natural sense* is what we call by the name of 'conscience.'[21]

The RO and Edwards have a similar outlook on the grounds of moral responsibility.

Muller on Compatibilism

In earlier writings on the topic of the freedom of the will, Muller resisted a straight comparison between the RO and compatibilists such as Jonathan Edwards, as in his lecture on Edwards and Turretin as constituting 'two ways'.[22] As we saw earlier, even to refer to Edwards as a 'compatibilist' is by Muller's standards an anachronism. But we have seen the readiness with which Vos and Muller use the modern terms 'synchronic contingency' and 'diachronic contingency', and this use may reasonably be taken as a warrant for referring to Edwards as a 'compatibilist', that is, a determinist who holds that it can be compatible with personal responsibility.

However, questions posed at the end of his book *Divine Will and Human Choice* suggest a willingness, at the risk of anachronism, to make

---

21. Edwards, *Freedom of the Will* , pp. 357-8.
22. Muller, 'Jonathan Edwards and the Absence of Free Choice' (2011).

comparisons between compatibilism and indeterminism, the latter position that he himself favours, as the view of freedom that is favoured by the RO.

Edwards was certainly influenced by the early Enlightenment, by John Locke and George Berkeley,[23] in particular, but he retained sufficient of the theological outlook of Reformed Orthodoxy to make himself rather an exception to any latitudinarian precedents that emanated from Locke. Rather, he was influenced by new developments in philosophy and of the natural science of the seventeenth century, without being blown away by them. Paradoxically, he defended much of Calvinistic orthodoxy using some of the same tools that others used to weaken or attempt to demolish it. Edwards was something of an anomaly, therefore.[24]

The issues raised in what follows pose a challenge for what Muller claims was the RO adherence to two-way contingency as the central activity of the will, a way of characterising indeterminism. As we know by now, Edwards adhered to no such concept. Such contingency was the central feature of the libertarianism and indeterminism that he strongly repudiated as irrational, if not as incoherent. In what now follows, in order to address problems of continuity and discontinuity between RO and Edwards, we shall concentrate on the nature of free will, with issues involving indifference, the relation of the intellect and the will, and the nature of contingency.

In *Divine Will and Human Choice*, Muller summarizes the alleged differences between the RO and the Edwards position, determinism, in a number of assertions. Here are three of Muller's conclusions embodying our interests. It is here that he refers to compatibilism. All are on page 323 of *Divine Will and Human Choice*.

> If determinism is taken to mean that there is no contingency in the world order such that human acts and effects, as willed by individual human beings, could not have been otherwise (or in view of resident potencies, could not be otherwise), then Reformed thought is not determinist.

The short answer to this is that compatibilism states that in their freedom human acts and their effects could have been otherwise, had there been an overriding reason for doing otherwise, and it was within the agent's

---

23. Edwards quotes Locke *verbatim*. On Berkeley see, for example, Scott Fennema, 'George Berkeley and Jonathan Edwards on idealism: considering an old question in light of new evidence' (*Intellectual History Review*, 2017).

24. Edwards, *The Freedom of the Will*, p. 430 ff.

grasp. In the passage note the stress on contingency, and the test of contingency as what 'could have been otherwise'. We shall consider the use of such phrases in more detail later. Part of the RO picture according to Muller is that there is contingency in the world when considered from the human level, but no contingency when viewed from the viewpoint of the all-encompassing divine decree, which is itself contingent, an expression of the divine sovereignty.[25]

> If compatibilism is taken to mean not only that the determination of all human acts and human freedom are epistemically compatible but also that this compatibility rules out genuine liberty of contradiction and liberty of contrariety in human choosing such that a choice at any given moment (given both divine and human freedom) could be otherwise, then Reformed Orthodoxy is clearly not compatibilist.

Here, as elsewhere, Muller uses the adjective 'genuine' to modify choice or liberty. To have 'genuine' liberty is another way of asserting indeterminism, I guess, for compatibilists are said to lack it. We shall see what this means later on. But there are places where Edwards discusses the liberties of contradiction and contrariety. We shall also consider them later. They are among the evidence that Edwards did not altogether free himself of scholasticism, and defends genuine choices in his determinism. If the presence of the liberties of contradiction (the liberty to perform A or not-A) and of contrariety (the liberty to perform A or B) are claimed by Muller as sure signs of the presence of contingency, and so inconsistent with compatibilism, then how does it come about that Edwards refers positively to them? It is because of his compatibilism, while not using the scholastic terminology.

Here's a further paragraph of summary:

> If, further, compatibilism is taken to mean the ontic (as well as epistemic) compatibility of the divine determination of all things with freedom of will, but not with freedom of choice understood as freedom of contradiction and contrariety, then the Reformed Orthodox were not compatibilist.[26]

The short answer is that the Reformed compatibilist takes free choice to be compatible with freedom of contradiction and contrariety.

---

25. Turretin, *Institutes,* I. pp. 210-11.
26. *Divine Will and Human Choice*, p. 322-3.

These statements in the Conclusion of the book are evidence of a belief that in supposing that the RO are compatibilist in their outlook, and so in line with Edwards, their avowal of contingency is overlooked or airbrushed away. Edwards's compatibilism allowed for contingency in other senses: in (a) epistemic contingency, that is, contingency as surprise; and (b) the belief in an agent's mind that she could have done otherwise had reasons to act thusly been uppermost, that is, with her choice, and even (c) that such contingency is consistent with the possibility of not knowing in advance of how one's mind will be made up, which alternative course of action one will choose.

In what follows we shall note that care needs to be taken with expressions such as 'could have done otherwise', 'genuine liberty', and particularly with 'contingency', in order that their use does not from the outset beg the question against compatibilism. What follows is concerned with teasing out all these senses, and doing so first by examining Turretin's discussion of human liberty, and making a detailed comparison of it with Edwards's outlook.

Turretin and Edwards on Free Will

Little will be said here about free will and its relation to the divine decree other than to note that Reformed views on the divine decree could hardly be expected to create a difficulty for the view that human freedom is compatibilist, as my opening comments on Turretin made clear. The compatibilism of human choice is one means by which the divine decrees are brought to pass. Edwards does not say much about his views of the freedom of the will and the divine decree except in his discussion of the charge that divine sovereignty makes God the author of sin.[27] We shall shortly consider this, another topic which the RO and Edwards had each to face, further evidence that they occupied the same theological niche.

While Muller is of the view that the RO are committed to *contingency* in human freedom, on the other wing of this debate, the contributors to the *RTF*[28] are united in the novel view that the RO are allegedly committed to *synchronic contingency*. As we have seen, synchronic contingency is the idea that the will is such that the requisites for action A to be performed

---

27. Edwards, *The Freedom of the Will*, p. 397f.
28. *Reformed Thought on Freedom*, p. 33

being present, an agent has the power to choose either A or B at that very moment, hence 'synchronic'. One of the great strengths of Muller's book is the historical case he makes against the influence of this novel supposition.

The RO certainly used the terminology of 'contingency' in respect of free human action, though not frequently, and only in a diachronic fashion, as we shall see. Yet Muller, despite his criticism of compatibilism, in his account of the RO retains a residual place for two-way contingency as an element in their view of human freedom, which is presented in compatibilism as a conditioned alternatively, nor of the libertarianism of what we have called 'Franciscan freedom'. And so Muller holds that the RO did not commit themselves to compatibilism on the one hand nor to the unconditional alternativity of synchronic contingency on the other, but to a third way. So the central question for us is, what did the RO mean by freedom and contingency if Muller is correct in his view that they did not favour either synchronic contingency or compatibilism? Edwards avoided the use of 'contingency' because it is used to mean 'something which has absolutely no previous ground or reason, with which its existence has any fixed and certain connection'.[29]

There is need to go over some of the ground that leads Muller to the positions implied by his assertions above, particularly given the tendency (as we have been showing) that RO discussions appear to be compatibilistic rather than libertarian. Their position favours the Edwardsean position, one similar to Muller's views of them. In pursuit of an answer to the question of whether the anthropology of the RO permits or requires compatibilism, what follows is a further discussion of Francis Turretin's understanding of human freedom in his *Institutes*, a book that Edwards recommended, and to which Muller gives extensive attention in *Divine Will and Human Choice*. Here we shall consider what Turretin says on indifference, and then on contingency, and later on, on what Edwards has to say.

Turretin, Indifference and Contingency in Human Choice

The way in which Turretin frames his discussion of free will in the Tenth Topic of his *Institutes* is itself of importance for our comparison between him and Edwards. Here is how he begins.

---

29. Edwards, *Freedom of the Will*, p. 155.

IV The subject of free will is neither the intellect, nor the will separately, but both faculties conjointly. As it belongs to the intellect with regard to the decision of choice, so it belongs to the will with regard to freedom. Hence you may rightly call it a mixed faculty, or a wedlock and meeting of both – the intellect as well as the will. Nevertheless you would not properly say it consists rather in each faculty; for as the decision of the intellect is terminated in the will, so the liberty of the will has its roots in the intellect.[30]

He proceeds to affirm that the will and intellect are necessarily connected and combined, and so are inseparable, but with logical and temporal priority being assigned to the intellect. This implies a fairly unified conception of the soul, though perhaps not quite as unified as Samuel Willard's, who in his *A Brief Reply to Mr George Kieth* maintained 'that *not the understanding, nor the will in the man, but the whole man is a free cause*'.[31] We shall glance again at Willard later.

Turretin's basic stance is therefore that freedom does not *consist in* indifference in which the will alone is sufficient, but in the intellect and will combined, the will being a *constituent* in such freedom, along with the intellect or understanding. Though throughout this discussion he rarely uses the terminology of contingency, the discussion of indifference is a related way of coming at the issue of contingency. Compatibilism is of theological importance for the RO because of the position of the Jesuits and Arminians, in the view of whom freedom *does* consist in indifference in the manner of Franciscan freedom. In his *Institutes* Turretin explicitly distanced himself from the Jesuits, and by implication from the Arminians.

Turretin says that freedom does not *consist in* indifference but in 'rational spontaneity' or 'rational willingness', the combining of intellect and will that we have noted. These phrases are handy because they help us to keep in mind both the role of the intellect ('rational') and of the will ('spontaneity', 'willingness'). The English translator of Turretin's *Institutes* uses these two words to translate the phrase *lubentia rationis*. It

---

30. Turretin, *Institutes,* I. p. 660.

31. Samuel Willard, *A Brief Reply to Mr George Kieth,* p. 15. I refer to Willard because he was a New England RO, and the Edwards family had connections with this popular preacher and voluminous author. Jonathan's father, Timothy Edwards, was one of the public subscribers to the author's *A Compleat Body of Divinity* (Boston, 1726).

is an essential feature of the operation of freedom that free acts are willed by the agent, and so are uncoerced, and so spontaneous, yet not acts of pure indifference. Once again the coincidence with compatibilism is evident.

At this point Turretin distinguishes between indifference understood *in sensu diviso* and *in sensu composito,* a scholastic distinction also used by Willard and other RO theologians. He claims that the 'willingness' in the expression 'rational willingness' involves indifference *in sensu diviso.* That is, indifference is an essential feature of the will as such, and denotes the power of the will usually to move frictionlessly in accordance with the judgment of the intellect. If the judgment is of the practical intellect, in considering an end that the agent wishes to gain, the intellect engages the will to take one direction, though if it had been required by the intellect to take a different direction, or no direction at all, the will could have acted on such judgments appropriately. This reference to the will alone is the will's indifference *in sensu diviso,* considered in abstraction. A will that lacks such a power of indifference is thus a contradiction in terms, an impossibility. For the will is simply an executor of the desires or appetites and decisions of the practical reason. The role of the will is to make to happen (assuming there are no external impediments to action) whatever the intellect overall prefers to be done.

In response to the question, 'How does indifference play a part in free action?', Turretin discusses three cases. It is at this point that the freedom of contrariety and the freedom of contradiction are introduced as kinds of choice, and therefore, as Muller puts it, kinds of freedom. Bear in mind that Muller claims that compatibilism 'rules out genuine liberty of contradiction and liberty of contrariety in human choosing such that a choice at any given moment (given both divine and human freedom) could be otherwise'.[32] He gives no reason. The three instances of the will's operating are as follows: The will can elicit or suspend an act X, i.e. do it, or not do it, what Turretin calls 'the liberty of exercise or contradiction'; or it can do either, following the intellect in choosing X or in choosing Y, called the 'liberty of contrariety and specification', as directed in each case by the intellect. And the third type of case is that as long as the intellect remains doubtful and uncertain as to what

---

32. Muller, *Divine Will and Human Choice*, p. 323 (See para. (2) above).

to choose, and the mind is not made up, the will retains its essential willingness, in the sense that it remains poised to fulfill whatever the intellect next finally directs, once the mind or intellect is made up. The decision of Joe to wear a tie, and not to go out tieless, is a case of the liberty of contradiction; his decision to wear a yellow and not a green tie, is an instance of the liberty of contrariety; and an indecision as to whether to wear a tie or not is his will remaining in a state of readiness, a state of doubt and indecision.

And so Turretin goes on to state,

> We do not deny that the will of itself is so prepared that it can either elicit or suspend the act (which is the liberty of exercise and of contradiction) or be carried to both of opposite things (which is the liberty of contrariety and specification). We also confess that the will is indifferent as long as the intellect remains doubtful and uncertain whither to turn itself. But concerning indifference in the second act and in a compound sense (as to simultaneity of power called objective and subjective) – whether the will (all requisites to acting being posited; for example the decree of God and his concourse; the judgment of the practical intellect etc.) is always so indifferent and undetermined that it can act or not act. This our opponents [that is, Jesuits and Arminians] pretend in order that its own liberty may be left to the will. We deny it.[33]

What these three cases have in common is that in each of them indifference, or alternativity, plays its part, but in different ways, and in each case it is subordinate to some condition of the intellect, either the mind as made up or as not yet made up. So indifference is an essential property of the free will, hence Turretin's use of the phrase that freedom is 'rational willingness'. Turretin does not say that these three types of case exhaust all the possible alternatives, but it would be reasonable to think that they do.[34]

So indifference *in sensu diviso* refers to a power, a potentiality of the will, the power intrinsic to the will, to execute what the practical reason may decide as an end in action. In coming to make the mind up from a state of indecision, the intellect typically weighs alternatives in the light of what they are believed to deliver. In determining one alternative, the

33. Turretin, *Institutes*, I. pp. 665-6.
34. ibid., I. p. 665.

intellect acts with spontaneity or willingness (*lubentia rationalis*). This is indifference *in sensu composito*. And the point that Turretin emphasizes against the Jesuits and Arminians, is that when the will carries out the dictates of the intellect, it has in that case rested its willingness in that particular case, since it has decisively chosen an alternative. By contrast, were the intellect to remain in a state of indecision, then it would remain in suspense. At no point does Turretin recognize the presence of what Muller refers to as a 'root potency' *in sensu composito*. We shall return to the significance of such root potencies for Muller's case later on.

Jonathan Edwards and Scholasticism

What of Edwards at points like these? Here it is to be noted that though due to his dislike of scholasticism Edwards abandoned the scholastic style, he nevertheless has his own way of describing the matter of several relevant scholastic distinctions, including in accepting a modified Aristotelian four-fold causality. In this way he follows Turretin fairly closely, as we shall see.

Towards the end of the *Freedom of the Will*, Edwards defended himself from the charge that his own style was metaphysical and abstruse.

> If the reasoning which has been made use of, be in some sense metaphysical, it will not follow, that therefore it must be abstruse, unintelligible, and akin to the jargon of the schools. I humbly conceive, the foregoing reasoning, at least as to those things which are most material belonging to it, depends on no abstruse definitions or distinctions, or terms without a meaning, or of very ambiguous and undetermined signification, or any points of such abstraction and subtlety, as tend to involve the attentive understanding in clouds and darkness. There is no high degree of refinement and abstruse speculation, in determining, that a thing is not before it is, and so can't be the cause of itself; or that the first act of free choice, has not another act of free choice going before that, to excite or direct it; or in determining, that no choice is made, while the mind remains in a state of absolute indifference ....[35]

Edwards's position is that while he is occasionally caustic in his descriptions of scholasticism, nevertheless from time to time he uses scholastic distinctions seemingly without blinking.

---

35. Edwards, *The Freedom of the Will*, p. 424.

Causation

In one place Muller says that Edwards 'neglects' formal and final causes in his account of causation.[36] That is, he suggests that Edwards abandons the scholastic understanding of action in terms of four-fold causation – material, efficient, formal and final – and that this has serious consequences for his view of freedom; as a result it is 'mechanistic'. But Edwards can be thought of as providing answers to the 'Why?' questions posed by three if not of these four scholastic terms, in ways of his own. For example, although he does not use those scholastic terms, he repeatedly refers to the *ends* or *purposes* of action (final causes), and to *apprehensions*, a way of referring to formal causes, and to efficient causes, of course.[37]

Edwards also fails to defend a mechanistic, linear application of causation in these words, despite Muller's repeated charges to the contrary, as is clear here,

> But the dependence and connection between acts of volition or choice, and
> their causes, according to established laws, is not so sensible and obvious.
> And we observe that choice is as it were a new principle of motion and
> action, different from that established law and order in things which is most
> obvious, that is seen especially in both corporeal and sensible things; and
> also that choice often interposes, interrupts and alters the chain of events
> in these external objects, and causes 'em to proceed otherwise than they
> would do, if let alone, and left to go on according to the laws of motion
> among themselves.[38]

And so Edwards sees human choice as teleological, purposive, and interrupting rather like the RO, certainly not as linear or mechanistic.

The radical character of Edwards's choice of terms signals some dissatisfaction with the formal language of scholasticism and with all terms that are as 'void of distinct and consistent meaning [as found]

---

36. Richard Muller, 'Jonathan Edwards and Francis Turretin on Necessity, Contingency, and Freedom of Will', p. 272.

37. See, in his *Freedom of the Will*, instances of the 'desired end' (p. 138), and the 'means and end' (p. 366) as formal or final causes, and his appreciation of an efficient cause as 'antecedent dependence' (pp. 180-1). Given the subject matter, it is understandably more difficult to find a use for 'material cause' to characterize the stuff out of which a mental object is made.

38. Edwards, *Freedom of the Will*, pp. 158-59.

in the writings of Duns Scotus, or Thomas Aquinas'.[39] Nonetheless, in so far as he judges terms to have a meaning, he has a set of parallel expressions of his own.[40] So he does not use the term 'synchronic' but instead the phrase 'same time'.[41] But nowhere does he criticize any RO theologian and their view of human freedom, saving his energy for the 'Arminianising' views of his contemporaries such as Thomas Chubb and Daniel Whitby.

It is clear to any reader of his *Freedom of the Will* that the willing of an end, the prospect of future pleasure or 'agreeableness', has degrees, a point emphasized in a passage such as the following:

> [I]f several future enjoyments are presented together, as competitors for the choice of the mind, some of them judged to be greater, and others less; the mind also having a greater sense and more lively idea of the good of some of them, and of others a less; and some are viewed as of greater certainty and probability than others; and those enjoyments that appear most agreeable in one of these respects, appear less so in others ....[42]

Such a way of thinking is perfectly consistent with recognizing there are situations in which the will hesitates because the mind is not yet made up, or that the mind unexpectedly and suddenly changes.

In the case of indifference *in sensu composito*, the supposed capacity of the will to possess freedom even when its choice has been made, the *Freedom of the Will* may be said to present an at-length critique of this notion, favoured by Jesuits and Arminians, which the RO Gisbertius Voetius called a 'chimerical indifference',[43] and Turretin refers to as a pretension.[44] A chimera is the product of an unchecked imagination. A pretension is an idea spun out of nothing substantial. Whether by these epithets Voetius and Turretin meant that such an idea was formally self-contradictory, or not, is unclear. They certainly thought of it as a

---

39. ibid., p. 228.

40. Helm, 'Turretin and Edwards Once More' (*Jonathan Edwards Studies*, Vol. 4 No. 2, 2014), p. 288.

41. Edwards, *Freedom of the Will,* pp. 196, 207.

42. ibid., p. 146.

43. See *Reformed Thought on Freedom,* p. 150.

44. Turretin, *Institutes,* 'This our opponents pretend in order that its own liberty may be left to free will. We deny it', I. p. 666.

fantastic, nonsensical supposition. In making this criticism, the RO had the Jesuits and Arminians in view,[45] that liberty *consists in* the will.[46]

Let us next consider how Edwards stands in connection with other scholastic distinctions used by Turretin, that we mentioned earlier, between the freedom of contrariety and of contradiction. Does he have a use for it? Here again he does not use this terminology. In his summary paragraph cited earlier, Muller refers to these as the 'genuine liberty of contradiction and liberty of contrariety in human choosing'.[47] Turretin refers to them as the liberty of exercise and of contradiction respectively.[48] But it is clear that Edwards also cites examples of contrariety in his own way. 'If it be now, on the whole of what at present appear to him, most agreeable to speak, then he chooses to speak: if it suits him to keep silence, then he chooses to keep silence.'[49] 'All that fact and experience make evident is, that the mind chooses one action rather than another'.[50] And he cites examples of the liberty of contradiction, 'So whatever names we call the act of the will by – choosing, refusing, approving, disapproving, liking, disliking, embracing, rejecting ... all may be reduced to this of choosing.'[51]

In virtue of this evidence it is premature to claim that, as Muller claims, 'compatibilism rules out genuine liberty of contradiction and liberty of contrariety',[52] and therefore that the recognition of these types of choice is a sure sign of a non-compatibilist freedom. This begs the question. Recognition of these types of choice is equally evident in Edwards's compatibilism. As we see here:

> [F]or in every act of will whatsoever, the mind chooses one thing rather than another; it chooses something rather than the contrary, or rather than the want or nonexistence of that thing. So in every act of refusal, the mind

45. ibid., I. p. 665.
46. Edwards, *Freedom of the Will*, e.g. p. 203.
47. Muller, *Divine Will and Human Choice*, p. 323.
48. Turretin, *Institutes*, I. p. 665.
49. Edwards, *Freedom of the Will*, p. 147.
50. ibid., p. 201.
51. ibid., p. 137.
52. Muller, *Divine Will and Human Choice*, p. 323. Unless, of course *'genuine* liberty of contradiction and liberty of contrariety' mean that such liberties were treated as indeterministic by definition.

chooses the absence of the thing refused; the positive and the negative are set before the mind for its choice, and it chooses the negative; and the mind's making its choice in that case is properly the act of the will: the will's determining between the two is a voluntary determining; but that is the same thing as making a choice …. For the soul to act voluntarily, is evermore to act electively'.[53]

Muller suggests,

> But isn't it the case that Edwards's voluntary determining is a matter of spontaneity (and not genuine alternativity), given that the will, with its predispositions, is only going to will one thing and that, given the denial of faculty psychology, there is no deliberation such that could bring about a different determination?[54]

In this sense any system of human choice is going to end in one thing. Edwards certainly has a place for deliberation, as we have seen. He also has a place for alternativity in choice. Whether this is what Muller calls 'genuine alternativity' is what we are in the process of discussing. The expression 'genuine alternativity' is tantalizing until Muller demonstrates what it is to be contrasted with, what a case of 'bogus alternativity' would be. So, the use of scholastic terminology does not of itself entail a rejection of compatibilism. Even the materialist Thomas Hobbes uses scholastic terminology.[55] What establishes non-compatibilism is not whether the contingency is 'genuine' or the use of the language of alternativity such that in doing X a person 'could have done Y', but what particular senses attach to such expressions, and other expressions such as 'could have done'.

God's Perfection

Both Turretin and Edwards were classical theists, and adherents to Chalcedonian Christology. They were therefore committed to God's infinite knowledge, power and wisdom, and to the impeccability of the human nature of Jesus Christ. And both were explicitly committed to the freedom of God and of the Son of God incarnate, Jesus.

---

53. Edwards, *Freedom of the Will,* p. 137.
54. Muller, email, December 1, 2017.
55. Thomas Hobbes, *Human Nature: or The Fundamental Elements of Policie* (1650). Chapter 7, 'Of Delight and Pain; Good and Evil', Sections 3-8.

Turretin argues in the following way. The element of indifference in free action (the scope of willingness) is qualified by reference to the nature of the agent acting. This is illustrated from the cases of God's perfections, that of the Incarnate Son of God, and thirdly, that of the glorified saints. God is most free and yet immutably good.[56] How this works is as follows: in regard to divine choice, God can possess a liberty of contrariety that is consistent with His nature, but presumably does not possess any liberty of contradiction at all, since there is no need for God to take time, nor to make up His mind, since in view of His eternity and omniscience there cannot be hesitancy or an indecision due to ignorance or other such factors. So God's perfections result in a further qualification to the place of indifference in freedom. Here are some representative paragraphs of Turretin's.

> First, such an indifference to opposites is found in no free agent, whether created or uncreated, neither in God, who is good most freely indeed, yet not indifferently (as if he could be evil), but necessarily and immutably; nor in Christ, who obeyed God most freely and yet most necessarily because he could not sin; nor in angels and the blessed.[57]

> {J]ust in proportion to God's liberty being more perfect than ours, so ought it to be farther removed from indifference (which instead of being a virtue is a defect in liberty). (2) That Christ, although he never sinned, and was not absolutely unable to sin; and that it is not repugnant to his nature, will or office to be able to sin? This blasphemy Episcopius[58] and other Remonstrants have not blushed to put forth. We answer that far be it from us either to think or to say any such thing concerning the immaculate Son of God whom we know to have been holy, undefiled, separate from sinners, who not only had no intercourse with sin, but could not have both because he was the Son of God and because he was our Redeemer (who if he could have sinned, could not also have saved us).[59]

And similarly with Christ's human nature, and with the glorified natures of the redeemed in heaven.[60]

---

56. Turretin, *Institutes,* I. p. 666.

57. ibid., I. p. 667.

58. This is a reference to the Remonstrant Simon Episcopius (1583–1643).

59. Turretin, *Institutes,* I. p. 666.

60. The authors of *RTF* stress the synchronic contingency of God's freedom. It is the view on which they pivot their entire critique of a 'predestinarian' Reformed theology.

Edwards says in a similar way,

> I say, that this being, according to this notion of Dr Whitby, and other Arminians, has no virtue at all; virtue when ascribed to him, is but 'an empty name'; and he is deserving of no commendation or praise; because he is under necessity, he can't avoid being holy and good as he is; therefore no thanks to him for it.[61]

And in the following Section, containing a long survey of biblical data, he concludes,

> Thus it is evident, that it was *impossible* that the acts of the will of the human soul of Christ should be otherwise than holy, and conformed to the will of the Father; or, in other words, they were necessarily so conformed. I have been the longer in the proof of this matter, it being a thing denied by some of the greatest Arminians, by Episcopius in particular ...[62]

And even more plainly and provocatively,

> So that, putting these things together, the infinitely holy God, who always used to be esteemed by God's people, not only virtuous, but a being in whom is all possible virtue, and every virtue in the most absolute purity and perfection, and in infinitely greater brightness and amiableness than in any creature; the most perfect pattern of virtue, and the foundation from whom all others' virtue is but as beams from the sun; and who has been supposed to be, on the account of his virtue and holiness, infinitely more worthy to be esteemed, loved, honored, admired, commended, extolled and praised, than any creature; and he who is thus everywhere represented in Scripture.[63]

Interestingly both Turretin and Edwards refer to the learned Arminian Episcopius, whose views were judged to be at fault here.

Muller comments further on creaturely freedom,

> Choice is therefore free from coercion and physical necessity, but remains under the extrinsic necessity of a dependence on God and under the intrinsic determination by the intellect .... The spontaneity and willingness

---

But if they had checked Turretin's view of God's freedom they would surely have come to a different view.

61. Edwards, *Freedom of the Will*, p. 278.

62. ibid., p. 289. This sort of circumstantial evidence can be extended to what Edwards referred to as human ability and inability (*Freedom of the Will*, III.3, p. 4) and to what Turretin referred to as 'moral necessity'. (e.g. I. p. 663).

63. Edwards, *Freedom of the Will*, p. 278.

requisite to choice rest, therefore, not on an indifference in the will but on the rational judgment that is in all human beings.[64]

Quite so. Edwards would agree. This is another key passage in the argument that what the RO mean by contingent action, compatibilists, when they use the term, mean uncoerced, spontaneous, reasoned choice, the exercise of the rational judgment, to use Muller's terms. In addition to this passage, which is hard to judge other than as compatibilistic, is more plausible to understand in a compatibilist manner. A similar passage, perhaps even more supportive of compatibilism, is where Muller paraphrases Turretin as follows:

> Turretin's insistence here that the will, as a rational faculty, cannot resist the practical intellect and must follow the last judgment of the practical intellect frames his argumentation clearly in a more Thomistic than a broadly Franciscan or specifically Scotistic manner – he in no way implies the possibility of the will rejecting the intellectual judgment. This necessity of following the judgment of the intellect does not, however, impede freedom. Rather, it defines freedom as a matter not of indifference but as the free determination and free election or rejection of an object by the conjoint action of intellect rendering judgment and will freely electing or rejecting the object presented by the intellect.[65]

Muller does not seem to recognize the compatibilistic tenor of Turretin's language here.

Unfortunately, however, to characterize contingencies as 'finite causes that can either produce or not produce their effect'[66] does not by itself settle whether or not Turretin is a compatibilist. For such locutions may also be used by compatibilists to describe the way in which a person could have acted otherwise had he possessed a stronger reason to do so. This also is a capacity unique to humans, distinct from those effects that are determined by 'necessary causes', such as occur in sheep, for example, or flames, and it is perfectly consistent for Turretin to have a place for them in characterising animals who operate by instinct. Muller may be making the assumption that human freedom follows the contours of divine freedom. But why would that be so, given the dependent, finite

---

64. Muller, *Divine Will and Human Choice*, p. 292.

65. ibid., p. 253.

66. ibid., p. 248.

character of the human creature, subject to external influences and to the decree of God? As Muller goes on to note, for Turretin such freedom is not autonomous or independent.[67] So could it not be compatibilist? Turretin's words can certainly be read that way.

In his discussion of free and necessary actions, which we considered at the beginning of the chapter, Turretin occasionally amplifies what he means by a free and contingent action and that 'physical and coactive [i.e coerced] necessity' which is inconsistent with freedom. Free acts are performed 'spontaneously and by a previous judgment of reason'.[68] What is not found here is any reference to 'the simultaneous presence in the human will of genuine potencies to different effects',[69] which misses the subordination of the will to the intellect that directs it, which Turretin is so clear about. The possibilities can become actualities only insofar as the practical intellect makes a judgment; the will has no independent power of making a choice actual. As Turretin puts it, 'For since the will is a rational appetite, such is its nature that it *must* follow the last judgment of the practical intellect ….'[70]

The above discussions have provided evidence that RO such as Turretin, and Jonathan Edwards, occupied a similar theological niche.[71] This is then presented as indirect evidence for Turretin having a similar outlook as Edwards as regards free will, that of a fellow-compatibilist.

Other evidence could be given. For example, both Turretin and Edwards take seriously the objection that their views entail that God is the author of sin. It is said to be a merit of non-compatibilism that it removes this charge. Edwards deals with it in his treatment of objections in Part IV Section 9 of *The Freedom of the Will*, 'Concerning that objection against the doctrine which has been maintained, that it makes God the author of sin'. Turretin takes it on in his treatment of God's knowledge of future contingents and of divine providence.[72] But I hope that an indirect argument has been made for Edwards and Turretin being compatibilists

---

67. ibid., p. 252.

68. Turretin, *Institutes*, I. p. 211.

69. Muller, *Divine Will and Human Choice,* p. 251.

70. Turretin, *Institutes,* I. p. 663, italics added.

71. It is possible to add further features to this niche.

72. Turretin, *Institutes,* I. pp. 206-121, on future contingents. Other parallel places are on the decrees of God, I. pp. 311-329, 509-11, on divine providence and evil, I. pp. 513-5.

in the absence of a direct argument which requires a more direct claim about 'determinism' or being a 'determinist' or 'compatibilist' than Turretin was able to offer. But we must remind ourselves at such a point that neither did Edwards make such claims in *The Freedom of the Will*. He too did not use either 'compatibilism' or 'determinism'!

According to what Turretin says in his discussion of free will, the alternatives presented to the will are reduced to one by the deliverance of the (last) judgment of the practical intellect. Which of the alternatives has the will of delivering the judgment of the practical intellect? It cannot be decided by any of the alternatives of the will itself, but only by the judgment of the intellect that informs the will. And of course a compatibilist can accept this subordinate view of the will without demur.

Compatibilism and Scholastic Accounts of Freedom

Here is some evidence of an admission from Muller that the distinction between compatibilism and scholastic accounts of freedom can come quite close.

> The compatibilist can allow for choice, indeed, for a version of alternativity on the assumption that the will can and in fact will choose a different end or object if something, whether in the background or in the circumstances surrounding the choice, is different. All things being equal, however, both the past and present situation being identical, the choice will be the same. The older Reformed view and the modern compatibilist view are, admittedly, very close at this point. There is, however, a difference that can be identified in the retention of the fourfold causality in the older Reformed view and its loss, specifically, the loss of an inwardly determined final causality in the classical compatibilist view.[73]

Potency

As we have already noticed, Muller's interpretation of RO as being committed to a two-way contingency runs into the following difficulty: In the transition from indifference *in sensu diviso* to indifference *in sensu composito*, where is there a place for such contingency as he recognises? Even if Muller's resident potency *in sensu composito* is allowed, there can be no work for it to do. What could it now contribute to the

---

73. *Divine Will and Human Choice*, p. 295.

past freedom of the act? It looks to be nothing more than a useless, counterfactual appendage forever left dangling in the mind. Muller seems to think that in order to do justice to the simultaneity of potencies as the sufficient condition of contingency a place must be found for it in the compound sense. But this does not appear to RO's such as Turretin and to Willard, whose position appears very similar to Turretin's at this point. As Willard puts it, in a passage already referred to,

> How far there is an *Indifference* to be acknowledged in the Will, respecting *Voluntary* actions, needs not be curiously discussed; only we may observe, that though there may such a thing be allowed to the Will, *in actu primo*, which the Schools call *Simultas potentiae*, by vertue whereof the Will, according to its own nature, is capable of acting or not acting, or acting thus or contrarily; and is capable of acting thus now, and is afterwards capable of revoking that act; nay indeed, this is the root of the liberty of the Will. Nevertheless, *in actu secundo*, which the Schools call *Potentia Simultatis*, which is in the Wills applying it self to its act, it doth not then act *Indifferently*, but upon choice, by which it is Determined.[74]

Another way in which Muller's account could have been clearer is for him to have distinguished unambiguously between a conditional versus unconditional alternative. As we saw earlier he refers a few times to 'genuine contingency' and 'genuine liberty', which as long as they are not spelled out, are question-begging, impeding discussion. If it refers to unconditional alternativity then it is hard to see how he distinguishes his account of RO such as Turretin from the position of Vos, the Jesuits and the Arminians, those committed to Franciscan freedom. But if by using the phrase he is tacitly referring to conditional alternativity then this is the hypothetical necessity of compatibilism. Muller does not seem to relate compatibilism with hypothetical necessity anywhere.

Providence and Freedom

It might be asked what attracts Muller to indeterministic freedom. It is hard to say. According to the Reformed, providence is a continuous creation, the result of God's decree. Such providence is traditionally said to comprise three elements – preservation, concurrence, and government.[75] The objects

---

74. Willard, *A Brief Reply to Mr George Kieth*, p. 15.
75. Louis Berkhof, *Systematic Theology*, p. 166.

of providence may be said to be 'all created things'. Yet in some of his writings, Muller has restricted these actions to God's salvific activity. Is this an argument for holding that some if not all human actions are indeterminate?

> The issue debated between the Arminians and the Reformed was not philosophical determinism but soteriology ... It was never the Reformed view that the moral acts of human beings are predetermined, any more than it was ever the Reformed view that the fall of Adam was willed by God to the exclusion of Adam's first choice of sin'..... This overarching providential determination (which includes the determination of and concurrence in freedom and contingency) is, moreover, distinct from predestination: predestination is the specific ordination of some to salvation, granted the inability of human beings to save themselves. Again: this is not a matter of philosophical determinism, but of soteriology.[76]

From this formulation it seems that for Muller, providence (as distinct from predestination) is the preserve of freedom and contingency. I think that it is fair to say that many Reformed, and their confessions, were more decisive than this, holding that the divine decree covers the 'all things' of Ephesians 1.11, for example, covering both soteric and non-soteric happenings, in one decree or in the totality of the decrees. The actions that are predestinarian, enabled by God's saving grace, form a subset of the actions that are governed by divine providence, and which 'fall out according to the nature of second causes, either necessarily, freely, or contingently'.[77] The Westminster Confession has it that the Creator of all things, 'doth uphold, direct, dispose and govern all creatures, actions, and things, from the greatest to the least ....'[78]

As further evidence of the closeness of compatibilism to his indeterminacy Muller acknowledges that there are places where a compatibilist version of determinism touches the language of the RO.[79]

---

76. Richard, A. Muller, 'Grace, Election and Contingent Choice: Arminius's Gambit and the Reformed Response', in *The Grace of God, The Bondage of the Will*, 2 vols. Edd. Thomas Schreiner and Bruce A. Ware (Grand Rapids, Mich. Baker, 1995), p. 2.270.

77. WCF V.II. For more on divine providence entailing hypothetical necessity, see Michael P. Preciado, *A Reformed View of Freedom*, Ch. 3 'Decree, Foreknowledge, and Providence'.

78. *Westminster Confession of Faith*, p. V.I.

79. For example, Muller, *Divine Will and Human Choice*, p. 295.

The Argument over Compatibilism

At the end of this chapter we are some way on our indirect argument for the compatibilism of the RO. It has been largely a matter of assembling circumstantial evidence. Turretin and Edwards each inhabit the same theological niche, with the same doctrinal emphases and having the same opponents for similar reasons. This conclusion takes us only so far, however. Besides, since compatibilism is a view about causation, we need to examine that side of things. This we attempt to do in the remaining chapters.

There is a residual question that someone may ask of Turretin, namely, why, if he is a compatibilist, is his style not more like that of Edwards? If he is a compatibilist why is that fact not more obvious? We shall consider this question in the next chapter.

CHAPTER 6

Causation in Doctrine

The last two chapters will discuss causal matters, compatibilism being a causal thesis. In this chapter, I want to suggest an answer to the question of why an RO such as Francis Turretin, a compatibilist, does not make all his views on the freedom of the will very apparent. Some of what he states is immediately and obviously compatibilistic. At other times he is less clear. Then the reader has to try and piece data from condensed and cryptic language, language of a highly analytic character. There is less attention paid to causes, despite the fact that the four-fold causation of Aristotelianism is central to scholasticism, a point which Muller emphasises. The comparison of Turretin's style with Edwards's is sometimes stark. In what follows I shall try to make an attempt to assess the price that this scholastic style paid regarding the clarity of a compatibilist free will position.

Before I begin on causation, it is worth saying that part of the answer to these difficulties may be due to the general outlook of the RO. In surveying the field, it seems that the theology of the RO had the following features. They were opponents of the Arminians and Molinists, who espoused Franciscan freedom, and who (let us say) occupied one end of the spectrum of views regarding free will. The fatalistic and deterministic other end of the field was taken by two groups. One was by Stoic and other fatalisms, with the conviction that even God or the gods were products of cosmic nature. The RO, with a clear commitment to the Christian doctrine of *creatio ex nihilo*, could not be attracted to such a view. Another class was occupied by various kinds of created beings and living things who possessed, as Turretin put it, 'physical and brute necessity, occurring in inanimates and brutes who act from a blind impulse of nature or a brute necessity and innate appetite, without, however, any light of reason (as the necessity in fire to burn, a combustible object being supplied; the necessity in a horse to eat the straw or grass put before him) and without any choice.'[1]

Human beings have what those possessing brute necessity lack, the light of reason, and of choice, and a compliant will, and a conscience. But at this point, the middle ground between extremes, so to speak, the RO were in general either reluctant or unable to articulate the power of 'rational spontaneity' in terms of causal power, efficient causation. Nonetheless, there is some clear evidence that they did hold this position, as we shall see.

The Effect of Scholasticism

However this may be, we shall now examine RO scholasticism as a theological method with a view to distilling the estimate of efficient causation within it, and asking why efficient causation is not presented as prominently in RO anthropology as it is in that of Edwards. To make the case for this it is necessary that we look not only on human action on its own, but also (later on) on the intersection of divine willing and human willing. This takes us into the area of divine providence, touched in the previous chapter, which Muller also considers in his book. He gives attention to this, and so must we.

What I shall suggest is that while the tools of the scholastic philosophy of the RO as expounded by Vos *et al* are extremely useful in delineating one theological view from another, they also have the unintended consequence of masking whole areas of anthropology, particularly the causal language of Scripture and of our ordinary talk about human actions. The tendency of RO is to make logical points of an analytic kind on the basis of this or that scholastic distinction, as the basis of analysis of such a topic as the freedom of the will. Indisputably, logical and metaphysical distinctions can be of value. These gave its external relations, not always its inner nature. Most of the distinctions are concerned with propositions or assertions, and of different senses of contingency and necessity. But human freedom is not an *assertion*. It is an *event*, one which connotes the exercise of causal powers.

---

1. Turretin, *Institutes*, I. p. 662.

So far in the book we have concentrated on certain distinctions prominently employed by scholastics, notably the two necessities, for Vos the hallmark of contingency, and synchronic contingency. And the habit of treating expressions in the primary and secondary sense (*in sensu composito* and *in sensu secundo*), and the distinction between *simultas potentiae* and the *potentia simultatis,* as we have seen. These are largely metaphysical and logical distinctions to do with time and possibility, diachronic or synchronic activities, and with necessity and contingency, enabling the student to analyse the results of the practical reason. To move from scholastic to non-scholastic modes of interrogation and investigation involves a change in method, as we have seen already. Perhaps Jonathan Edwards's repudiation of scholasticism, and the adoption of the language of the 'vulgar', as he emphasized, brings with it this change of emphasis.

We have seen that Edwards mostly uses ordinary, everyday language to make the same substantive position on a range of theological matters. He writes his book on free will with ordinary men and women in mind, though he is often interrupted by the language of the learned, including some of his contemporary opponents, such as Chubb, Whitby and Watts. This is because in the book on the freedom of the will he is very much interested in the connection of free will with the practical business of praising and blaming people for what they do, and of the conscience and its judgments. Nevertheless, as we saw in the last chapter, he takes it that ordinary language is flexible enough for his purposes, only occasionally complaining of its limitations.

The suspicion that the theology of the RO as portrayed in *RTF* is constructed in predominantly logical terms rather than in any other, is fed by the doctrine of synchronic contingency which its contributors claim as a characteristic feature among the RO. It is certain that synchronic contingency and indeterminism go together, for the following reason: as already noted, Vos and company formulate a logico-theology that is largely *a priori* in its foundations, based on Scotus's doctrine of God and a rather dubious thesis about the implications of human beings being created in God's image. In this, the historic Reformed theological balance between special revelation, human reasoning, religious experience and sensory observation is in danger of being lost, becoming lop-sided in favour of logic and metaphysics.

While synchronic contingency is definable, its absence or presence in human action is undetectable and unverifiable, as is the role or remaining root potency in Muller's diachronic contingency to which we shall devote some more attention in the last chapter. Vos uses synchronic contingency in the case of God as Andreas Beck defines it: 'God does *p*, and he has simultaneously the possibility of not doing *p*'.[2] Another definition is 'Synchronic Contingency means that for one moment of time, there is a true alternative for the state of affairs that actually occurs'.[3] And so it is an ideal datum for the logico-theologians, as is its anthropological version 'John chooses P, and he has simultaneously the possibility of not choosing P but *Q* or not-P instead'. This is a state of affairs that makes the ascription of responsibility entirely conjectural. How can the agent or the onlooker or other person know which of such simultaneous alternatives were in play at any one time?

For synchronic contingency to be true of a person entails the following counterfactual: if John freely chooses P then it is possible that if he had freely chose alternatively, at the same moment he could have freely chosen not-P or Q. At that very moment everything in his outer and inner world being exactly the same, there would have been such alternatives. Such libertarianism is spurred on by an *a priori* truth of the form, if a person is responsible for an act *A* it must have been possible to perform not-A or B unconditionally, by the use of a libertarianly free will. So synchronic contingency is accepted theologically not because it is true to the facts of Scripture, or of inner reflection, or of observation, or more likely to be true than not. It is treated in a largely *a priori* fashion, not witnessed or discovered or grounded by a combination of the exegesis of special revelation and of human experience.

Muller has argued in *Divine Will and Human Choice* that the idea of synchronic contingency in RO anthropology has been exaggerated, even though, as we have seen, he himself has a role for metaphysical diachronic contingency.[4] I am suggesting that scholastic anthropology was in general rather different, with its focus on deductive arguments

---

2. Cited in Paul Helm, 'Synchronic Contingency in Reformed Scholasticism: A Note of Caution', *Nederlands Theologisch Tijdschrift*, 2003, p. 208.

3. *Reformed Thought on Freedom*, p. 41.

4. *Divine Will and Human Choice*, pp. 298-9.

and inferences in theology, characteristic of the genres of *questiones* and *disputationes* that had a prominent place in the theological education of the RO academies. Such education gave prominence to the mastery of certain distinctions, as exhibited by the teacher and his respondent. For the student there is a premium placed on the making of logical distinctions to avoid (or evade) an unwelcome logical consequence of a term in use, or of affirming its heterodoxy. So the teachers' and students' theological skills lay in the ability to disambiguate certain terms in theological thought, such as instances of the assertions of necessity, potency, and contingency. They held that unless these distinctions are borne in mind, logical fallacy in argument and wrongness in theology would result, as such theology is attested by the confessions of the various Reformed churches. In such a situation the theological value of human and biblical narratives of human action, with their emphasis on causation, was neglected.

Here I wish to no more than suggest that such education had a masking effect on the awareness of efficient causality in human life, though not a total rejection of it. The concentration on logical distinctions, of necessity or contingency, when applied to human freedom, had the effect of under-emphasizing the underlying causality that is embedded in narratives of human thought and action, including biblical narratives. Not that efficient causality is completely ignored by scholastics, but it is downplayed. I shall try to show this first by considering what is said about causation in the Introduction to *RTF*.

Reformed Thought on Freedom

The *masking* of causation, I suggest, seems to be evident in the concentration by the RO on propositional and modal logical language and ideas, to the exclusion of other factors, particularly the place of belief and desire, and habit in the formation and executing of human actions. In a way this is surprising when the prominence of the vegetative, sensory, and intellectual appetites in Aristotelian anthropology are remembered.

In the Introduction to *RTF* a great deal of time is spent in discussing the various relations between truth and falsity, and especially of the modal terms necessity and contingency. In a heading 'Ontological Distinctions', our old friends the two necessities are prominent. And extracted from these discussions are several diagrams anatomically displaying divine and human causation in the style of the square of opposition table of fundamental formal logic.[5] In the course of this discussion the contributors say that cause and effect are ontological concepts. They rather sketchily distinguish between *natural* and *free* causes. 'In distinction to the effects of natural causes (which were called natural or necessary effects), the effect of free causes was called contingent or free'.[6] Everything that is not causal is free. So, a logical distinction of causes.

In the scholastic scheme from Thomas Aquinas onwards God is the primary cause and creaturely causes are secondary causes. In this instance without much more ado the contributors to *RTF* illustrate how free causes, both Creatorly and creaturely, bring about free effects, 'contingent effects'. In this theism, contingency is used primarily in the sense of 'could not have been caused', though Vos's influences are seen in assuming that causes are indeterminate, and that rather question-beggingly, causes which are indeterminately free necessarily beget free effects. 'The secondary causes are contingent themselves, as they are dependent in their existence on him', that is, on God.[7] This clearly needs qualifying, regarding God's free creation of powers that are regarded as not contingently free, such effects as are necessarily causal, such as the movements of the Earth and the Moon in relation to the Sun, to take an obvious example. The secondary cause and the primary cause of a human action are 'ontologically distinct'. Necessity and contingency in these senses are contradictory, and said by the Reformed contributors to be 'irreducible',[8] which means that it is not profitable or possible to study the operation of such causes in terms of other factors, such as their causal origin.

What is striking, especially in a discussion that is intended to elucidate human freedom, is that there is not a better, fuller, analysis of causation in their literature, than this rather spare one. This omission is perhaps what the contributors refer to, the fact that 'an exact answer to the question would require a separate study',[9] but perhaps not. There

5. *Reformed Thought on Freedom*, p. 32.

6. ibid., p. 32.

7. ibid., p. 32.

8. ibid., p. 33.

9. ibid., p. 33.

is no discussion of the endowment of creatures with powers (*potentiae*), such as habits or virtues or appetites, or this instance of the working of a faculty or that, except for the one case of the distinction between *simultas potentiae* and the *potentia simultatis*.[10] A *potentia* is a power 'in the sense of efficacy or efficiency in action'.[11] According to faculty psychology, the soul of a human being possesses an ensemble of such *potentiae*. But without a fuller discussion of their place in human action, taking in the fact of the complexity of human action, the diagrams illustrating necessity and contingency found throughout the Introduction of *RTF* have very limited value. Linked with the focusing in such distinctions is a corresponding disregard for actual instances of human motivation.

As we have noted, the only substantive theological issue offered in *RTF* regarding the nature of human freedom is a rather unsafe appeal to humans created in the *imago dei*. It is asserted by the contributors that since God is indeterministically free *à la* Scotus, then His creatures created in His image are similarly free.[12] This is an obvious begging of the question against compatibilism, with no support in special revelation. If anything the RO place the *imago* to the possession of the will.[13] Also, it must not be forgotten that for Christians the creation is an exercise of God's power over a formless mass, inanimate and animate and human, angelic, and so on, and the upholding and governing of them. According to the early modern Reformed confessions, God is immaculate and immutable while human beings, not yet fallen, were created mutable. They recognize categories of mutability, from that of rocks and vegetation through insects and the like, lower animals, to higher animals possessing sensory appetites only, and finally to mankind possessed of a soul having intelligence and will, and a conscience, and a closely connected body. Does not mutability signal change, and of the forces that make change? And the Aristotelian teaching on the hylomorphic unity of, and influence of, body and mind. Creatures of all these categories are created contingent in an obvious sense, in that

---

10. ibid., p. 47.

11. Richard A Muller, *A Dictionary of Latin and Greek Theological Terms*, p. 201, art. *potentia*.

12. *Reformed Thought on Freedom*, p. 15.

13. For Turretin on the *imago dei*, see *Institutes,* I. p. 446.

they do not exist as a matter of necessity, from a logical or metaphysical point of view, and so may not have been created. Rocks and sheep are not created in the image of God. And it is begging the question of free will to assume that the freedom of an eternal God is present in His human creatures, who necessarily make changes in time. In the introductory material of *RTF* which we mentioned, there is not one reference to the causal influences of the passions (or emotions) on action.

In their debates with the Arminians and Jesuits the RO were forced to consider the nature of human freedom, and with it of divine freedom. The contributors to *RTF* start with the claim that to understand human freedom *requires* an historical and an analytical examination.[14] This is certainly true. In their case, however, the historical is largely subsumed under the analytic. The 'exact definitions, detailed distinctions and profound arguments' that the authors of *RTF* celebrate are undoubtedly scholarly. But by concentrating almost exclusively on them at the expense of instances of causal power in Christian anthropology, the understanding of readers who are not scholastics is cramped, as they familiarise themselves with RO writings, by empirical observation become aware of the frequency and significance of a range of human *potentiae*, which can be expressed in terms of beliefs and desires and their relations, but never are.

We have seen earlier that Muller stresses that scholasticism is a method, not in itself an ideology. If so, it should be possible to transpose scholastic meanings into non-scholastic versions of them, even if such transpositions are not perfect. The contributors of *RTF* recognize that 'Many [scholastic] concepts cannot be understood apart from the medieval background from which they originated'.[15] As Muller says, this is largely the influence of Thomas, and furthermore it concentrates their attention almost exclusively on the presence of 'Franciscan freedom'.

An interlude: John Owen on the Limits of Scholasticism

A recognition of the limits of scholasticism that I have been stressing is reminiscent of an approach that we find the Puritan John Owen making in his writing on justification by faith. Something of a scholastic himself,

---

14. *Reformed Thought on Freedom,* p. 16.
15. ibid., p. 16.

Owen realized that analytical and subtle distinctions have their place, but that they carry their own dangers as well, and are often subordinate in value to other ways of description that can be used in theology. He says in his introduction to *The Doctrine of Justification by Faith*,[16] that in connection with the analysis of the place of faith in justification there were in circulation in his day 'twenty several opinions'.

> When men are once advanced into that field of disputation [that is, scholasticism], which is all overgrown with thorns of subtilties, perplexed notions, and futilious [futile] terms of art, they [the scholastics teachers] consider principally how they may entangle others in it, scarce at all how they may get out of it themselves. And in this posture they oftentimes utterly forget the business they are about, especially in this matter of justification, – namely, how a guilty sinner may come to obtain favour and acceptance with God. And not only so, but I doubt they oftentimes dispute themselves beyond what they can well abide by, when they return home unto a sedate meditation of the state of things between God and their souls.[17]

What to do? Owen's response to the making of even finer scholastic *distinctions* is instead to offer *descriptions,* descriptions of causes. So he advises his readers not to forget that,

> [E]very true believer, who is *taught of God*, knows how to put his whole trust in Christ alone, and the grace of God by him, for mercy, righteousness and glory, and not at all concern himself with those loads of thorns and briers, which, under the names of definitions, distinctions, accurate notions, in a number of exotic pedagogical and philosophical terms, some pretend to accommodate them withal.[18]

Owen goes on,

> It is, therefore, to no purpose to handle the mysteries of the gospel as if Holcot and Bricot, Thomas and Gabriel, with all their Sententiarists, Summists and Quodlibertarians of the old Roman peripatetical [Aristotelian] school, were to be raked out of their graves to be our guides. Especially will they be of no use unto this doctrine of justification. For whereas they pertinaciously adhered unto the philosophy of Aristotle, who

---

16. Owen, *The Doctrine of Justification by Faith*, *Works*, ed. Goold, V. p. 11.

17. ibid., V. p. 11.

18. ibid., V. p. 12.

knew nothing of any righteousness but what is a habit inherent in ourselves, and the acts of it, they wrested the whole doctrine of justification unto a compliance therewithal.[19]

And so he observes in the first chapter of his book, that the causes and objects of faith have to do with the grounds and reasons of them, and also of their effects, in their different degrees. Faith may produce great effects in the minds, affections, and lives of people.[20] Note that these expressions—grounds, reasons, effects—are all causal in character, and are a matter of describing experiences or of drawing inferences from special revelation. Living off a diet of scholastic distinctions may have a flattening effect when applied to the 'vulgar' language of human intention and action, and have distracting consequences.

The Language of Causes

It is true that in the introduction to *RTF*, the contributors note that an act is comprised of cause and effect. They distinguish between natural causes, in which a cause produces the same effect. They go on to contrast 'a free cause was held to act variously, not only in different times, but also structurally at one and the same moment ... the effect of free causes was called contingent or free'.[21] They go on,

> The distinction between natural and free cause is given with the way they 'determine' their act. This technical term 'determination' should not be associated with the *modern* term 'determinism', because that term did not exist yet; the concept of determinism was denoted by other terms like 'Stoic fate'. Rather, determination means that a cause gets directed to one effect. A natural cause is determined by its *nature* to the act, a free cause determines itself by *freedom* to one of possible acts. Hence, determination refers to the state of a cause: being undetermined means that the (free) cause has not yet determined itself to a certain effect. A determined cause will produce a determined effect, but still the effect can be either contingent (determined by a free act) or necessary (determined by a natural act).[22]

---

19. Owen, *The Doctrine of Justification by Faith, Works*, ed. Goold, V. p. 12. Robert Holcot (1290–1349), and Thomas Bricot (1490–1516) were scholastics, a Summist is the writer of a *Summa,* and a Quolibertarian is a pedantic reasoner.

20. ibid., V. pp. 72, 73.

21. *Reformed Thought on Freedom*, p. 31.

22. ibid., p. 31.

This understands 'determination' to be near to 'assignment' in meaning, except for its last use in this quotation. Making determinations, decisions, is certainly making applications of the verb *determinare,* but the assumption that such decisions are synchronically contingent begs the question, prejudging the way in which human beings in fact come to make decisions.

It is true that, as we saw earlier, in the seventeenth century and before, Stoic fate was distinguished from Christian concepts of divine and human action because for the Stoics' god was himself subject to natural causes. As Calvin noted,

> The nature of the Stoics' supposition is known. They weave their fate out of a Gordian complex of causes. In this they involve God himself, making golden chains, as in the fable, with which to bind Him, so that He becomes subject to inferior causes. The astrologers of today imitate the Stoics, for they hold that an absolute necessity for all things originates from the position of the stars. Let the Stoics have their fate; for us, the free will of God disposes all things.[23]

Undoubtedly this fact affected how RO saw human freedom. But it does not follow that they had no place for causal determinism, though they did not use the word 'fate' of God's will without qualification, to avoid any suspicion of God being subject to His creation.

Yet while the word 'determinism' was not used, yet we see that various constructions of *determinare* certainly were. The introductory material in *Reformed Thought on Freedom* is biased in favour of one understanding of 'free' as having an indeterminate sense. This begs the question against compatibilism, and skews terms like 'necessity' and 'contingent'. It is the authors' further understanding that contingency and necessity are not to be understood causally but logically, according to which a necessity is a logical necessity and a contingency is a logical possibility, and so non-necessary. The dominance in the treatment of the logical difference of terms is why thinkers schooled in this way of analysis find it to be against the grain to articulate human action in causal terms. As Sir Arthur Eddington joked, 'what my net can't catch isn't fish'.

---

23. John Calvin, *Concerning the Eternal Predestination of God*, 1542, p. 170.

We have seen how the contributors of RTF take away the causal connotations of 'determine', and reduce it to the assigning of a truth value. At another point the contributors say this further about 'determine'.

> It is perhaps useful to point out here that 'to determine' in scholastic usage, often simply means 'to assign a truth-value to a proposition.' For example, if a scholastic author claims that the truth of a future contingent proposition is determined, mostly all that is meant is that it has a truth-value, in distinction from lacking it (being neither true nor false). The content we often hear in 'determined' is 'could not but be so-and-so.' This necessitation element, however, is only attached to the meaning of 'determined' in a basically non-Christian, Aristotelian paradigm. Even if we keep in mind that a 'determination' may mean in this context that God performs his eternal act by which all creaturely states of affairs exist, nothing deterministic has happened. God assigns a truth-value to propositions.[24]

But Turretin says that God determines a creature to determine itself because God so moves creatures as to leave their own motions to them, and 'although the will is free, this does not prevent its being determined by God and being always under subjection to him'.[25] Who can doubt that here 'determines' is being used causally? If I want to ensure the proposition 'Helm is eating an apple' is true, then I do so by taking the apple and biting it, *taking* and *biting* being causal notions. And if 'Helm is eating an apple', then it will be at least partly the outcome of my desire or appetite, and so the eating may be causally determined, free in the compatibilist sense.

These efforts by the editors to evacuate 'determine' of any causal force are what we called earlier the 'masking' of causality with logic. They are extreme cases of scholasticism. The RO were not as extreme, recognising that God's decrees are not arguments, assigning truths to sentences, nor are human actions. According to the RO God creates, upholds, and governs His creation, His creatures and all their actions. We may say that the divine decrees and acts of creation have effects, states of affairs, the bringing to pass of what the Creator has decreed. The divine

---

24. *Reformed Thought on Freedom*, pp. 189-90.
25. Turretin, *Institutes*, I. p. 668.

decrees are causal in character, bringing states of affairs to come to pass. By steadfastly avoiding or severely downplaying this fact, the authors of *RTF* are excluding or minimizing causality in their theology, and making it almost a purely logical exercise.

So somewhat similar to Owen's remarks on studying justification in his day, I suggest that the scholastic distinctions we have been involving ourselves in earlier on in the book, in scholastic expressions, and in scholastic distinctions, do not help us very far insofar as our enquiries about the causes of human freedom are concerned. The most insightful way to compare Edwards with the RO is to avoid their various scholastic distinctions applied to human action, and to concentrate instead on the scholastics' working of the practical reason, particularly the identifying the end of a good, and the choice of the means to that end, which involves the judgment of the intellect and the moving of the will. Edwards, not a friend of scholastic language,[26] mostly uses the language of the vulgar or of 'common usage' rather than that of the learned, which he did his best to avoid, as he repeatedly stresses.[27]

Elsewhere Owen has this to say about the four-fold causes of scholasticism.

> Between both these, *end* and *means*, there is this relation, that (though in sundry kinds) they are mutually causes one of another. The end of is the first, principal *moving cause* of the whole. It is that for whose sake the whole work is. No agent applies itself to action but for an end; and were it not by that determined to some effect, thing, or manner of working, it would no more do one thing than another .... And manifest, then, it is, that the whole reason and method of affairs that a wise worker or agent, according to the counsel, proposeth to himself, is taken from the *end* which he aims at; that is in intention and contrivance, the beginning of all that order which is in working.[28]

---

26. Edwards's references to scholasticism in *The Freedom of the Will,* include that it is 'more unintelligible, and void of distinct and consistent meaning, in all the writings of Duns Scotus or Thomas Aquinas' (p. 228). Of course against this sweeping language must be set his warm estimate of Turretin and Petrus Van Mastricht, as theologians. See Paul Helm, 'A Different Kind of Calvinism?' in *After Jonathan Edwards,* p. 91f.

27. Edwards, *Freedom of the Will,* pp. 150, 151, 154 etc.

28. Owen, *The Death of Death in the Death of Christ, Works* ed. Goold, X. pp. 160-1.

Here is a rather different account of scholastic causes, more compatibilist. Causal language present in our talk of human actions is not totally absent in scholastic writings, however, as we see in what Turretin says about the phenomenon of making up one's mind,[29] and the way it affects human responsibility, and in his account of the relation of intellect and will.[30] And that is true of the RO more generally. For the scholastics do not, by and large, focus on a description of the soul in preparing to act and in acting, or in rejecting a choice, and on what it believes, and how what a person believes affects other states of his mind. As Owen puts it, 'to say that faith is "the flight of a penitent unto the mercy of God in Christ", has more sense and faith in it than in twenty others that seem more accurate.' Owen cites from a quotation of Louis Le Blanc,[31] though we are not given a reference. In a parallel way, Turretin's remarks about making up the mind, and on compulsion, and the causal priority of the intellect over the will, tell us more about the causal character of freedom than what he has to say about *potentiae*. And what he says about compulsion taking a causal effect that is beyond the limit of responsibility.[32]

The impression gained by the project of *RTF* is that scholastic analysis was given a bold, independent role, the chief role, in thinking about theological issues. But if so this was to overvalue these distinctions. The question of free will and its place in nature and grace, to which a great deal of thought was given in the 17th century, is a biblical and philosophical matter which has to be decided by study and argument about the primary data, the text of the Bible. Substantive questions about human freedom are to be settled by the exegesis of Scripture and by theological reasoning regarding such first-level theological data. The difference between the Reformed, and the Jesuit and Arminian, and Socinian positions, are theological, and as

---

29. Turretin, *Institutes*, I. pp. 665-6.

30. ibid., I. p. 662.

31. This is Louis Le Blanc de Beaulieu (1614–75) a theologian of the Sedan Academy. His *Thesae Theologicae* was published in London, 1675. Owen does not give us the reference to Louis Le Blanc, who likely drew his attention to Jean Mestrezat (1592–1657) in his *Des Fruits de la foi en Vertus Chrestiennes* (Geneva, 1655). Interestingly, Edwards refers to him once in his book on freewill, p. 263.

32. Owen, V. p. 75. Owen cites a reference that is likely to be that of the Huguenot preacher Mestrezat. Of course Owen's strictures are intensified by the subject he is considering, justification by faith alone, and the debates that it gave rise to.

far as anthropology is concerned, they are by and large to do with the generation, character and extent of human causal power in the exercise of faith in Christ.

Turretin has astute remarks about why the Jesuit Molinist theory of middle knowledge was significant in the defence of,

> [T]he semi-Pelagian heresy of foreseen faith and good works in election, and to support their figment of free will in order the more easily to free themselves from the arguments of the Dominicans who rejected such a foresight (principally for this reason – that since there is no knowledge in God [unless either natural – of things possible – or free – of things future] all foreknowledge of faith and of the good use of free will ought to depend upon, not to precede the decree). This argument they supposed could be escaped in no other way than by inventing this middle knowledge.[33]

The contributors of *RTF* shirk the task of arguing about human freedom, despite the book ostensibly being on the concept of free choice; instead they assume its indeterministic, Franciscan character. Yet there is no awareness that this must lead to a comparison made between it and the Franciscan freedom of the Molinists and Arminians, the antagonists of the RO. This is but one of the agenda of problems left largely untouched, even unnoticed, by the authors of *RTF*. The commentators inaccurately engineer Turretin and the other RO's they consider into holding to human indeterministic freedom, apparently not being interested in the theological consequences of doing so.

Compulsion and Responsibility

As noted earlier, both Turretin and Edwards have similar criteria for praise and blameworthiness. So Turretin says in compatibilistic fashion that, 'The nature of obedience is not placed in this – that man can obey or not obey; but in this – that man obeys freely and without compulsion from previous reason.'

> So far is the use of exhortation and commands from being taken away by our opinion, that it is the rather more strongly asserted. For if it is certain that the will is determined by the intellect, the intellect must first be persuaded before it can influence the will. And yet how can it be persuaded except by reasons and exhortations? Although a compliance with the exhortation is

---

33. Turretin, *Institutes,* I. p. 213.

impossible by us without grace; still not the less properly can it be addressed to us because it is a duty owed by us.[34]

Compulsion or its absence has to do with the presence or absence of the rational will. Compulsion is causal, it is, in serious circumstances, a gun to the head, an injection, or the effect of psychological pressure such as blackmail. Or at the presentation of that degree of evidence that we call 'compelling'. These 'compellings' are interruptions of a causal kind, blockages to the normal course in which the mind is made up voluntarily, either singularly, or as a matter of habit. In such passages as the above Turretin steps clear of metaphysical and logical distinctions at which he is so adept to clearly reveal something of the causal nature of freedom or its denial, so revealing his compatibilism.

Compare this with this example of Muller's heroic efforts to expound his understanding of Turretin's view of contingent human action.

> Turretin's argument places the possibility of the event taking or not taking place primarily in terms of the potencies resident in finite or secondary causality. In the case of an individual human being making a choice, the indeterminacy of the future event arises not merely from an absence of knowledge concerning what the choice is going to be or, as Helm puts it, from an unexpected or fortuitous result, but the indeterminacy itself as well as the absence of foreknowledge arising from it rests on the simultaneous presence of potencies to contrary effects belonging to the human will. What Helm's analysis does not consider is the simultaneous presence in the human will of genuine potencies to different effects and the resultant issue that all choices, as contingencies or necessities of the consequence, could be otherwise.[35]

Clearly, this language is abstract, scholastic. Muller's judgment that the position of Turretin and compatibilism is near seems absent. I venture to suggest that what is happening here is that the theorizing is striving to identify indeterminism where it is not to be found.

Edwards's account of human culpability is more straightforward, less circuitous.

> The common people, in their notion of a faulty or praiseworthy deed or work done by anyone, do suppose that the man does it in the exercise of

---

34. ibid., I. p. 668.
35. Muller, *Divine Will and Human Choice*, I. p. 251.

liberty. But then their notion of liberty is only a person's having opportunity of doing as he pleases. They have no notion of liberty consisting in the will's first acting, and so causing its own acts; and determining, and so causing its determinations, or choosing, and so causing its own choice. Such a notion of liberty is what none have, but those that have darkened their own minds with confused metaphysical speculation, and abstruse and ambiguous terms. If a man is not restrained from acting as his will determines, or constrained to act otherwise, then he has liberty, according to common notions of liberty, without taking into the idea that grand contradiction of all the determinations of a man's free will being the effect of the determinations of his free will. Nor have men commonly any notion of freedom consisting in indifference.[36]

So there are times when Turretin's account of human freedom in his *Institutes* is masked by his engagement in scholastic refinement. But there are other occasions, such as his comments on freedom and responsibility, where he shows clearly that human responsibility is a matter of whether or not free choice is or is not obstructed or nullified by 'brute necessity' or 'the necessity of coaction' i.e. compulsion; 'the things done by force and compulsion cannot be done voluntarily'.[37]

Edwards on Causation

Edwards's definition of 'cause', is as follows,

> I sometimes use the word 'cause,' either natural or moral, positive or negative, on which an event, either a thing, or the manner and circumstance of a thing, so depends, that it is the ground and reason, either in whole or in part, why it is, rather than not; or why it is as it is, than otherwise; or, in other words, any antecedent with which the consequent is so connected, that it truly belongs to the reason why the proposition which affirms that event, is true; whether it has any positive influence, or not.[38]

This is a somewhat expansive definition. Edwards needs something other than the Aristotelian four-fold causation, because, as he tells us next: 'Having thus explained what I mean by cause, I assert, that nothing

---

36. Edwards, *The Freedom of the Will*, pp. 358-9.

37. Turretin, *Institutes*, I. p. 662.

38. *Freedom of the Will*, I. pp. 180-1.

ever comes to pass without a cause'. It is a fundamental premise of his compatibilistic reasoning: every event has a cause.

In considering human action, its antecedences and consequences, we are dealing with what the RO refer to as cases of practical reason. Such reasoning is analyzed by them in terms of the Aristotelian four-fold causal character – material, efficient, formal, and final causes. Edwards does not operate in this Aristotelian way overtly, though as we have seen there remain several traces of that way in his *Freedom of the Will*. So, to remind ourselves, Edwards can be thought of as providing answers to three of the four 'Why?' questions posed above by the four scholastic terms, in ways of his own. For example, although he does not use the scholastic terms, he repeatedly refers to grounds of action and their *ends* or *purposes* of action (final causes), and to the agent's *apprehensions*, ways of referring to formal causes.[39] Just as with the operation of practical reason, when that four-fold causation is in operation, it is interconnected with another distinction, between means and an end, and possibly in some cases also of intermediate means to the realization of the end. The last three causes, material, efficient and formal, comprise the various means, and the final cause the end. The different instances do not amount to a causal chain as in Newtonian science, but the final cause conditions (or causes) the character of the other three. Their paradigm case is obviously the work of a sculptor or of some other artist or workman. But this schema does not fit every account of a cause. So the scholastics recognized that the divine creation *ex nihilo* has no material cause—there is no pre-existing stuff that the Creator shaped—so it cannot be a case of four-fold causation, and in a similar way some cases of human acts do not have a readily-identifiable material cause.

So we see Edwards deliberately not employing scholastic terms, but covering similar ground using the language of the 'vulgar' instead, using everyday rather than learned speech. It is true that he is not wholly consistent in this, partly due the language that he was forced to use in his rebuttals of the various claims of his philosophical antagonists who were by and large not scholastics. But his use of the language of ordinary people provides the heart of a narrative of distinctly human activity.

---

39. We earlier noted in *Freedom of the Will*, the expressions 'desired end' (p. 138), and 'means and end' (p. 366), and now note Edwards's appreciation of a cause as an 'antecedent of an event' (pp. 180-1).

After all, how could Edwards write a treatise on free will, 'essential to *Moral Agency, Vertue* and *Vice, Reward* and *Punishment, Praise* and *Blame*' (part of the long title), if it were not written in common language? I don't say that he is making a universal prescription here, stipulating that his is the only way for a compatibilist to operate. But Edwards's use of common speech enables the use of the language of freedom and of compulsion, of motives, intentions, desires, appetites, fears and so on, and of the terms in which we call an action fit for praise or blame.

There are some exceptions. As already mentioned, in the case of some of the RO some of the time, there is occasional evidence of use of causal language in human action. It is more evident in Turretin than in others, perhaps due to the fullness of his treatment, as in his section on the definition of freedom as rational willingness, by which a person does what he pleases by a previous judgment of reason. So, intrinsic to freedom is not a brute impulse or a basic instinct, but what occurs from choice, and by the previous light of reason, and the judgment of the practical intellect. Its voluntariness is to be seen in its spontaneity, the absence of compulsion. It elects this or that end because it is determined to do so by a judgment of the intellect. The intellect must first be persuaded before it can influence the will, by reasons and exhortations.[40] Such passages of discussion of the prominent RO is relatively free of scholastic distinctions between various kinds of cause, though not completely so.

The best chance of understanding the relationship of the RO and Edwards, then, lies not in focusing on one or more of the scholastic distinctions cited earlier, which prove not to be finally illuminating on the issues of causation, but in concentrating on the RO position as affording instances of practical reasoning, in which intellect and will cooperate in the project of gaining an end.

It has to be remembered that the scholastics regarded the faculties of the soul as so many forces or powers, *potentiae*. Among the energies of such powers was enabling a person to formulate or appraise ends and to take means suitable to the gaining of such ends, a matter which has to be learned from a teacher or by trial and error. These energies involved the expending of the soul's powers, such as forming and focusing of mental and material means, above all (for the RO) the work of the intellect,

---

40. Turretin, *Institutes*, I. p. 667-8.

which for the RO was the seat of the *imago dei*.[41] The language of the faculties is routinely causal. When they appeal to the *imago dei*, the RO sometimes have the intellect, at other times have the will, in mind. And they do not forget that the Creator is an independent reality, possessed of *aseitas*, while those who possess the image of God are creaturely, whose actions are routinely the effect of external causes, for which they are dependent on God their Creator and conserver.

It was suggested in chapter 2 that whatever the wrongs and rights of the Vosian use of human freedom as synchronic contingency, affirming it in a Reformed context creates an agenda of other problems: the consistency of such a view with the divine decrees, with providence, and the bondage of the will, with regeneration and so forth. I agree with Richard Muller on this, though of this agenda he seems only to concentrate on providence. I think he concentrates on that because the decrees of God and the bondage of the will, and regeneration are or involve topics in soteriology, with divinely gracious operations, whereas providence is more straightforwardly metaphysical, though I do not remember him saying as much about this.

In the foregoing we have considered the significance of compulsion for the genuineness or otherwise of compatible free action. For compulsion is an application of a force that limits or wholly exempts voluntariness in action. It is vital for assessing responsibility. I was not making the argument that compulsion is strong evidence of compatibilism only. Indeterminacy no doubt also uses compulsion as a reason for the absence of responsibility. Rather, I have been arguing that compulsion is causal in character.

Agency in Providence

When we come to the treatment of the distinction between primary and secondary causation in *Divine Will and Human Choice*, they have a more central place than in Vos's work and that of his group. The theological importance of causality is here given its due. Muller says that the sharpness of Edwards's break with the RO can be seen in his unwillingness to use the language of primary and secondary causation.[42]

---

41. ibid., I. pp. 667-8.

42. Paul Helm, 'Jonathan Edwards and the Parting of the Ways?', *Jonathan Edwards Studies*, 4.1. 2014, p. 57.

But in fact Edwards did use this distinction, in spite of his generally occasionalistic outlook.[43] In his discussion of the relation between divine concurrence and continuous creation he was in dialogue with William Ames (1570–1633), not a minor figure in the development of RO. Edwards does not demur from Ames's use of the primary-secondary distinction.

First, primary and secondary causes figure in Turretin's account of providence. He is concerned with preserving a proper place for what the *Westminster Confession of Faith* referred to as the 'contingency of second causes' and seems to be saying that there are at least two ways in which a 'thing' can be contingent. Human beings and (say) insects are both contingent beings because their existence depends upon God the first cause. They exist contingently because their Creator may not have created them, and even though created, they die. Their Creator causes them to exist in this sense, and returns them to the dust. If there are human beings and insects then it is only with respect to the will of God that they may be said to be contingent. Both the workings of insects and of human beings are necessary in the sense that the RO called 'hypothetical necessity', necessary only in virtue of the prior 'hypothesis' that God had willed their existence, and their natures.

The *second* way in which something can be said to be contingent is in virtue of a secondary cause having the power either to produce an effect or not. Turretin's point is that the divine decree does not take away contingency with respect to second causes 'because the same decree which predetermined also determined the mode of futurition, so that the things having necessary causes should happen necessarily and those having contingent causes, contingently'.[44] Note the reference to causes here. The basic idea is that the divine decree does not smother or collapse or override the distinction between necessary causes and contingent causes, but respects and preserves it. So that while all things that are decreed are necessitated by the decree, and so they are hypothetically necessary, 'taken according to themselves' they retain their distinctive

43. S. Mark Hamilton refers to over 100 references of the distinction between primary and secondary causation in Edwards's writings, including in his well-known sermon 'A Divine and Supernatural Light'. *A Treatise on Jonathan Edwards Continuous Creation and Christology* (JE Society Press, 2017), p. 48-51.

44. Turretin, *Institutes*, I. p. 321, also pp. 217, 218.

character. In this connection Turretin cites Aquinas 'Every effect in necessity and contingency follows the proximate cause and not the first'.[45] So the liberty and spontaneity of actions possessing these properties is not compromised. This is 'extrinsic and hypothetical' necessity, extrinsic because it secures the happening of an action or event but only through the outworking of its own nature, freely and contingently in the case of a thing that has such properties or powers, such as human beings, necessary in other cases, such as sheep.

So in Turretin's view, obviously insects do not possess the power of rational choice, for example, but human beings do, possessed as they are of reason and will. So now there is the contrast Turretin wishes to draw, between a contingent effect and a necessary effect. For instance, insects act and react not from choice, but by instinct, likewise a flame does not have a choice whether or not it flares up and produces heat. Applying a thumbscrew produces pain in the victim; it cannot produce pleasurable feelings, anymore than a sheep can choose to eat ham and eggs. In the absence of choice, the occurrence of all such events are necessary, not contingent, even though the insects, fire, a thumbscrew, and sheep, have contingently-possessed powers, in the sense that each depends on God. Though sheep, along with other higher animals, possess appetites, and may have the power of choice in a rudimentary fashion.[46]

Further, many events are capable of having consequences that may not be foreseen by human beings. Many sorts of agents are capable of producing effects that as far as their human bystanders are concerned are not intended or expected. They are unintended consequences that are often unforeseen. A tree may fall in the wind, and a freak wave may appear, an insect may suddenly sting, and so on; and Joe may surprise himself by deciding to wear his new tie this morning. Each change, including human actions, it may seem, are capable of bringing about changes that surprise us, and in the case of human actions, the human agent himself may be surprised at himself.

But are there contingent things whose powers and the effects they produce, are contingent in a second sense, a case of Franciscan freedom? No one doubts that God can know that the occurrence of physically

---

45. ibid., I. p. 311.
46. ibid., I. p. 662.

necessary events will or will not take place. But what of those contingent events in the second sense, the actions of human beings, that possess reason and will? Scripture teaches that God nevertheless has infallible knowledge of contingent effects, effects which 'have a free cause'.[47] Free, here, surely, must be rational spontaneity, compatibilism.[48]

So far, so straightforward, or so it may seem. Within the contingent, i.e., dependent, world order, certain classes of event are necessary, not the outcome of choice, certain kinds of other events are contingent on account of choice, 'free'. But to make things a little more complex for the interpreter, Turretin also employs a different expression to cover this second sense of contingency, or at least provides some more explanation of what he has in mind. He says,

> But future contingent things are not such [not absolute and in every respect indeterminate]. For if they are indeterminate with respect to the second cause and in themselves, they are not so as to the first cause which decreed their futurition. If their truth is indeterminate with respect to us (who cannot see in which direction the free second cause is about to incline itself), it is not so with respect to God to whom all future things appear as present.[49]

So God's *decree*, a causal term if ever there was one, besides being that to which the existence of human beings as a class are due, reaches to all future events, including free human actions. In respect of the divine decreer, therefore, to whom the future appears as present, God knows each created agent from an eternal standpoint. But to us, the human agents, the creaturely knowers of human actions, Turretin says we 'cannot see in which direction the free second cause is about to incline itself'.[50]

That is, while God who decrees a future creaturely free action and thereby knows it, those who possess creaturely free actions (who cannot usually know for sure the direction in which the free second cause is about to incline itself) don't know, *for they are contingent*. I have added the italicized words of explanation, for that is what Turretin is implying. He says a few paragraphs later,

---

47. ibid., I. pp. 208-9.
48. ibid., I. p. 665.
49. ibid., I. pp. 210-11.
50. ibid., I. p. 211.

[T]here remains always this distinction between necessary and contingent things. The former have an intrinsic necessity because they arise from necessary proximate causes and are such in themselves, while the contingent, although they have an extrinsic necessity by reason of the event, [here Turretin is referring to the fact that contingent events are nonetheless decreed by God and foreknown by Him] yet in their nature take place by contingent causes.[51]

Contingent causes are those causes that may or may not occur depending on the action or inaction of a human agent.

In the case of those things which possess both understanding and will, powers to make contingent choices, they take place in such a manner that we the observers may not see in what direction the cause of the action is about to incline itself. By his use of these expressions does Turretin think that this ignorance is a feature of a person's lack of knowledge of *others'* actions only, or may it include his lack of knowledge of *his own* actions? Surely he must be referring to both. We are frequently unable to tell for sure how people are going to make up their minds, and are similarly unsure about how we are going to make up our own minds. Until we do so, the decision as to what to do may go either way, to choose A or not-A, or to choose A or B. And anyway our knowledge is not like God's, infallible, at best it is an educated guess. Not until we have finally and irrevocably made up our minds can we ourselves be said to know what we have decided to do.

So maybe the following represents the position: Turretin holds that an agent is frequently in the condition of not knowing the outcome of his own and others' deliberations. So long as action is being performed as a result of past deliberations there is not much of a problem. But with the prospect of new choices there are new indeterminacies (e.g. suspensions of judgment, states of indifference).[52] Until these choices have been made, minds are not irrevocably made up, and then new deliberations are made, and the choices may surprise us, even if they are our own choices. These activities are contingent in Turretin's second sense.

So as I understand things Turretin is here explaining further a phrase he uses in his earlier discussion of contingency: 'their truth is

51. ibid., I. p. 211.
52. ibid., I. p. 669.

indeterminate with respect to us (who cannot see in which direction the free second cause is about to incline itself)'.[53] The contingency we are referring to here (i.e. a contingency that arises in connection with a choice because the mind has not been made up and so the choice has not been finally made) is an intrinsic feature of someone who is freely making up their minds (i.e. whose action is not the result of coaction or of brute necessity, like horses eating hay). All this is from Turretin's discussion of the divine foreknowledge of human free acts.

A *third* discussion arises in Turretin's treatment of providence in the Sixth Topic, the Third Question: *Do all things come under providence – small as well as great, contingent and free, natural and necessary? We affirm.*[54]

> Scripture in many places asserts that contingent and fortuitous events fall under providence. Nothing is more contingent than the killing of a man by a woodcutter, contrary to his own intention, and yet this is ascribed to God, who is said to deliver him into the hand of the slayer (Exod. 21:22, 13; Deut. 19:4f). Nothing is more casual and fortuitous than lots, and yet their falling out is referred to God himself …. Nothing was more contingent than the selling of Joseph and his incarceration and exaltation, yet Joseph himself testifies that these were all ordered in the providence of God. (Gen. 45:8)[55]

And further, as far as free acts are concerned, 'whose mode of action is contingent', the agents may not know what choice they are going to make.

> For that infallibility of the event from the hypothesis does not take away their contingency from the condition of second causes and from their mode of acting (in which there is always an intrinsic faculty and indifference to the opposite). So it was necessary for Joseph to be sold by his brethren and to go down to Egypt because it had been so determined by God for the preservation of Jacob's family. Yet it was contingent with respect to the brothers of Joseph who might either have killed him or have sold him.[56]

So Joseph's brothers had a choice, whether to sell him or to kill him. Before they made up their minds they did not know what that choice

---

53. ibid., I. p. 211.
54. ibid., I. p. 497.
55. ibid., I. p. 499.
56. ibid., I. p. 500.

would be, and so they did not know how things were going to turn out. (Had they been coerced, by being bribed, say, into making one choice, the matter would have been significantly different). So the outcome was contingent, not in the sense of being fortuitous, but in that it involved the settling of indecision. (Once again, we need to bear in mind Turretin's understanding of freedom as rational spontaneity.) Here he underlines what he had previously discussed, and what we have been trying to understand. All events are capable of producing unintended consequences. The tossing of a coin, the turning of a card, the choice of a straw, may be necessary, fixed through shuffling or tossing, and yet have surprising and significant consequences. For example it may turn out that after the shuffle, the top four cards turn out to have a sequence of a 1, a 2, a 3, and a 4 of Spades. And free human actions may have unintended and unforeseen consequences, which add to their contingency. It is such free acts that Turretin is here interested in, in this discussion, and the part that settling an indecision plays in the genesis of an action. In the next paragraph he writes, 'Therefore, nothing in the nature of things can be granted as so fortuitous and casual as not to be governed by the providence of God and so not happening necessarily and infallibly with respect to the divine decree'.[57]

By 'more contingent' Turretin refers to an action whose performance depends upon the outcome of other free actions and so is doubly or multiply contingent.[58] For example the dilemma of Joseph's brothers as to what to do with him was intensified and ultimately solved by the sudden, unexpected appearing of the Ishmaelite caravan on its way to Egypt (Gen. 37:29). Turretin uses the phrases 'contingent and fortuitous' (*contingentia et fortuita*)[59] and 'fortuitous and casual' (*fortuitum et casualia*)[60] to refer to events that are unexpected and yet may have an explanation, such as the woodcutter's chopping of wood, or the time and rate of travel of the Ishmaelites, which are contingent acts.

---

57. ibid., I. p. 499.

58. ibid., I. p. 499. Compare Owen on such doubly contingent circumstances, *Vindiciae Evangelicae* (1655), *Works*, ed. Goold, XII. pp. 128-9.

59. ibid., I. p. 499.

60. ibid., I. p. 497.

And there is this:

> Third, it follows, since providence does not concur with the human will, either by coaction, compelling the unwilling will, or by determining it physically (as a brute and blind thing without judgment), but rationally (by turning the will in a manner suitable to itself), that it may determine itself as the proximate cause of its own actions by the proper judgment of reason and the spontaneous election of the will so that it does no violence to our will but rather kindly cherishes it. These two are the only kinds of necessity which destroy liberty and are incompatible with it: natural and coercive necessity. The others (arising from God's decree and the motion of the first cause or from the object and the last judgment of the practical intellect) so far from overthrowing liberty, rather defend it, because they turn, do not compel, the will and make it willing from unwilling. For whoever does spontaneously what he wills from a judgment of reason and a full consent of will cannot help doing that freely even if he does it necessarily (from whatever source that necessity flows, whether from the very existence of the thing [because whatever is, when it is, is necessarily] or from the object efficaciously moving the mind and the will or from a first cause decreeing and concurring).[61]

This language seems to be fully consistent with compatibilism.

It seems that in the case of free actions there are two factors for us to bear in mind. '...[M]an is always free in acting and many effects are contingent'.[62] Here the focus is not on the free action itself, but on its effects, the outcomes of the action. Not all effects, but many of them, including those that are unknown until the very need for a decision arises and the decision is made. Turretin's interest in the outcomes of a free action suggests the following question; if mere ignorance of the outcome of a future choice is contingency to some degree, maybe such an as-yet undecided choice is contingent in this sense, for a person does not know the outcome of his own action until he has made up his mind to act in a certain way. And maybe this is the chief thing to note about those effects that are free, that many of them may be presently undecided and when the choice is made it may be unanticipated by the agent, and may be surprising to him. '...[W]ith the indefinite and free, however, they also determine themselves by the proper judgment of

---

61. ibid., I. p. 513.
62. ibid., I. p. 512.

reason and the free disposition of the will ....'[63] This is a good example of how the components of a free act are laid out by Turretin in a little more detailed narrative.

In this section I have offered an interpretation of Turretin's employment of the distinction between primary and secondary causes that is consistent with his account of freedom as spontaneous willingness. This has involved understanding 'contingency' as 'spontaneous choice', and not as 'indeterministic' as found in Vos and in Muller. The point has been to show its consistency with compatibilism.

God and Contingency in Providence

Muller makes the important point[64] that it is God's action to create the world that gives birth both to necessities and contingencies. Edwards construes God's freedom somewhat differently, he does not stress the divine indifference, but nonetheless God alone freely brings to pass individuals who possess both natural and moral inabilities and abilities, and indifferences of various other kinds, as we have seen. Muller's schema for the intertwining or concatenation of divine free will and human free will in providence is rather different, but all recognize that imputing to God a human-like freedom, whatever their view, is a risky business.

In using this schema in respect of God's providence and human action, Muller says things that leave void an account of how these two come together in a providential order of the sort that the Reformed confessed. Given contingency in God and in his human creatures, Turretin (as Muller construes things) can ring the changes about the *sensus diviso* and *sensus composito*, but[65] spelling these out does not come near to indicating *how* it is still that when 'God wills that *p*' He does so in a way that preserves entirely the present indeterminate freedom of the human creature's choice, and the next *and* the next, in such a way that the successive free acts of the creature can be said to be such that they are 'according to the will of God', in accord with His plan, His purposes. Invoking divine premotion, which according to Turretin [as

---

63. ibid., I. p. 513.
64. Muller, *Divine Will and Human Choice,* p. 304.
65. Turretin, *Institutes,* I. p. 305.

Muller understands him] is another notion that we are extremely taxed in trying to understand.[66]

When Muller sets out the meshing of the divine will and the human [allegedly] indeterministic free will it seems that his desired and willed providential order comes to pass by sheer coincidence! This is because Muller's account is in terms of God's contingent free indeterministic will and the person's own contingent free indeterministic willing. What seems to be strangely absent is an account of *how God carries out* His upholding of the creature's condition that secures and guarantees His ability to do just those successive divine actions without impinging on human autonomy, but as expressing it.

Potencies

In an earlier paper I argued that scholastic distinctions such as the two necessities, and of the two potencies, *potentia simultatis* and *simultas potentiae*, can not only be applied to men and women, but to non-human animals, to artefacts and natural objects such as apples.[67] My point was to show the general character of such distinctions. Their use can enlighten as to human free contingency only if such free contingency is assumed. It follows:

> It is hard to see how these various distinctions, taken by themselves, suggest an ontology of synchronic contingency, or presuppose a particular view of contingency, synchronic contingency, as is claimed. And even when the examples considered are those of human action, it does not follow that a writer in using them has synchronic contingency in mind. He may simply be disambiguating certain expressions to avoid possible misunderstanding. These various distinctions could not be the criteria of the presence of the freedom of synchronic contingency.[68]

Muller later says 'Whether some of these distinctions can be used to develop a view of synchronic contingency and can also have ontological implications (and I agree that several of them can); whether they support a particular ontology is an entirely different matter.'[69] The state of affairs

---

66. ibid., I. p. 505.

67. Paul Helm, '*Reformed Thought on Freedom*: Some Further Thoughts', pp. 189-90.

68. ibid., p. 191.

69. Muller, *Divine Will and Human Choice*, p. 301.

that the scholastic theologian is in—his tools—does not serve to explain the issue of the executing of the divine plan. The solution is surely not yet more logical distinctions. We need the evidence of the understanding and the will in action.

In the era of RO, there was considerable animosity between the scholastic theology as represented and headed up by Voetius, and the developers of covenant theology such as Herman Witsius and Johannes Cocceius. One was topical and logical in its emphasis, the other stressed a historical narrative and diachronic 'flow' in its emphasis. I reckon that the issues of human free will fare better in the employment of the second method than in the first.

'Christian Fate'

Earlier I set out an informal hierarchy of causal forces that the RO observed. First there is God, who has alternativity, not being subject to any external causes. Of His creatures, some have one-way causal power, like natural forces such as flames and the pull of gravity, some have natural appetites and instincts, like insects and sheep. And mankind, made in the image of God, is capable of rationally spontaneous choices and courses of action. And there are angels, fallen and unfallen. To this list should added the term 'fate' or 'Christian fate' as a term to refer to the entire network of causal powers as willed by God. Earlier we saw Voetius as one who used the term. But some of the RO were reluctant to use it because of its pagan associations.

The Reformed had this ambivalence to the use of 'fate' as a name of all that God wills, an attitude that they inherited from Augustine, who was similarly ambivalent. In his *City of God*,[70] he discusses the view of the Stoic Cicero [Tully] in his work *De Divinatione*, that it was inconsistent with either divine or human foreknowledge. 'Thus denies he God's foreknowledge, and idly seeks to subvert the radiant lustre of true prophecies, by propounding certain ambiguous and fallible oracles, whose truth notwithstanding he does not confute.'[71] Augustine says that in his book *De Divinatione* Cicero denied that divine foreknowledge was consistent with fate, with the absolute

---

70. Augustine, *The City of God*, V.IX.
71. ibid., V.IX.

necessitation of all changes, and that it was therefore inconsistent with freedom of choice.

Augustine sets against this his own belief in God's foreknowledge. God knows beforehand what we will do by our own will, against the Stoic claim that such foreknowledge required fate.

> And if they come so to pass, then God knows the certain order of things beforehand, and consequently the certain order of the causes; and if He knows a certain cause in all events, then are all events disposed by fate; which if it be so, we have nothing left in our power, nothing in our will': 'which granted', says he [Tully], 'the whole course of humanity is overturned'; law, correction, praise, disgrace, exhortation, prohibition, all are to no end: nor is there any justice in punishing the bad and rewarding the good.[72]

But Augustine reckons that there is no such need for the denial of foreknowledge in order to prevent the genuineness of the working of the human will, and the place of rewards and punishments. 'But the religious mind chooses them both'. God both knows all things as they come to pass, and we do all things by exercise of our will, which we are not compelled to do. ['Not directly enforced to'.] [W]e neither deny an order of causes wherein the will of God is all in all, neither do we call it by the name of fate, unless 'fate;' derives from *fari*, 'to speak'…. For our very wills are in that order of causes which God knows and hath in his prescience; human wills being the cause of human actions; so that He that keeps a knowledge of the causes of all things, cannot leave men's wills out of that knowledge, knowing them to be the causes of their actions'.[73]

So there is a fate that is the divine foreknowledge, but this is not the outcome of, say, the movement and position of the stars, which is unacceptable to the religious mind. 'So men good and bad have all their wills: and hereby it is apparent that the efficient causes of all effects are voluntary causes and nothing but the decrees of that nature which is "the spirit of life".'[74]

Among the RO Peter Martyr Vermigli picks up these Augustinian themes.

---

72. ibid., V.IX.
73. ibid., V.IX.
74. ibid., V.IX.

If as we have said before, by the word 'fate' or similar words they understand the connection of causes over which God himself rules, moderating and governing, then there is no harm in that opinion. Although because of the abuse of the word, it is better to abstain from it. There are also some who dream of a kind of fatal necessity (mighty and strong) fixed to the stars and natural causes, which even God cannot change. This is false, impious, and far from the wise men of old. They explicitly declared that by fate they understood the will and governance of God.[75]

When we speak of foreknowledge we do not exclude the will, for as we admonished at the beginning. God cannot foreknow something will happen unless that he chooses that it will happen. Nothing can exist except what God wills, and what God wills he also brings about for us. It is as Paul says 'He works in us both to will and to perform.' (Phil. 2:13)[76]

Turretin in the next century discusses what he calls 'Christian fatalism': he is of course against pagan fatalism, according to which the stars (or some other source) determine everything that occurs. In contrast 'Christian fate' is 'the order of series and order of causes depending on divine providence by which it produces its own effects', following Augustine closely. He notes the fathers used the term 'fate', as did Thomas Aquinas.[77] But he observes that the term 'fate',

[I]s now taken actively for the divine decree itself ... then passively, for the very complexion and disposition of all causes to their own effects (according as they depend upon the immutable providence of God). Thus it is distinguished from providence by reason of the subject because providence is in God, while fate is from God in second causes and by reason of order (because fate depends on providence, not the contrary) and in the object (because all things lie under providence, but not under fate; those for instance which take place immediately by God).[78]

So in 'Christian fate' God is not subject to created events, but events, including voluntary actions, are subject to God. Yet because the word 'fate' has such strong associations with the Stoic versions, and with

---

75. Peter Martyr Vermgli, *Predestination and Justification*, The Peter Martyr Library, 8 ed. and trans. Frank A. James III (Kirksville, Mo. 2005), p. 72.

76. Vermigli, *Predestination and Justification*, pp. 72-3.

77. Thomas Aquinas, *Summa Theologiae*, Ia. p. 116.

78. Turretin, *Institutes*, I. p. 497.

astrology, Vermigli thinks it safer to be cautious, like Augustine, on the grounds that such fate as defined by Cicero, were it to be received, entails the denial of divine foreknowledge. Because 'all things lie under providence, but not under fate; those, for instance, which take place immediately by God'.[79]

Passages like this from Turretin do not seem to raise any interest in the minds of his synchronic contingency interpreters in *RTF*. They make several references to Stoic fatalism,[80] but in pursuit of their novel libertarian interpretations of the RO, not once do they take into account the positive features of such passages as these on 'Christian fate'.

Summary

In this chapter we have looked at those contexts in which causes are deployed and discussed by the RO, and should have been, and have shown that they are consistent with compatibilism, the relationship between the reason and the will. We have also noted how primary and secondary causality as used by Turretin are instances of divine and human efficient causation. Here, clearly, contingency is a matter of causal efficacy. Such views are consistent with compatibilism and open an aperture into the working of causality, which the compilers of *RTF* have little time for.

In the third of our arguments, in the last chapter, we will attempt to open this window of understanding further in paying more attention to the interaction and cooperation of the faculties of the mind in furthering the working of the practical reason. In this last chapter we shall have reason to consider both aspects of causation, the interactions of the faculties, and the efficient causes of human agency.

---

79. ibid., I. p. 497.
80. *Reformed Thought on Freedom*, pp. 15, 17, 31, 38, 40.

CHAPTER 7

The Evidence of the Faculties

This chapter presents the last of the three central, circumstantial (and therefore indirect) arguments for the compatibilism of the RO, and it will focus on another causal side of RO anthropology. The first argument (Chapter 5) had to do with the fact that Turretin and Edwards occupied the same theological niche. The second (Chapter 6) had to do with how the scholastic mind has principally to do with logical distinctions, arising from the place that *disputationes* had in RO education. This outlook is prized by Vos and his group and as a consequence narratives and everyday discussion of the place of the mind in the production of actions takes second place. In this last chapter we focus on what the RO and Edwards each has to say about the connection between the intellect and the will, and finally with how Muller in *Divine Will and Human Choice* and in his later article of 2019, defends Turretin and other RO as being indeterminists, and the problems his argument entails. Some repetition in these chapters has been inevitable, because in each chapter we are concerned with the same causal side of things in RO anthropology, as well as in their doctrine of God.

The argument of this chapter has to do with the character of human freedom when this is understood in terms of the faculty psychology that was a central part of the anthropology of the RO, but about which Vos and his group have little to say. This last chapter has prepared for this by the two other arguments, in which the factor of causation has already raised its head.

We shall assemble this causal evidence by looking at a range of the RO treatment of the faculties in the extracts displayed in *RTF,* and also discussed by Muller in Chapter 6 of his book, augmented by one or two other sources. Scholastic *disputationes* particularly majored on questions of consistency and self-contradiction about which the various questions were interrogated. In disputing, the RO more often than not disambiguate some expression, which otherwise appears to be contradicting some revealed truth, or is ambiguous, or some other claim that has been made. The distinctions they offer as conclusions to their disputation provide two or more readings, one of which is consistent with revealed truth.

It is the great merit of Muller's *Divine Will and Human Choice*, and other of his writings[1] that he has provided evidence that undermines to some extent the importance of Scotus in the formation of the RO tradition as seen in *RTF*. It is puzzling therefore that Muller himself sees the RO as what we might call mildly libertarian, a sort of semi-indeterminism, not committed to Franciscan freedom, but neither compatibilist either. Instead, he grants a residual place for contingency in their diachronic (not synchronic) view of freedom, which we shall come to later in this chapter.

We shall largely follow Muller in his historical survey in Ch. 6 of *Divine Choice and Human Will* in a search for diachronic and synchronic contingency and its allegedly crucial place in the thinking of RO. I shall add examples that Muller has later added.[2]

The thinkers that are surveyed in this chapter understand the working of faculties of the mind, particularly the mental acts that express the ends towards which they move the agent. We shall include some of the same thinkers that appear in *RTF*. In that book the introductory statements of the relation between intellect and will are question-begging, as we shall shortly see. But the fact is that the contributors of *RTF* pay little attention to the behaviour of the faculties, largely ignoring the relationships of the intellect and will, the appetites, vices and virtues, and their contribution to the nature of human free agency. This is a significant gap in a book the subtitle of which is, 'The Concept of Free Choice in Early Modern Reformed Theology'. This mismatch is due to the fact that it is assumed that human freedom has to do

---

1. Richard A. Muller, 'Not Scotist: understandings of being, univocity, and analogy in early-modern Reformed thought' (*Reformation and Renaissance Review*, 2012).

2. In 'Neither Libertarian nor Compatibilist', *Journal of Reformed Theology*, 2019.

solely with indifference. The difference between their outlook and that of compatibilism is that for them the issue of 'free will' has primarily to do with the will, whereas compatibilists highlight the will in its subordination to the working of other faculties, chiefly the intellect, or in the case of Edwards, what he calls the understanding.

Faculties and Potencies

Faculties are powers, some of them what Muller calls 'resident', others more fleeting. In his discussion of RO indifference, Muller says the following,

> The will also, however, continues [after its exercise] to possess its essential character and, therefore, it retains its *actus primus* indifference both with regard to other objects and, indeed, with regard to this particular object in another temporal moment – just as the unactualized potency to do otherwise also remains, but as potency.[3]

Muller says something that seems different from this in his latest article.

> Helm's argument embodies a series of misconceptions concerning both the early modern Reformed understanding of freedom and my approach to the theory identified as 'synchronic contingency' and argued in *Reformed Thought on Freedom*. These misconceptions arise largely out of a failure to grasp the basic distinctions used by scholastics to argue the case for contingency and freedom. In the first place, Helm improperly describes synchronic contingency as 'the idea that the will is such that the *requisites for action* A to be performed being present, an agent *has the power to choose* either not-A or B at that very moment, hence "synchronic," and then comments that one of the strengths of my work is my rejection of "this novel supposition."'[4]

> Better to identify synchronic contingency as 'the idea that the operation of intellect and will is such that the *requisites for choice* being present, an agent *simultaneously (or synchronically) has the potencies to choose* A; *to refuse it, choosing not-A; or to choose B* ….' Once the concept is better defined, it becomes considerably more comprehensible, considerably less novel, and, clearly, not rejected by me.

---

3. Muller, *Divine Will and Human Choice*, p. 294.

4. Muller, 'Neither Libertarian nor Compatibilist' (*Journal of Reformed Theology* 2019), p. 273.

For the compatibilist the will can follow the judgment of the understanding. A compatibilist does not introduce synchronicity, however defined. 'The term 'synchronic contingency' may be novel, but the concept it references is not. My preference is to hold, as much as possible, to the language used by the Reformed orthodoxy, namely 'simultaneity of potency'.[5]

I have discussed potencies earlier and so I shall only consider them tangentially here.

So there is some support in Muller for the idea of synchronic contingency, though he prefers the scholastic expression 'simultaneity of potency', though he does not venture to say why this is better. A question is why he nevertheless plays down the influence of Scotus on the RO in Chapter 6. It is certainly absent in the treatment of the texts of the various RO theologians in *RTF*.

At the heart of Muller's view is that there must be a moment of genuine indifference for the will, pure indifference, that exists before a free choice takes place, which he thinks distinguishes genuine freedom from the spurious freedom of the compatibilist. For the compatibilist, the agent has a choice, to wear his yellow tie or not, say. He may falter in his choice, or make it immediately, or have another end in mind. But in no case does he have before him a purely indifferent will. He could choose for the yellow tie for a reason, or the green tie for a different reason, or no tie for yet another reason. In each case the will is subordinate to the understanding or intellect. There may be some reason to take one or other possibility, but genuine indifference, pure indifference, of this kind is another word for stalemate or randomness. He will choose that outcome at a time that he has the strongest reason to take at that time. Not every situation of choice is a possible choice already invested by a 'pre-determining bias or preponderation'. Whether there is such a preponderation may be due to habit, or a person's situation—for the tired, rest; for the thirsty, water, and so on—or for the relatively passive, say, the choice between an apple or a pear; no choice yet, or no choice at all. In the passage from which this wording is taken, Edwards is taking a perfectly indifferent choice to absurdity.[6]

---

5. Muller, 'Neither Libertarian nor Compatibilist' (*Journal of Reformed Theology* 2019), p. 273.

6. Edwards, *Freedom of the Will*, p. 201.

I wonder if some of Muller's outlook on creaturely free will is due to the assumption—not in so many words but as revealed by his procedure—that a consideration of it has to focus first on the will, its potencies and the like, and then its relations to other factors. But, paradoxically, in compatibilism, the will is governed by what factor or factors generate the will's action, what has been called 'the primacy of the intellect'. As Edwards put it, 'it is that whereby the soul either chooses or refuses ... for in every act of will whatsoever, the mind chooses one thing rather than another ....'[7] The approach of RTF is *a priori*, whereas that of determinism is *a posteriori*.

Muller cites the Puritan Stephen Charnock (1628–1680) as saying, 'Man hath a power to do otherwise than that which God foreknows he will do'. What this comes to for Muller is that 'inasmuch as God foreknows free acts as free, there is to be acknowledged a power or potency (albeit no longer realizable) exists in the very moment that God foreknows an act to occur, and that because of this potency the act could have been otherwise'.[8] Note the primary stress on indifference. To which a compatibilist may retort, 'Yes, certainly, if he had a stronger reason at the point of choice, then he would not merely have the possibility to choose, but would choose'.

Turretin's antipathy to indeterminism is seen in his discussion of the place of the intellect in free action, and also, from the other side, from his view that indifference is not necessary or sufficient for freedom. As evidence for this that we have not yet considered is Turretin's discussion of Middle Knowledge, in the Third Topic, Question XIII, held in common with the RO generally. The Molinists, including Jesuits and Arminians, held that the free will *consists in indifference*, whereas the RO saw it as a combination of the will and the intellect. Turretin thought that the idea of God's middle knowledge, between God's knowledge of simple intelligence, and His knowledge of vision, of the future of His creation, was to be rejected.

Middle knowledge by its practitioners was supposed to be a new source of divine knowledge between the two, hence 'middle' knowledge.

---

7. ibid., p. 137. Note Turretin's, 'the will follows the last determinate judgment of the practical intellect', *Divine Will and Human Choice,* p. 297.

8. Muller, *Divine Will and Human Choice*, p. 296.

It was the knowledge of what indeterminately free individuals would do in various hypothetical situations. The Reformed had several arguments against this: that it was a form of divine knowledge outside the scope of the divine decree. It is not divine knowledge, because it is purely indifferent. '[W]here then is the indifference of the will? If it foresees it as certain, how could the foresight of an uncertain and indifferent thing be itself certain? ... the certain necessity of the event cannot be founded on the contingent ends ....'[9] Not even God could foresee the outcome of pure indifference. Knowledge rests on evidence and in the case of pure indifference there cannot be any.

The Vos Approach

Among several remarks of the contributors to *RTF,* when they come across the phrase 'rational spontaneity', they seem to forget the reason for that term given by the RO themselves.

As we noted earlier, these various Reformed theologians are said (by Vos and company) to uphold indeterminism in statements such as, 'It is important to note that the will is *not determined* (*determinari*) by the intellect when it *follows* (*sequi*) the intellect: the will keeps its own task of choosing'. [10] But Turretin, for example, more than once notes a stronger connection between intellect and will than merely being 'followed by' the will, and it is these stronger connections and their implications that we shall first focus on. For him the will's role in choosing is by *necessarily* executing the goal or goals of the intellect. Turretin states that the liberty of the will has its roots in the intellect. If I believe that the way to Blackpool is via Preston (a judgment of my intellect), and I have Blackpool as my destination, my will follows my intellect, under usual circumstances, such as that I have not in the meantime fallen asleep, or changed my mind.

It is true that the RO writers say, the intellect and will 'work together'[11] in free choice, but this expression is weaker or vaguer than the facts warrant. This activity of the will is the effect of the last judgment of the intellect. It follows the judgment, of course, as effects follow their

---

9. Turretin, *Institutes*, I. p. 215.

10. *Reformed Thought on Freedom*, p. 46.

11. ibid., p. 46.

causes. The question of the relation cannot be settled *a priori*, but it is a matter of the ways in which that relation is expressed. In Turretin, for example, it is clear that the intellect *necessitates* the will. As we have already seen, this corresponds precisely to what Edwards asserts, that 'the will always follows the last dictate of the understanding', or 'the will is always determined by the strongest motive, or by that view of the mind which has the greatest degree of previous tendency to it.'[12]

Hence in Turretin's understanding of freedom as 'rational spontaneity', the intellect and will work conjointly, the intellect energizing the will to a particular end. So Turretin elaborates as follows. 'Here are two principal characteristics of free will in which its formal nature consists: (1) the choice, so that what is done by a previous judgment of reason; (2) the willingness, so that what is done is done voluntarily and without compulsion.' 'For since the will is a rational appetite such is its nature that it must follow the last judgment of the practical intellect'. So, on the question of the divine decree, 'Although the will is free, this does not prevent it being determined by God and being always under subjection to him'.[13]

> The will can be viewed either in relation to the decree and concourse of God or in contradistinction to the intellect. In the former sense, it is rightly said to be so determined by God as also to determine itself (because, as was seen before, God so moves creatures as to leave their own motions to them). But in the latter sense, it cannot be said to determine itself (because it is determined by the intellect whose last judgment of practical intellect it must follow).[14]

The compatibilism of these statements could not be clearer. Note the use of 'necessitates' and 'determines' here. The way in which they are carefully discriminated by Turretin is sufficient to warrant compatibilism. It is an intellectual necessitating. It is sufficient to cast doubt on the *RTF*'s compilers pointed assertion that

> The technical term 'determination', should not be associated with the modern term 'determinism', because that term did not exist yet, the concept of determinism was denoted by other terms like 'Stoic fate.' Rather determination means that a cause gets directed to one effect, A natural

12. *Freedom of the Will*, p. 148.
13. Turretin, *Institutes*, I. p. 664.
14. ibid., I. p. 664.

cause is determined by its nature to one act, a free cause by freedom to one of possible acts.[15]

Well, yes and no. As we found earlier, 'determine' can take an object such as 'I have determined that the lighthouse is higher than I at first thought' by the information of the relative positions of two places on the map. This is 'determined' as in 'discovered', or 'judged', acts of discrimination. Discovery in this sense is an act of the theoretical intellect rather than of the practical intellect, when the agent has in view the choice of the means to an end. Turretin, in the quotation above, writes of the determining of the intellect in an act of preference, the choice of an alternative, a characteristic expression used by compatibilists.

Turretin's account in the Tenth Topic of the *Institutes* is very like Jonathan Edwards's account of the causal activity of the mind. Edwards says, for example,

> By 'determining the will', if the phrase be used with any meaning, must be intended, causing that the act of the will or choice should be thus, and not otherwise: and the will is said to be determined, when, in consequence of some action, or influence, its choice is directed and fixed upon a particular action. As when we speak of the determination of motion, we mean causing the motion of the body to be such a way, or in such a direction, rather than another.[16]

For Turretin, that the relation between intellect and will, distinct faculties, is one of causal necessity, is shown by the limited vocabulary that is used to characterize these faculties, all of it causal in character, as we saw in the last chapter. This is a case of efficient causation. There is an alternativity at work here, but it is a causally-produced one, a conditional alternativity. The faculties are constitutive powers of the soul that together go to make up human choice. In practical means-end reasoning, the desiring or 'appetitive' part, included in the working of the appetite of the intellect, causes an activation in the will or willingness, so one element is in an asymmetrical causal relation with another part. So suppose that as a result of a change in my intellect on my beliefs in my current end or ends, I change my mind as to where I am going, then I would have pointed my bicycle in the appropriately different direction. Isn't this so?

---

15. *Reformed Thought on Freedom*, p. 31.
16. Edwards, *Freedom of the Will*, p. 141. The entire section is an expansion of this position.

The RO utilize Aristotle's distinction between 'the appetite of the senses' or the 'appetitive intellect'; the will has rational or intelligent appetites that express themselves in the intellectual activity of the will, as distinct from the *appetitus sensitivus*, the appetite of the senses. The activity of the intellect and of the will express these appetites or combinations of them. The work of the appetites is thus causal in character.[17] Muller does not seem to introduce this scholastic distinction.

For Turretin, when we are considering the nature and operations of the free will, we are in the area of the operation of the practical reason, as distinct from that of the theoretical or contemplative reason, the two theatres of the operation of the reason according to scholasticism, the theoretical having to do with the true, the practical reason with the good.[18] The reason is theoretical when it has concern only with truth for its own sake, as when I investigate the distance between Blackpool and Preston, say. A practical reason is formed when the person's concern is with the achieving of some good identified by the agent, such as going to Blackpool, or avoiding it. This is what he or she regards as a good, as a desirable end to be enjoyed now or shortly. The intellect, informed by the senses and by what a person already knows or believes, judges what it regards as true. So in the case of some practical need, the intellect judges what it is good to do, what steps to take, to respond to or fulfill that need. So the reasoning of the practical reason is means-end reasoning. Once the end is judged, overridingly desired, and the means to that end, the will then executes the achieving of the end, which may be trivial or momentous. If not overridingly, there is a pause, a hesitation.

Here are some of Turretin's further remarks about what he calls rational necessity. The Second Question of the Tenth Topic is: *Whether every necessity is repugnant to freedom of will. We deny against the papists and Remonstrants.* 'Repugnant' is equivalent to 'opposed to' or 'incompatible with' or 'at odds with'. So, unlike these groups, Turretin (like Edwards) holds that some necessities, what he (and others) call moral necessities, are consistent with free will. In all he distinguishes six kinds of necessity, four of which are consistent with free will, among them hypothetical, rational and moral necessity. Rational necessity has

---

17. Aristotle, *Nicomachean Ethics*, I. p. 13.18.

18. For more detail, see Paul Helm, *Human Nature from Calvin to Edwards*.

to do with the determinations of the practical reason. 'For since the will is a rational appetite, such is its nature that it *must* follow the last judgment of the practical intellect.'[19]

> Fifth, moral necessity or of slavery arising from good or bad habits and the presentation of objects to their faculties. For such is the nature of moral habits that although the acquisition of them be in our power, still when our will is imbued with them, they can neither be unexercised nor be laid aside ... Hence it happens that the will (free in itself) is so determined either to good or to evil that it cannot but act either well or badly. Hence flows the slavery of sin or of righteousness.[20]

> For as the will can be called 'free' if it is devoid of habit, so it can rightly be called 'slavish' if by habit it has been determined to a certain manner of acting. Still this servitude by no means overthrows the true and essential nature of liberty.[21]

'Habit' is another Aristotelian term appropriated by the RO. These are all matters that at least have an empirical, observable thread. Turretin is ready to use 'determine' of the faculties when he thinks this is called for. He also provides his reader with a wider array of examples of the faculties and also a wider range of applications of 'free' than is usual in the literature we are examining.

'Although the will can oppose the theoretical judgment of the intellect or the absolute judgment and of simple practical intellect, whither pertain those words of Medea in the poet – "I see the right and approve it too, and still the worse pursue"'.[22] 'Yet it can never oppose the decided and last judgment'.[23] Here he is discussing 'weakness of will', much debated in classical times.

So Turretin is clear that the intellect and will are not distinct parts of the soul, as the heart and liver are parts of the body. They are different sets of powers, and they act by the operation of the intellect as a means to an end and in the generation and satisfaction of desires with regard to the attraction to a goal, or to its repudiation.

---

19. Turretin, *Institutes,* I. p. 663, italics added.
20. ibid., I. p. 662.
21. ibid., I. p. 663.
22. Ovid, *Metamorpheses* 7. pp. 20-1.
23. Turretin, *Institutes,* I. p. 664.

In his section on the place of indifference in the will in action is one of the few places in which Turretin refers to the narrative of actions. The will is indifferent in its initial phase (in a divided sense). This indifference is continued so far 'as the intellect remains doubtful and uncertain whither to turn itself.' But when the mind is made up (in the compound sense) it is no longer indifferent, as the Molinists claim, who maintain that the will is always indifferent, even if the mind is made up. Turretin denies this. [24] So here Turretin takes a snapshot of action as he sees it from the familiar experience of making up one's mind. Once the mind is made up there is no indifference in it. Hence for him liberty consists in rational willingness, not in indifference, which is at best a necessary condition, willingness.

'The will can never be without determination as well as extrinsic from the providence of God, as intrinsic from the judgment of the intellect (as has been shown).' [25]

And again, 'For if it is certain that the will is determined by the intellect, the intellect must first be persuaded before it can influence the will.' [26] 'And so far is the determination to one thing (made by the reason) from taking away from free election, that it rather makes it perfect', [27] complete as a free action.

He goes on to state that Adam's liberty was not a liberty undetermined by the practical intellect, 'for this would have changed the will into an irrational appetite, so that he would have sought evil as evil.' Adam had essential liberty which Turretin identifies as preference and will, 'so that what is done may be done by a previous judgment of the reason and spontaneously.[28] For in this way it [the will] cannot but be *in subjection* both to God *and to the intellect.*' [29]

It is worth remembering here that the term 'intellect' is not confined to the 'pure intellect', but an apprehension and judgment of some fact or situation which is informative.

In such passages Turretin discusses freedom as a compatibilist.

---

24. ibid., I. pp. 666-7.
25. ibid., I. p. 666.
26. ibid., I. p. 668.
27. ibid., I. p. 668.
28. ibid., I. p. 570.
29. ibid., I. p. 664.

The Powers of the Soul

We have seen that the RO were faculty psychologists, working with the assumption that the rational soul is where the *imago dei* resides. The human soul has the faculties of intellect and will, and other separate powers including the conscience, the memory, the imagination, the affections, and so on. We now look at the operation of these powers from a range of RO theologians.

To avoid the charge of special pleading I have selected some of those theologians treated by Muller in Chapter Six of *Divine Will and Human Choice*, and others he has added in his 2019 article, and one or two of my own.

Peter Martyr Vermigli (1490–1562)

Vermigli was a contemporary and friend of John Calvin, but unlike Calvin he had a scholastic education, which he actively continued following his move to the Reformed position. He was an accomplished theologian. In his locus on free will in his *Loci Communes,* we note the account he gives of the relation of the intellect to the will. Vermigli says, in words that Muller quotes,

> Choice seems to consist in this, that we follow things that are appointed by reason, as they are deemed good. Then, without doubt, the will is free when it embraces those things that are approved on the part of the knowing soul. The nature of free choice, therefore, although it appears to belong mostly to the will, has its root in the reason.[30]

His point is that despite the suggestion of the phrase 'free will', freedom is not a direct state of the will but is the outcome of the operation of the judgment in deliberation. It is conditioned. Muller notes that Vermigli stresses deliberation and alternativity, as indeed he does. This is another place that it is necessary to distinguish between unconditional and conditional versions of alternativity. Alternativity by itself is not sufficient for non-compatibilism, since for a compatibilist freedom of the will arises from the operation of some state of the reason, hence the alternativity, a choice, is grounded in some state of the intellect.

Vermigli states that the Latin for free will, *liberum arbitrium*, means the judgment made by one who has authority over himself, and so is not

---

30. *Divine Will and Human Choice*, p. 195.

compelled. 'Judgment belongs to the function of understanding, but desire belongs to the will. Reason or understanding has the place of an adviser, but the will desires, accepts, or rejects'. [31] The will is subservient to the intellect, or understanding. It is its executive, hence the reference to the will accepting or rejecting. Acceptance but then rejection can occur when the intellect takes into account a second view, and either changes its goal, or keeps the goal and changes its mind regarding the means to be taken to gain the goal.

> Thus it appears that we have free will when the appetite is moved by itself toward what the understanding or power of knowing reveals to it. It is indeed in the will, since it takes root in the understanding since it is appropriate that something is judged and measured first, and then follows either refusal or endorsement. [32]

Note here the various terms that Vermigli uses are all causal in their character – such as move, reveal, refuse, endorse, deliberate, choose, and identify. Regarding the different spheres of the will, Vermigli says that,

> They are of two kinds. Some are of a lower order, subject to the senses and human reason, not exceeding our capacity or requiring supernatural light, such as whether I am teaching or not teaching, whether I stay or not, whether war is undertaken or not. Other things are higher, of which we cannot even dream: for instance, to believe in Jesus Christ; to obey the commandments of God, to trust in him ... [33]

The understanding is a power (*potentia*) of the soul. On recognizing this the RO will at once think of the distinction between a simultaneity of potencies and a potency of simultaneities. As we noted before, the commentators of *RTF* are fond of this distinction because it warrants them to introduce 'simultaneity', which is for them short for Scotian simultaneous contingency and a sign of its operation. It is certainly in the eyes of some a valid distinction between powers. But it turns their attention away from considering that the powers of the soul have between instances of one exercise and instances of another. The mere fact that the distinction can be made, if it can, and made in the case of

---

31. Vermigli, *Philosophical Works, The Peter Martyr Libr*ary (Vol. 4., trans Joseph C. Mclelland, Kirksville Mo, 1996), p. 272.

32. ibid., p. 272.

33. ibid., p. 273.

the human will, tells us nothing about the nature of the freedom of a person. After all the distinction can be drawn between the powers of an animal and even an artifact, as we saw earlier. The dog has the power (or possibility) to bark and to growl. The camera has the power to shoot in black and white, and in colour. This is a case of a scholastic distinction that adds nothing distinctive to the account of the human will.

In common with the RO in general, Vermigli calls the will 'blind', that is, it follows the dictates of the understanding, having no active perception of its own.[34]

John Calvin (1509–64)

> Let the office, moreover, of understanding be to distinguish between objects, as each seems worthy of approval or disapproval; while that of the will, to choose and follow what the understanding pronounces good, but to reject and flee what it disapproves … [after addressing Aristotle and appetitive understanding] … Not to entangle ourselves in useless questions, let it be enough for us that the understanding is, as it were, the leader and governor of the soul; and that the will is always mindful of the bidding of the understanding, and in its own desires awaits the judgment of the understanding … Indeed, in another place we shall see how firmly the understanding now governs the direction of the will.[35]

Calvin, though not a scholastic by education, shows that he readily became appraised of scholastic distinctions. Here he characterises the relation of the intellect and the will as its leader and governor.

Franciscus Junius (1545–1602)

Junius was a learned and innovative Reformed scholastic. He distinguishes three kinds of freedom, freedom from obligation, freedom from necessity, and freedom from coercion, what he calls 'simple coercion', as when the will is immediately informed of a particular good, the judgment of the will. '[I]t should be possible to define free choice as the faculty of the discrete will free from necessity, by which a mind-gifted nature chooses one thing above another from the things which are shown by the intellect, or, choice facing one and the same thing, accepts

---

34. ibid., p. 277.
35. Calvin, *Institutes of the Christian Religion*, I.11.7.

it as being good, or rejects it as being bad. [36] So we are free when we are free from coercion, when with respect to a choice we can will it, or will it not, not will it not, or not will. [37] We are free when our will relates to a goal 'in a contingent and free way'.

What does Junius mean by 'freedom of necessity'? Is that freedom from *causal* determinism? It would be hasty to draw that conclusion. Junius divides freedom into two alternatives: either freedom from coercion, and freedom, as necessarily (and instinctively?) willing the good. [38]

In a passage like this it is usual for the commentators in *RTF* to assume that 'in a contingent and free way' obviously refers to an indeterminist Scotian sense of freedom. But a compatibilist can use these expressions, taking freedom to be an alternative choice grounded by the reason. It is unfortunate that there is a tendency of Vosians to summarily beg the question against compatibilism.

Junius has some interesting remarks on freedom and necessity, and freedom from compulsion.

> Considered in themselves they are free from coercion only, not from necessity. For they are willing freely and according to their internal principle, but necessarily. This is by reason of their nature, according to which this free necessity of willing is imposed on them … Some of the *objects*, according to their nature, are determined to one such as those natural and self-evident ends …. Other objects are not determined … Of this kind are all the means as well as some subordinate and unknown ends. The first ones exclude only coercion, the latter one excludes every kind of necessity. [39]

Junius seems to be a very inventive scholastic, that is to say, he is a great multiplier of distinctions, as the reader of the Junius extract in *RTF* will discern. Muller makes a valiant effort to make a consistent and intelligible picture of the relationship between intellect and will in Junius's 1601 disputation. [40] According to Muller, Junius stresses freedom as spontaneity, and its actions 'subserve' God's providence, that is, they are in accord with it. Willing is essentially spontaneous,

---

36. *Reformed Thought on Freedom*, p. 100.

37. ibid., p. 100.

38. ibid., p. 99.

39. ibid., p. 100.

40. Muller, *Divine Will and Human Choice*, p. 217.

that is, not forced, or coerced. '[A] person can will freely according to his nature, namely, according to who and what he is, but his nature delimits his willing: a person who is five feet tall cannot [rationally] will himself to be six foot tall ....'[41] In the midst of scholastic distinctions, the insistence of Junius on making basic points such as these suggests his willingness to make distinctions for their own sake. He is not very clear in his distinctions, however. To conclude in one discussion of his mentioned by Muller, it is frustrating to have as a conclusion that the will stands in a fully 'contingent and free relation to its objects', that is, is able to direct the fulfilling of the object(s) of the intellect. One gets the impression that Junius is interested principally in definitions, not in narratives. How illuminating it would have been to have from him an account of a sequence of the courses of understanding and choice.

Franciscus Gomarus (1563–1641)

According to Muller, Gomarus holds: 'Specifically, absence of coercion identifies the act as spontaneous, but to be free in the proper sense of a *liberum arbitrium*, the act also is free from necessity, an act such that "by itself is indeterminate; and determines itself by an intrinsic potency to elicit its own act".... The choice itself is a free act or relative self-motion in which a power is engaged and the indifference overcome by the act of the rational agent or *natura intelligens*.'[42]

We have seen that for the RO there are various kinds of necessity. In the context of choice the necessity to be avoided is brute necessity as distinct from the intelligence of the will. Such other creaturely necessities are hypothetical necessities, flowing from the agency of second causes. For Gomarus '[F]ree choice is a potency or faculty flowing from the essence of a soul' and the free act, *liberum arbitrium*, belongs to the human being as a rational agent or intelligent nature whether or not he acts. As a faculty, free choice functions as the ruler (*domina*) of its act and accordingly capable of judgment (*arbitrium*) whether to act or not act'.[43] This is an apt characterization of a creaturely hypothetical necessity, a secondary cause. It is a contingency in the sense that it is a

---

41. ibid., p. 218.
42. ibid., pp. 221-2.
43. ibid., p. 223.

choice that could be different if the intelligence had made a different judgment of the means and the end, as in the case of Joseph and his brothers, a favourite case, cited by Gomarus.

Muller goes on to make further comment on Gomarus's statements. 'Gomarus concludes that if one looks to "the things of nature & secondary causes (which God does not remove, but ordains)," recognizing human ignorance of the divine work, "there are innumerable contingencies"' – and 'equally so, if one conjectures concerning the divine decree and foreknowledge, "all things are necessity by hypothesis, by a necessity, so called of immutability and of the consequence."'[44] This is the language, 'hypothetical necessity', of a compatibilist.

The point of Gomarus' discussion seems to be to argue for the conclusion that this freedom is a case of the necessity of the consequence. But all that shows is that this is rooted in the divine decree. Such hypothetical necessity is what the Reformed compatibilist understands by the necessity of determinism.

And this is made even plainer by the case of the death of Ahab,[45] who was said to be killed 'contingently & fortuitously on consideration of the secondary causes', accidently, we may say, but 'necessarily by reason of the decree & prediction of God'. Similarly with Gomarus's 'freedom as a potency or faculty flowing from the essence of the soul'. This does not tell us the whole story of the character of this flowing, until we have an account of it. Gomarus does not address this, suggesting in this account of free will that he was not really interested in the spelling out of causal factors.

Gomarus cites the contemporary Roman Catholic scholastic Robert Bellarmine (1542–1621) as follows, 'I add, *in accordance with what reason deems best to fit*, not because the judgment of reason determines the will; as Bellarmine wishes, Book III, *Free choice and grace*, chapter 8, but only because reason judges the goodness or badness of a means.'[46] This is of interest for being a case of the use of the language of determination, here the determination of the practical reason. But for the judgment being practically rational, it must surely judge for a reason, so that the will is

---

44. ibid., p. 222.
45. Cited in Muller, *Divine Will and Human Choice*, p. 223.
46. Gomarus, quoted in *RTF*, p. 131.

determined by the intellect's choice of the end identified by the reason. And so Gomarus joins the RO chorus of the intellect as the necessitator of the will, by which Edwards also understands the freedom of the will.

Gisbertius Voetius (1589–1678)

What follows next is from a disputation of Voetius' 'Containing Two Questions, the Distinction of the Divine Attributes and The Freedom of the Will'.[47] Handling such questions was part of a theological education, to sharpen the students' distinction-making abilities.

Voetius states,

> Although God is the efficient cause of the acts of this faculty, he is not their formal cause or even partial formal cause, namely inasmuch as these are free acts, since otherwise it would not be the will of man who wills, but God in it, which is an absurdity in theology. Note that this mode of acting of the free potency that fits its nature requires a two fold indifference, viz. (1) *Objective* indifference viz, indifference of the means that is displayed by the intellect as something that can be chosen and does not have a necessary connection with the intended end as such. And (2) *Vital, internal and choosing* indifference, which belongs to the free potency that is not yet finally determined by the practical judgment.[48]

This is the first time we have come across a reference in our survey of various RO theologians to 'efficient cause' and 'formal cause', two of those four kinds of cause that the RO observed. This is not surprising, as Voetius was known as a scrupulous devotee of scholasticism. He is here explicating an aspect of the divine concourse of free human actions, saying that in such a situation God is the efficient cause of the human will, for it is by His power that the human agent is able to act, but God is not the formal cause of the action. Say there is a case of the human act of requesting, then God by His power ensures the person make a request, but in such a case it is not God that is requesting, but the person. So, for Voetius, for an action to be a free human act there are two indifferences involved: what he calls an objective indifference of the means to an end, the end of *requesting*, say, and a vital, internal and choosing indifference necessary for the particular request to be accomplished.

---

47. Muller, *Reformed Thought on Freedom*, p. 148.
48. ibid., p. 149.

This is a good example of the way that, by adding a qualifying adjective or adjectives to a noun, the scholastics do some justice to the intricacies of human action. It is clear from the terms chosen, that Voetius understands the indifferences to exercise a causal role upon the last act of the practical judgment. It is not that indifference is an element, some passive ingredient in all free acts, but it is in this case a vital, internal and choosing indifference. These terms, 'vital, internal, and choosing indifference' involve movements in the body, and so on.

It is interesting to note that in his discussion of Voetius's views on providence, Aza Goudriaan finds it natural to discuss Voetius's thought in terms of determinism.

> God is the sovereign Cause of the whole range of created being – including the particular mode of every being, namely *of contingency* in contingent causes and effects, *of necessity* in necessary causes and effects .... It is especially this free determination of everything by God which makes this doctrine completely different from Stoic fate that represents a comprehensive regime of necessity. Yet as we saw earlier, the term 'fate' can be used in a theologically correct manner, Voetius argues, if it is taken to mean 'virtually the will of God that disposes everything formally ... the disposition of second causes to an infallible effect, traced to the Divine will.' The kind of fate that Voetius understands, with reference to Thomas Aquinas, as a *fatum mobile* is different from the Stoic fate refuted by Aristotle.[49]

John Owen (1616–83)

Owen's first book was *A Display of Arminiansm*, written when he was a young minister, aged 26. Over a decade later in his work on Socinianism, *Vindiciae Evangelicae* (1655), he discussed indifference and freedom in connection with the Socinian views which limited God's foreknowledge. (Rather similar to the 'open theism' of our own day.) He refers to the sense of free will that the Socinians use which is in critically the similar terms to what he had previously referred to as Arminian liberty, as 'that latitude and absoluteness as none before him had once aimed at.'[50] By

49. Aza Goudriaan, *Reformed Orthodoxy and Philosophy, 1625-1750* (Leiden, Brill, 2006), pp. 152-3. See also pp. 177-8.
50. Owen, *Vindiciae Evangelicae*, in *Works*, p. 12:116.

now, he seems to have developed the habit to use the term "absolute" to qualify the strong sense of free will as the Arminians and now the Socinians understood it, Franciscan liberty.[51]

Owen also uses 'indifference' in what he takes to be the orthodox view: 'It is true, in respect of their immediate causes, as the wills of men, they are contingent, and may be or not; but that they have such a cause as before spoken of is evident from the light of this consideration: in their own time and order they are.'[52] What Owen means, I take it, is that if in the situation of a choice between A and B (a situation of indifference) the choice is for A, then the will can carry it out, and if it is for B, then it could also carry out B. However, until such a choice is made irrevocably, by the judgment, a person does not know which way he will go. The choice is made 'in their [the agents'] own time and order'. Such indifference is not absolute, unconditioned, but contingent on the judgment for which the action is chosen. This is a clear case of 'hypothetical indifference'.

> That which is so contingent as to be also *free*, is contingent both in respect of the *effect* and of its *causes* also. Such was the soldier's piercing of the side of Christ. The effect was contingent – such a thing might have been done or not; and the cause also, for they chose to do it who did it, and in respect of their own elective faculty might not have chosen it. That a man shall write, or ride, or speak to another person tomorrow, the agent being free, is contingent both as to the cause and to the effect.[53]

From such a statement we gain a fascinating window into Owen's understanding of contingency. A man might on an occasion be faced with either spending some time reading, or with writing, and which he does is up to him, up to his desires or purposes. He chooses, exercising his 'elective faculty', say to read instead of to write, or as we might say, he has a power of choice. This also is indifferent, in the sense that what is at issue is a choice between the two activities. It is a case of what we have called 'conditioned alternativity.' The person can choose or not choose, and if he chooses he can chooses to read or to write, depending on his preference. So there is a double contingency, like the soldier's piercing

---

51. ibid., p. 12:116.
52. ibid., p. 12:129.
53. ibid., pp. 12:128-29.

of Christ while he was on the cross. Such an action was chosen. In this situation, Owen draws the curtain away from the customary modalities, necessity and contingency, to disclose some of the choosing itself and its psychology.

Owen says more than once that given freedom of the will, a person is,

> free in his choice from all outward coaction [that is, compulsion], or inward natural necessity [necessities arising from physical operations on the will; e.g. spasms, or other workings of the body], to work according to election and deliberation, spontaneously embracing what seemeth good unto him.[54]

> Most free it is in all its acts, both in regard of the object it chooseth and in regard of that vital power and faculty whereby it worketh, infallibly complying with God's providence, and working by virtue of the motion thereof; but surely to assert such a supreme and independently and every way unbounded indifferency as the Arminians claim, whereby, all other things requisite being pre-supposed, it should remain absolutely in our power to will or not to will, to do anything or not to do it, is plainly to deny that our wills are subject to the rule of the Most High.[55]

There is more of this in the following from a later book:

> The difference, therefore about free-will is reduced unto these heads –
> 1st. Whether there is a power in man *indifferently*, to determine himself his choice and all his actings, to this or that, good or evil, one thing or another, of the will, power, and providence of God, and his disposal of all future events? This, indeed, we deny, as that which is inconsistent with the prescience, authority, decrees, and dominion of God, and as that which would prove certainly ruinous and destructive to ourselves.[56]

So for Owen, as for Turretin, there are two kinds of indifference and, correspondingly, two kinds of contingency. There is the 'absolute indifference' of the Arminians, expressed in various of their articles of faith, that we have referred to as 'Franciscan freedom', and secondly the freedom of willingness and spontaneity. Owen's chief concern here

---

54. We need to bear in mind that Owen has a number of pieces which deal with the workings of the soul, studying its motives and plans. For example, the *On the Mortification of Sin*, *On Temptation*, and so forth (in *Works*, volume 6), which flesh out these rather spare descriptions. *(Works* 6, pp. 158-9, 166-7, 170-1).

55. Owen, *Works*, X. p. 119. Note the similarity between Arminians, and Molinism, as Owen notes.

56. ibid., III. p. 495.

is with the problem of the consistency of such indifference with the divine decree, with the Creator-creature relation insofar as this involves a decree in concurrence with the will of the Creator. Owen sometimes uses scholastic language but prefers to use more paraphrastic language conveying rational spontaneity.

Muller says from time to time that to be a free choice an alternativity cannot be reduced to mere spontaneity.[57] Choice that is deliberate, according to Owen,[58] is a case of alternativity that is grounded in the agent's goals or ends in compatibilist fashion. In such a case a person can be possessed of a reason for making a choice, and be able as a matter of course in the next second to choose oppositely, having suddenly becoming aware of the relevance of some previously unaware factor. Such grounded alternativity, usually spontaneous, a case of freedom from coercion, is clearly consistent with compatibilism. So alternativity is not necessarily a sign of indeterminism, just as necessity is not necessarily compulsive. It is the RO reluctance to discuss such everyday alternatives, and seemingly to confine their instances of alternativity, that makes the account of free, contingent acts so under-described. The RO, more generally, seem to generally dislike giving descriptions of the sources of action, and for this reserve sometimes appear to equate freedom as nothing other than metaphysical contingency. Owen is certainly an exception. This is what was hypothesized as due to their preference for logical as against causal distinctions. Owen's style is an exception, though he is not the only one to adopt it, of course.

Turretin and the others so far discussed subscribe to a standard account of faculty theology, the faculties referring to distinct, separable powers in causal action. But some RO have a more unified view of the self. We shall next consider three examples of these: firstly the Puritan William Pemble, secondly the New England theologian Samuel Willard, and finally the late RO figure, Bernardinus de Moor.

William Pemble (1592–1623)

Pemble was a fellow of New College, Oxford, tutor to Edward Leigh, author of *A System or Body of Divinity*, 1654. He is one of the clearest

---

57. ibid., pp. 236, 239.
58. ibid., p. 237.

writers of the Puritans. If Pemble held that sanctification precedes justification, his anthropology undoubtedly contributed to his account of the unified character of the soul.[59] He died in 1623, aged 31.

This is part of Pemble's account of faith:

> In every Intellectual nature there are usually made two Distinct Faculties: First, the Understanding: Secondly. The Will. The Object of that is Truth: The object of this, Goodness. Now then Faith being an assent to the Truth and Goodness of Divine Revelation, we must see in which of these Faculties it is resident, or whether of both. Our adversaries teach that the Assent of Faith is an act of the understanding only, not of the Will. This opinion we reject as erroneous, because Divine Revelations are essentially as good as they be True, nor hath their truth any prerogative above their goodness: and so Faith is given but by halfs unto one part of the object, where there is not so well an election and Approbation of the Goodness of it by the Will, as an assent to the truth if it in the Understanding. Wherefore we affirm that this Assent of Faith is an act of the Understanding and of the Will, both together approving and allowing of the truth and goodness of all Divine things. In which assertion you are to note that we do not make the Habite of Faith to be inherent in two diverse subjects, nor this act of Assent to come from two diverse Principles, or two several Faculties of the minde, but we affirm the subject is by one and the same, namely the intellectual Nature. For I take it with diverse of the Learned, yet as they do under correction of the more Learned, that those speculations about the real distinction of Faculties in such Spiritual Substances as are the Angels and the souls of men, are but subtilties of the School, without any true ground in nature it self.[60]

We see here Pemble reflecting on the diversity of the faculties, yet in the case of 'Spiritual Substances' he goes on to claim that the two principle faculties of the mind, understanding and will, are of one essence, the will essentially including the understanding.

> Our senses have in this case deceived our reason; and because we find in compounded bodies diverse actions and motions to flow from diverse qualities, we have therefore imagined, that in simple Spiritual Substances

---

59. Interesting details are in J.V. Fesko, *The Theology of the Westminster Standards* (Wheaton, Ill. Crossway, 2014), pp. 255-8.

60. Pemble, *Vindiciae Gratiae, A Plea for Grace, More Especially Grace and faith*, in *The Workes of that Late Learned minister of God's Holy Word, Mr William Pemble* (Oxford, Henry Hall, 1659), p. 111.

the case must be alike, and there is no remedy, but we must Understand by one Faculty, Will or Nill by another. Remember by a third. Whereas all these severall actions flow immediately from the body and active essence of such a Spiritual Substance, without any such distinct facultie that neede come between the Agent and the Action. For our purpose, it appears that the Understanding and Will are not distinct faculties that have distinct actions.[61]

So, as Pemble goes on to state, the understanding essentially includes the will, and the will essentially includes the understanding, because each are powers of a simple substance, the soul without parts, and in the operations of the soul each involves the other. So he has a rather different emphasis on the operation of the understanding and the will than others who see them as distinct entities that have relations with the others. There is no danger in Pemble of treating individual faculties as if they were little people (*homunculi*) in their own right.

He has however to make other distinctions, if his views are to be clear. Differences in the will, in particular, need identifying. He needs two senses at least in which the will operates. In the case of a person who has a willing habit, covetousness, say, or the fear of God, his will is performing in an 'imperate' fashion, in contrast to making a conscious, deliberate, licit judgment, allowable or permitted. As we saw earlier, Turretin also distinguishes between imperate powers and elicit acts; 'elicit acts which cannot properly be said to be under the control of the will, since they are the very command of the will';[62] imperate acts are moral reactions, which cannot be said to be under the control of the will.

Pemble goes on to make some observations of the will and its freedom.

[F]or how is the Will free, but because it may choose this or that? How can it make choice, unless it do also compare, advise, and deliberate about the matter and consequences of things offered to its choice? Wherefore it is manifest, that *Intelligere* and *Judicare* are actions belonging unto the Will also, and that this proposition [*Volunta intelligit bonum aut malum*. 'The will understands good and evil'] is true and proper. Thus in regard of the actions *Volendi* and *Intelligendi,* we have no reason to make a distinction

---

61. William Pemble, *Vindiciae Gratiae*, p. 112.

62. Turretin, *Institutes*, I. p. 664. This distinction is I hope more accurate than in that given in *Human Nature from Calvin to Edwards*, pp. 109-10.

of Faculties, where the actions are common, and Indifferently agree to each of them.[63]

This is an account of differently-functioning powers of the soul that are tightly aligned (and even intertwined), from other intellectual powers in the business of the practical reason. Of interest to us is that as mental acts they have in common; comparing, advising, and deliberating, all effects of the mind, and also acts in which the will is involved. They are actions of the one unified soul in undertaking an end or ends, and identifying the means to them. Some thought of the will as blind, but for Pemble the voluntary powers may be infused with those of the intellect. What he writes is surely consistent with compatibilism.

Note the strongly causal character of his account of this arrangement of the intellect and the will. 'How can it [the soul] make [a] choice, unless it [does] also compare, advise, and deliberate about the matter and consequences of things offered to its choice?' There speaks the compatibilist.

Samuel Willard (1640–1704)

Here we return to the extract from his short work, *A Brief Reply to Mr George Kieth*, that we considered earlier, which stresses the unity of 'the whole man'.

> It is therefore to be observed, that *not the understanding, nor the will in the man, but the whole man is a free cause.* Man is a Reasonable Creature, and his Will is one faculty put into him as such a Creature; and so it acts according to the Influence of the Understanding on it; else it were not a Humane Will. As also, that in a free agent *Indifferency* may be taken away, but as long as he still acts *Spontaneously,* he acts freely; but if that be denied him, he ceaseth to be a free agent.[64]

Note that Willard subscribes to the view that in a reasonable creature his faculty of will acts according to the influence (surely a causal term) of the understanding. Otherwise it is not a human will. Also for Willard, if indifference is taken away, but an act is performed spontaneously, nonetheless such spontaneity may be a sufficient condition of the person's freedom. If the whole man is a free cause, how are we to understand this? He is free when his spontaneity brings it to pass. And, rather

---

63. William Pemble, *Vindiciae Gratiae*, p. 112.

64. Samuel Willard, *A Brief Reply to Mr George Kieth*, p. 15.

boldly, Willard adds that if indifference were expelled, still spontaneity would be sufficient for freedom. Perhaps he has in view the habits of the mind. If a person's action is the expression of a settled habit alone, not a newly occurring reason, then it follows that this action is nonetheless spontaneous, making it willingly free.

> How far there is an *Indifference* to be acknowledged in the Will, respecting *Voluntary* actions, needs not be curiously discussed; only we may observe, that though there may such a thing be allowed to the Will, *in actu primo*, which the Schools call *Simultas potentiae*, by vertue whereof the Will, according to its own nature, is capable of acting or not acting, or acting thus or contrarily; and is capable of acting thus now, and is afterwards capable of revoking that act; nay indeed, this is the root of the liberty of the Will. Nevertheless, *in actu secundo*, which the Schools call *Potentia Simultatis*, which is in the Wills applying it self to its act, it doth not then act *Indifferently*, but upon choice, by which it is Determined.[65]

Muller and I have different takes on the New England pastor. I take him to be stating that the will as such is capable as acting or not acting, that is, 'according to its own nature, [it] is capable of acting or not acting, or acting thus or contrarily; and is capable of acting thus now, and is afterwards capable of revoking that act; nay indeed, this is the root of the liberty of the will'. It has a variety of capabilities according to the lead of the intellect. But the same cannot be said of the intellect itself. When the mind is made up 'upon choice, again by an act of the intellect by which it is Determined' spontaneously. Rather like Turretin.

In his later article in 2019, Muller pulls me up on my view of Willard.[66] He says,

> Helm concludes that in the 'last sentence' of the quotation, where Willard indicates the absence of a potency of simultaneity in the will's operation or second actuality (*in actu secundo*), 'there is no suggestion ... of resident potencies. Quite true.'[67]

---

65. Cited in Paul Helm, 'Francis Turretin and Jonathan Edwards on Compatibilism', *Journal of Reformed Theology*, p. 12 (2018). Muller's 2019 article is a response to this article, which has been used in various places in the later chapters of this book.

66. Muller, 'Neither Compatibilist nor Libertarian', *Journal of Reformed Theology*, 2019, p. 277.

67. ibid., p. 277.

But in the preceding sentence, multiple potencies are not merely suggested, they are precisely referenced, namely, *simultas potentiae* as defined by Willard as the simultaneous presence of capabilities of acting or not acting in the will's primary actuality (*in actu primo*).[68]

This is the last sentence of the quotation.

.... which the Schools call *Simultas potentiae*, by vertue whereof the Will, according to its own nature, is capable of acting or not acting, or acting thus or contrarily; and is capable of acting thus now, and is afterwards capable of revoking that act; nay indeed, this is the root of the liberty of the Will. Nevertheless, *in actu secundo*, which the Schools call *Potentia Simultatis*, which is in the Wills applying it self to its act, it doth not then act *Indifferently*, but upon choice, by which it is Determined.[69]

Yes, but Muller does not give enough recognition to the fact that the will has a simultaneity of willings, of which one willing is the execution of the intellect, that is due to the particular influence of the intellect. Other possibilities are not willed, because of the actuality chosen. Are the other willings 'resident'? Perhaps they are.

Bernardinus de Moor (1709–1780)

The last example of a unified soul rather than one of separate faculties, of powers of the one soul, and not of distinct faculties, is given by Bernardinus de Moor, who lived into the second half of the 18th century, spending his adult life as a scholastic RO theologian at Leiden. By this time the influence of the Enlightenment was fully felt, especially in de Moor's case, the influence of René Descartes (1596–1650). The extracts are from de Moor's seven-volume *Continuous Commentary on à Marck's Compendium of Christian Theology* (1761–71).

---

68. ibid., p. 277. In correspondence Muller had stated that 'In Turretin's view, there cannot be indifference in the second act, since in the movement from first to second the choice has been made. But I think he also assumes that when one potency is exercised the other potency remains – i.e., a simultaneity of potencies but no potency of simultaneity. A person simply cannot exercise contradictory potencies at the same time. The point concerning the composite sense is that, even *in actu secundo*, by the time there is no indifference remaining, there are still multiple potencies in the will and the will, having willed A, retains in the same moment and continuing a non actualizable potency to not-A' (Muller, email, December 1, 2017).

69. ibid., p. 277.

De Moor's unified understanding of the mind is seen in a passage such as this:

> Yet, it is one and the same rational mind, which, when it judges something to be willed, determines itself to will that thing. But if the faculty of both intellect and will are here considered as mutually distinct, the will cannot be said to be *determined* by the intellect, but to *follow* the intellect, in such a way that the previous judgment of the intellect is followed by the inclination of the will.[70]

Here there is a more familiar reference to the following of the intellect. De Moor follows the compatibilist order. Writing of the judgment of the practical reason, he says,

> [I]t is often the case, that although somebody judges theoretically and absolutely and should be followed, still on the basis of the relative practical judgment he judges the same thing is to be neglected at this moment. And the other way round, he can judge that a thing is generically bad and must be fled, and still the pleasure or profit which one hopes to gain, may induce the mind to strive for it. He can judge that it is decent on the Lord's day to go to church and that therefore it is his duty to go to church, but in order not to offend worldly people, in whose company one finds oneself and of whom he fears the hatred or mockery, more than God, he can judge that he should neglect for himself that duty for this moment ....[71]

Reflecting on this interesting passage, we see De Moor emphasizing the operation of judgment, sometimes having a theoretical view that is supplanted by another act of the practical intellect, not a case we have discussed previously, while recognizing that its smooth working is conditioned by a number of factors. These have to do with motives or reasons which cause the operation of the practical reason to be held up, as there is reflection of what one judges in short-term as against the longer-term, or the pressure of competing loyalties, such as that between faithfulness to God's commands as against one's loyalty to friends and acquaintances. The resolution of such cases is perfectly consistent with compatibilism. De Moor generalizes as follows:

> Experience confirms this sufficiently for everybody: nobody wills something unless for that moment at which he wills it, he has estimated, that is, judged,

---

70. De Moor, cited in *Reformed Thought on Freedom*, pp. 204-5.
71. ibid., pp. 203-4.

that it should be willed in that way. So, as long as the vacillating judgment doubts, the ambiguous will remains also suspended. When judgment errs, the will also is dragged away soon in willing wrongly.[72]

His stress on the unity of the self is seen in this following comment.

> [A]s I said above, the faculties of intellect and will are not really separated from each other, nor from the mind itself, and the actions of both are connected to each other by a tight necessity [perhaps a mutual necessity] such that the mind is acting upon the same things in *understanding*, when it is occupied in cognition and judgment of these things; and in *willing*, when it is drawn to love or hate toward them.[73]

The relations between intellect and will, when exemplified in human actions by judging and comparing, the language is causal. The practical intellect has to do with the means-end relation, selecting and identifying the end, and the means to the end will involve activities that are causal in character, depending for their success in the estimating of what is the best means to a preferred end. This language is used un-self-consciously. It is the everyday language of the choice of ends and of the means to the end or ends. Even when the relations between intellect and will are discussed, the will is the subordinate, if not as a distinct faculty but as a set of powers which perform a close and yet distinctly identifiable executive function. It is perfectly consistent with, even redolent of, a compatibilist outlook. Synchronic contingency and with it Franciscan freedom, are a considerable distance from such language.

Edward Reynolds (1599–1676)

In his 2019 article, Muller shows his expertise in the history of this field by choosing a further number of the RO. Edward Reynolds was prominent in the work of the Westminster Assembly and later in the Commonwealth. Muller quotes the following from him in his 2019 article in an effort to ward off the appearance of compatibilism among Reformed scholastics. The passage is,

> [i]t may not hence be concluded that the Understanding hath any Superiority, in regard of Domination over the Will, though it have Priority In regard of Operation. The Power of the Understanding over the Will,

---

72. ibid., p. 204.

73. ibid., p. 205.

is only a Regulating and Directing, it is no constraining or Compulsive Power. For the Will always is *Domina suorum actuus*, the Mistresse of her own Operation.[74]

It seems uncharacteristically rash for Muller to continue: 'The act of willing the object must follow the determination of the understanding – quite so, but the free choice of the will is not caused by the understanding. It is the will that governs, moderates, and rules over all human actions, with the judgment of the understanding providing "some precedent guiding Acts" that are "proportioned to the Rules of right Reason" and identifying some mean to an end as more suitable than others.'[75] In this the intellect does not compel the will, which is receptive to it.

Muller states that Reynolds infers from this that, 'The act of willing the object must follow the determination of the understanding' – quite so, but the free choice of the will is not caused by the understanding.[76] It is Reynolds's position that the understanding is in a certain state as a result of information received by the intellect and the senses. Let us grant that possessing such information may not constrain or be compulsive, as Reynolds says. But it identifies a course of action apart from other courses of action as 'more suitable' than others, so willing that course. Is that not causal? The alternativity in this case is a conditional alternativity. It is hard to see how Reynolds' can be taken in any other way than asserting that the will follows the judgment of the intellect in the routine compatibilist fashion. To say that the will is not caused by the understanding, but governs, moderates, and rules over all human actions, is a case of finessing the account. All these are causal influences familiar to a compatibilist.

Gulielmus Bucanus (died 1603)

Bucanus, a Professor in Lucerne, Switzerland, quoted by Muller, says, 'It is *Liberum* with respect to the will which voluntarily and of its own accord follows or refuses the judgment of the intellect'. Yes, the understanding is the understanding and not the will, and the will is the will and not

---

74. 'Neither Libertarian nor Compatibilist', *Journal of Reformed Theology*, 2019, p. 281.

75. ibid., p. 281.

76. ibid., p. 281.

the understanding. Neither is reducible to the other. But it is a serious misunderstanding on Muller's part when he says that the free choice of the will is not caused by the understanding. The will is free, and if there is sufficient reason to act, a conclusion of the understanding follows, and that act is appropriately caused. As he quotes Bucanus, 'rather the faculty of willing or nilling something, or the free pleasure of the will, that follows the deliberation and consultation of the reason or the mind'.[77]

John Weemse (1579–1636)

Weemse (or Weemes) was a Scottish Reformed scholastic who followed Thomas Aquinas closely. According to Muller, 'According to John Weemse, the intellect is a deliberative, not an appetitive faculty. It provides the condition for the determination of the will but does not cause the free choice: "the *understanding* is not the *cause*"; rather, it provides "the *condition* without which [the will] could not chuse."'[78]

Muller draws the conclusion that 'Recent scholarship has added a significantly different dimension to the debate by looking more deeply into the complex distinctions made by early modern Reformed scholastics and arguing that a case can be made that this scholastic theology, in common with several lines of argument inherited from the medievals, found an alternative way of framing the issues of divine and human willing that is quite distinct from the modern patterns of argument.'[79]

Certainly the arguments put forth in what Muller calls the 'ground-breaking' volume *Reformed Thought on Freedom* and in a significant number of other essays, are the source of his anti-compatibilism. I shall not here re-visit the many errors in this book. But Muller's resistance to either any form of libertarianism, and any form of compatibilism, is not borne out in his latest essay on the issue.

It is a shame that Muller sees evidence for indeterminate freedom in Reynolds, and Bucanus, and Weemes. This can only be that, as noted

---

77. 'Neither Libertarian nor Compatibilist', *Reformed Journal of Theology*, p. 280.

78. ibid., p. 281. Muller cites from John Weemse, *The Portraiture of the Image of God in Man: In his three estates, of Creation, Restauration, Glorification*, in *The Workes of Mr. Iohn. Weemse of Lathocker in Scotland*, 4 vols. (London: T. Cotes for Iohn Bellamie, 1637), I.xvi (p. 98).

79. ibid., p. 268.

earlier, the understanding of free will for the RO is not an examination of either the logical or metaphysical character of the will highlighted by *RTF* and by Muller's later work. The key to a compatibilist understanding is to identify the will as an ancillary, subordinate to the intellect, or understanding. This basic position we have found to be set out in a variety of expressions among the RO, but making the same point.

Edwards on the Faculties

We conclude this chapter by looking at what Edwards has to say about the faculties. Instead of 'synchronic contingency', Edwards refers to what happens or does not happen, at 'the same time'.[80] Despite disavowing RO scholasticism, his language is in crucial respects very similar to theirs. Despite having a more unified sense of the soul than some RO, which he took from the English philosopher John Locke, he nonetheless continued to refer to the faculties more or less as they did. In the early pages of his *The Freedom of the Will* he sets out his view of the place of motives in human action.

> Things that exist in the view of the mind, have their strength, tendency or advantage to move and excite its will, from many things appertaining to the nature and circumstances of the thing viewed, the nature and circumstances of the mind that views, and the degree and manner of its view; which it would perhaps be hard to make a perfect enumeration of. But so much I think may be determined in general without room for controversy, that whatever is perceived by an intelligent and voluntary agent, which has the nature and influence of a motive to volition or choice, is considered *as good*; nor has it any tendency to invite or engage the election of the soul in any further degree than it appears such.[81]

And in the *Religious Affections* (1746) there is a distinct contrast between the understanding and the will.

> God has indued the soul with two faculties: one is that by which it is capable of perception and speculation, or by which it discerns and views and judges of things; which is called the understanding. The other faculty is that by which the soul does not merely perceive and view things, but is some way inclined with respect to the things it views and considers; either is inclined

---

80. *Freedom of the Will,* pp. 159, 196, etc.
81. ibid., p. 142.

to 'em, or is disinclined and averse from 'em by which the soul does not behold things, as an indifferent unaffected spectator, but either as liking or disliking, pleased or displeased, approving or rejecting. This faculty is called ... the inclination ... the will ... the heart.[82]

The Crux of the Matter?

What I have tried to show in this chapter, by interrogating a number of RO theologians, and comparing them with Edwards, is that for them the intellect (broadly understood) and the will are closely related, but that the connection between them is asymmetrical. In what sense? That the action of the intellect is prior to that of the will. (No doubt there are occasions in which there is there is a gap between the two.) We have seen that some of the RO had a more unitary understanding of the relation between these two faculties, or powers. They are the powers of a simple soul. To say that the intellect leads the will is not to say that the sequence is a temporal, causal one. The relation between means and end in the scholastic account of the practical reason is similar, a distinction of the reason. Turretin made a clear distinction between the intellect and the will, yet he called their action together a 'marriage'. That in such an arrangement there is action of the will at each stage which is covered by the distinction between the 'licit will' and the 'imperate will'.

The argument is that such a relation is compatibilistic. The voluntarist alternative, in which the will and has either synchronically simultaneous (Vos, the Franciscan voluntarists) or 'diachronically simultaneous' (Muller) is prior, and allegedly the intellect follows, is open to the obvious objections that the action acting first or alone, is irrational or random. Freedom is free from compulsion, not the occurrence of pure alternativity. And there is no middle position between these two kinds of freedom.

There is nothing in Turretin that indicates that if the past had been identical, the intellect could have judged differently, and the will likewise. For Edwards such a state of affairs would have been irrational or incoherent; not a strength of freedom, but a fatal weakness.

Another puzzling reaction is Muller's assertion that Turretin and the RO generally are committed to human choices that are to be

---

82. *The Religious Affections*, p. 96.

understood in terms of 'multiple potencies', 'resident potencies to do things that they are not doing'. 'Potency' is a general term for the powers of the soul. It muffles the particularities of the various powers of the mind even if it does not intend to. This claim persists in registering an allegiance to synchronicity, albeit of a diachronic kind, in a seemingly non-deterministic interpretation of Turretin and other RO. In the pages of *Divine Choice and Human Will*, Muller appeals to the significance of unactualized multiple potencies in a number of places, as here:

> What Helm's counter-argument fails to appreciate, however, is that even as there is a diachronic movement of one of the will's potencies into actuality, there is also the simultaneous presence of the unactualized potency to the opposite (which of course cannot be actualized simultaneously). What Turretin and Voetius indicate – and the authors of *Reformed Thought on Freedom* identify – is that at *t1* the will has two unactualized potencies, one actualized to *p* and the other at *not-p,* just as in the realm of pure possibility, there remain two possibilities *p* and *not-p,* one to be actualized at t2 as a contingent, and the other not to be actualized, remaining a pure possible.[83]

This complex style invoking *potentiae* has largely taken over the style of Muller's 'Parting of Ways' paper and the one that followed.[84] It is not Turretin's language. In these writings he uses the difference between the phrases 'the freedom of the will' as standing for Turretin's indeterminism and 'freedom of will' as standing for Edwards's determinism. But on inspection these phrases are not used consistently in the literature in this way. The preferred way of expressing the point is subject to the difficulty with the old way, that Turretin does not write in terms of the will having a mind of its own, but of executing the last judgment of the intellect. As was routine with the RO, the will is said to be 'blind' until enlightened by the reason or understanding.[85] Turretin's doctrine is that the will cannot self-trigger, but can trigger only at the behest of the intellect in an act of free will or free choice. His compatibilism generates hypothetical necessities.

---

83. Muller, *Divine Will and Human Choice*, 298-9. References to potencies, usually as 'unactualized' are found for example in pp. 294, 297, 298, and 299.

84. 'Jonathan Edwards and the Absence of Free Choice', and 'Jonathan Edwards and Francis Turretin on Necessity, Contingency, and Freedom of Will.'

85. See Helm, *Human Nature from Calvin to Edwards*, pp. 87, 152, 153-4.

This is the compatibilistic understanding of diachronic contingency, then, the agent having exercised his freedom of choice and determined its object, the will still having the unused potency. One actual, the chosen, the other remaining unchosen, a pure possibility. This seems to be Muller's way of characterising the moment of pure indifference, pure contingency, and its consequences.

This diachronic state of things is made clear, and this supports a compatibilistic outlook. But Muller's idea is that in the will there exists a residual potency that is present after the will has made a choice, and that this is relevant to the choice having been indeterministic. He understands a use of contingency not as an element in synchronic contingency but in diachronic contingency, as providing a vital element in Turretin's and others' understanding of contingency. But what is non-deterministically free about a diachronic free choice? It seems, only if the will is inherently two-fold, even after the choice is made. This is what Miller may call a 'root indifference'. But Turretin disavows this: 'For since the will is a rational appetite, such is its nature that it *must* follow the last judgment of the practical intellect.'[86]

A further critical question here is, is this interpretation of Turretin textually warranted? Muller says that,

> Turretin, arguably, assumed that the underlying requirement for freedom of choice, was a fundamental spontaneity of the will resting on this essential or root indifference in primary actuality – with the indifference defined in terms of a simultaneity of potencies, but rather than rest his understanding of freedom radically in this indifference, as did the Molinists, he rested it in the uncoerced or spontaneous passage, on the basis of an uncoerced judgment, from the indifferent *actus primus* to the determinate *actus secundus.*[87]

This is hard to follow, but here Muller's 'arguables', twice on the same page[88] look tentative and speculative. There is nothing in Turretin that corresponds to these phases, nor in any other ways of denoting resident, root potencies in Muller's sense. Turretin's view seems to be that this is not a case of the potency of simultaneity, but rather

---

86. Turretin, *Institutes*, I. p. 663 (italics added).
87. Muller, *Divine Will & Human Choice*, p. 297.
88. ibid., p. 297.

he is asserting that the potency of simultaneity has no application in the *actus secundus* except on pain of committing the person to the unacceptable Jesuit view of synchronic simultaneity, what we have referred to as 'Franciscan freedom'. Turretin says that this is the view that the will is 'always so indifferent and undetermined that it can act or not act. This our opponents pretend in order that its own liberty may be left to the will. We deny it'.[89] Isn't Muller here running headlong into the Jesuit view of freedom, despite his protestations to the contrary?

On page 297, towards the end of the page Muller states this,

> The freedom of choice is not constituted by the root indifference of the will, although clearly it could not exist without this indifference; one might say that, for Turretin, this root indifference which he views as a result of human mutability, is a necessary but not sufficient condition for human freedom. Freedom is constituted formally—its *ratio formalis*—by the willing response to a rational judgment made by the intellect. Arguably, Turretin grounds alternatively in the intellect, given that he does not assume that freedom resides in the ability of the will as it engages an object *in actu secundo* to refuse the judgment of the practical intellect.

This is close if not equivalent to determinism.

Second, had he asserted it, what would possessing a non-actualised potency amount to? Such a potency is one of two potencies, one of which has been exercised, and so is spent, in a choice. And so is not the remaining potency now unrealizable, because it is already in the past? The remaining non-actualized potency is presumably a vestigial power that it is impossible at this stage to realize, because the other potency has been actualized in the choice, whatever it was. What does this trace of the past contribute to indeterminism in the present? Possessing an unrealized potency appears to be a 'scholastic' expression in the worst sense, like possessing a potency to eat the ice cream when I have chosen and eaten the trifle!

This leads to another epistemological difficulty. According to Muller, for Turretin the will is a multiple-way power (perhaps two ways, perhaps many ways), freely intertwining with the intellect in pursuit of the end or ends of the practical reason. Suppose this is true. How different is

---

89. Turretin, *Institutes*, I. p. 666.

this state of affairs from the will possessing synchronic contingency, Franciscan freedom? How is this to be established? Apart from Muller's general view of freedom as diachronic, how can one be sure that for the RO the will behaves as Muller claims? Is this proposal the fruit of introspection, or is this yet another instance of how *a priori* theory masks awareness of the causal powers of the soul, the will and the appetites? What is the evidence for such a vestigial, un-realizable potency? I suggest that the only evidence tolerable is the *a priori* requirements of Muller's understanding of a scholastic theory of indeterminate choice. There is no empirical evidence, only what we might call the requirement of the demands of the purely theoretical evidence.

Where is the textual evidence that Turretin argues for *interaction* between the understanding and will, not only of the influence of the intellect on the will, but of the will on the intellect? I have not been able to detect it. As we have seen, Turretin is emphatic that the intellect and the will are two faculties in which the intellect dominates, that it identifies an end or ends, and the means to achieve or obtain the end or ends lie in the exercise of the will. What Muller says on the same page is nearer to Turretin's position. 'For intellective judgment to be completed in a choice or election, it must be engaged by the will—and for the will to act on its freedom it must receive a judgment of the intellect.' [90] The idea that the will acts freely in the sense of purely indifferently on receiving the judgment of the intellect goes considerably beyond what Turretin states. This is closer to what Muller asserts by maintaining: 'He [Turretin] in no way implies the possibility of the will rejecting the intellectual judgment.'[91]

In his work over the years Muller has stressed the point that scholasticism is not an ideology, but that it is a 'rather eclectic Christian Aristotelianism' a mix of several philosophical sources.

> Thus, the rather eclectic Christian Aristotelianism of the Protestant orthodox drew on rules of logic and devices like the fourfold causality in order to explain and develop their doctrinal formulae – and only seldom, if ever, to import a full-scale rational metaphysics or physics into theology. Contrary to what is sometimes claimed, the four-fold causality (i.e. first,

---

90. Muller, *Divine Will and Human Choice*, p. 252.
91. ibid., p. 253.

formal, material, and final causes) does not imply a particular metaphysic. Specifically it is not by nature 'deterministic'. One can use the model to delineate the soteriological patterns of the eternal decree of God and its execution in time; one also can use the model to describe the sources and effects of human sinfulness and human moral conduct: or one can use the model to explain how a carpenter makes a table.[92]

Well said in 1999, but by 2011 poor Edwards was criticized for being intellectually constrained by not having room for the four-fold causality of Aristotle, and so not being 'Reformed'. I hope that later Muller will find room in the canvas for the philosophical influences of Locke.

A Last Word

The view of the mind, the will, the judgment and the election of the soul, volition, choice, and their relation to what the agent takes to be the good, are very much as Turretin, and of any other scholastic RO divine held to. The will is subordinate to the understanding. But rarely do the RO weave as clear a narrative of choosing as Edwards did. As a result, in Edwards the compatibilism is apparent, that of Turretin and other RO it is less explicit, partly hidden. It's nonetheless clearly present, for all that. There's the rub.

---

92. Richard A. Muller, 'Ad fontes Argumentorum: The Sources of Reformed Theology in the 17th Century', Inaugural Lecture, University of Utrecht, 1999. Reprinted in *After Calvin*, New York Oxford University Press, 2003, p. 55.

Conclusion of Part Two

When Francis Turretin discusses the use of the terminology of 'free will' in the introductory section of the first question of Question Ten of his *Institutes,* in which most of the material on free will is to be found, he finds the phrase a bit awkward to handle. He says that 'free will' is a pagan term, originating in Plato. Strictly, the term belongs to God alone, who is perfectly independent, and is not accountable to any other. But human beings are accountable. Yet, he says, free will now has long usage in the church, so it should not be returned to the philosophers, and the RO by no means repudiate the phrase when it is properly understood. It is not analysed from the intellect alone, nor from the will alone, but from the operation of both together, bearing in mind that 'the decision of the intellect is terminated in the will, so the liberty of the will has its roots in the intellect', for 'the intellect and will' are mutually connected by so strict a necessity that they can never be separated from each other'. 'Thus what is in the intellect affirmation and negation, that in the will is desire and avoidance'. The decisions of the soul denote an act of the mind, therefore.[1]

Part 2 has been written in the light of Muller's strictures about anachronism, respecting that at no place does Turretin, nor the RO more generally say "I am not a compatibilist". The closest Turretin comes to writing directly in this vein is when he writes of God's determination. The Vos people have maintained that Turretin was not using the determinists' sense of the Latin *determinare*, but there is no real reason for this. We noted that Aza Goudriaan thought it was natural to refer to Voetius as a theistic determinist.

---

1. These quotations are taken from Turretin, *Institutes*, I. p. 660.

In Chapters Four, Five, Six and Seven, we have made an indirect case by giving further attention in Chapter Four to some of the general issues to follow. Then in the remaining chapters three indirect arguments in support of compatibilism have been presented.

In Chapter Five attending the common theological niche that Turretin and Edwards lived in, and its significance in being aware of certain doctrinal positions as presenting 'live issues' given that Muller and Edwards occupied the same theological niche, has the effect of each of them having to narrow their views, and to having the same option when it comes to free will. Depending on the niche that a theologian occupies, certain theological issues will be (to adopt William James's distinction) 'live options' or 'dead options'. For example, a unitarian will not find the nature of God's tri-unity a 'live option', but 'dead'. There is nothing at stake for him in such discussions. We might say that theologians who share several positions will have the same set of live options. In the case of the RO and Edwards, they agree on theism, trinitarianism, the Chalcedonian definition of the nature of Christ's person. And beyond these, they shared a post-Dordtian outlook on divine sovereignty, and on particular doctrines such as the bondage of the will to sin, the perseverance of the saints, and so on.

After Chapter Five, which is concerned with a survey of the issues at stake and necessary background issues, the first argument is the *theological niche argument*. The RO and Edwards held to the 'catholicity' of the Reformation, a robust theism, of the classical patristic trinitarianism and of the Chalcedon Christology. They held to the divine decrees, meticulous providence, and they held in common an Augustinian soteriology, and sustained polemics against Roman Catholicism, and during our period, also against Arminianism and Socinianism.

Chapter Six has to do with that a diet of scholasticism proves to have a masking effect over evaluating the causal dimension of doctrines. We saw that there is more at stake in the formulation of anthropological doctrines than logical distinctions. And we saw that despite scholasticism, the RO still find the data of the causal character of the flow of a personal agency, and so find it natural to give a compatibilist account of agency, supplemented by the criteria they recognize as an impediment to personal responsibility for the consequences of action.

Secondly, in Chapter Seven the causal functions of the faculties have been stressed. Then follows the third indirect argument for the compatibilistic tendency of the RO, far from taking the view that free action is a case of synchronic contingency, and we have already rejected this, not even indeterminism of the diachronic contingency adopted by Muller is other than Turretin's text. It is argued that when their account of the causal behaviour of the faculties is examined, which the contributors of *RTF* or Muller rarely do, they strengthen the evidential basis of their compatibilism. Compatibilism is the view that human action is a matter of cause and effect within the soul, not the outcome of logical factors which are classified using the idioms of scholasticism. In chapter six, having in mind that compatibilism is a causal thesis, I have surveyed the incidences of causation in Turretin's work involving human action that are efficient causes, noting that efficient causes find prominent expression in the work of the faculties.

In that chapter, the account of the relation between the activity of the intellect and will is closely causal, even allowing for the fact that accounts of the faculties are more distinct in some RO theologians than in others. These causes are efficient and are cases of hypothetical necessary since the causes are contingent acts of the intellect. Whether this state of affairs entails that the RO together with Jonathan Edwards are 'necessitarian' depends on the sense of that term, but they are certainly not fatalists.

In the book, and particularly in Part Two, we have been engaged in an aspect of Christian theology which is partly a work of nature, and partly of grace. The first because there is no revealed doctrine of human nature, and as a consequence from the beginning, Christian thinkers have been forced to rely on secular philosophies to provide a systematic account of it. In fact, when it comes to providing a systematic account of any Christian doctrine terms have been used whose original location was in paganism or secularism. But there is scriptural warrant for this, if one thinks of Paul's behavior when he was in Athens (Acts 17), then we may say, the greater reliance on philosophical terms and concepts, the greater the risk of corrupting Christian theology, and of being more tentative and undogmatic in one's theological conclusions. If we think of Christian theology as a circle, then the closer to the centre the more safe it is, as with the confidence in the usefulness of the term 'trinity', an unrevealed word, to characterize the revealed godhead. The nearer to the circumference of the circle we move the more tentative we must become in our conclusions.

We mentioned at the Introduction that issues of anthropology, of which human freedom is an aspect, are not in a similar way reliant on Scripture. It is an area in which the influence of philosophy is significant. To take some significant figures, Tertullian, Augustine, and Aquinas were influenced by a prevailing metaphysics of the human person, Stoic, Platonic or Aristotelian. The Reformed in addition endured the era of Descartes, and Edwards that of John Locke and other early enlightenment figures. For the Reformed tradition, all such influences were legitimate, as the tradition was not biblicistic, and held to Calvin's dictum that Christian theology could profitably use words and expressions not found in the biblical text. When it came to anthropology, both parties applied to it the four-fold state of mankind that Augustine had introduced – mankind as innocent, sinful, regenerate and glorified. The bearing of the nature of these states on Christian soteriology are certainly of first importance, as the attitudes of the RO and Edwards to Arminianism and semi-Pelagianism as their confession of the bondage of the will make clear. The will is in bondage not only in the fact that sin has affected the will, but sin has also affected the other faculties of the human soul, as grace is seen in the sovereign grace of God in Christ.

However, the lack of explicit deterministic terms has meant that the strategy we have been left to is to offer indirect, circumstantial evidence. This has the advantages of widening our attention to other passages from elsewhere in Turretin's *Institutes*. A second advantage is that in these three chapters there is a crossing and re-crossing of the data from Turretin and then from Edwards. Especially Turretin, because there has been more disagreement about him. This recrossing is, I hope, a help to those unfamiliar with the territory to understand more readily. In the first two chapters we are becoming familiar with the context in which the issue of free will is employed, while the third (Chapter Seven) is more directly on Muller on compatibilism towards the end of *Divine Will and Human Choice*.

The evidence is indirect insofar as it respects the fact that such as Turretin do not avow determinism by affirming it by that word. We cannot therefore catch him in the act of avowing determinism, or compatibilism (any more, it must be said, than we can catch Edwards in such an act, or scholastics avow the pagan Aristotle). Hence the need for a more round-about strategy. This has involved eliminating possibilities, and retaining others. In chapter 5 the possibilities have to do with showing that Turretin and Edwards inhabit the same theological niche. They are both post-Dordtian Calvinists. In this final chapter I have found further relevant evidence of their compatibilistic character in their account of the relations between the faculties. Each of the lines of evidence shown by the three chapters is consistent.

Besides this, in the final chapter I have argued directly against Richard Muller, the foremost contemporary expositor of the theology of post-Reformation Reformed theology, who in Chapter 8 of his latest book *Divine Choice and Human Will*, defends an indeterminism that is 'very close'[2] to a compatibilism by an argumentative appeal to radical potency. I have found reasons against this. It is a reasonable conclusion, therefore, to hold that Francis Turretin, as a representative, prominent theologian of the Reformed Orthodoxy in the Early Modern Period, is himself a compatibilist, in the line of Augustine before him,[3] and of Jonathan Edwards after him.

---

2. Muller, *Divine Will and Human Choice*, p. 294.

3. Katherin Rogers, 'Augustine's Compatibilism' (*Religious Studies*, 2004), 'It is hard to dissent from the view of O'Daly that 'there is little to distinguish the later Augustine's view of the will from that of the compatibilist Jonathan Edwards', G. O'Daly, 'Predestination and Freedom in Augustine's Ethics', *The Philosophy in Christianity* ed. G. Vesey (C.U.P. 1989).

Glossary

Compatibilism: that some determinate states of affairs are consistent with praise or blame. Freedom and responsibility are consistent with determinism.

Contingent: Neither impossible nor necessary. Senses are (i) an event that could logically have happened, distinct from (ii) 'contingent upon' as when one thing depends on another.

Determinism: The main categories are compatibilism and incompatibilism. A compatibilist holds that free will together with moral responsibility are compatible with determinism, a 'soft' determinism. The incompatibilist holds that free will/moral responsibility are incompatible with determinism. Libertarianism holds to incompatibilism and denies determinism. There is no third way between compatibilism and libertarianism.

Diachronic Contingency: an action that depends on something later in time to that which is changed, which could have the power to have been otherwise than it is, and so not deterministic. If there is something that has the power to make an alternative at the same time, this is said to be a case of synchronic contingency.

Fate: the position that whatever happens will happen. It may be applied to everything that will happen, or to particular events. It is distinct from determinism, which has a crucial place for human action, and for other factors.

Freedom of the will: Some, libertarians, ascribe to the will unconditional powers of choice. Others, determinists, ascribe to the will only conditional powers, as judged by the mind, the sources of motivation.

Hypothetical Necessity: 'When changes occur from a preceding state of affairs, it may *necessitate* them. This is known as the necessity of the consequence. In contemporary work determinism is defined as a conditional or hypothetical necessity. "Determinism is thus a kind of necessity, but it is a conditional necessity. A determined event does not have to occur, no matter what else happens (it need not be absolutely necessary). But it must occur when the determining conditions have occurred."' Robert Kane, *Contemporary Introduction to Free Will* p. 6.

Indeterminism: The view that some human actions are not determined by prior states or events, but are solely due to the activity of the will, and perhaps of some other factor or factors, which produce random choices.

Indifference: two or more events that are equally probable. The liberty of indifference envisages that two or more choices are possible but are not necessitated.

Libertarianism: The view that some actions are the outcome of the free will alone, in opposition to determinism

Middle Knowledge (Molinism): The theological claim that besides God's knows all possible truths and those possible truths that are true, he also has knowledge of 'counterfactuals of freedom', of what individuals would freely do under such and such conditions. It supported the view that preserves free will with divine grace. Such middle knowledge is rejected by those who hold that God ordains whatever comes to pass, and the actions of people are determined.

Necessitarianism: An older-fashioned way of characterising determinism or compatibilism.

Practical Reason: In scholasticism, practical reason is the intellectual operation of intending to bring about the attainment of an end, and the means that ensure it. It is what the agent regards as a good, to be desired. It is contrasted with the theoretical reason, which has to do solely with issues of truth and falsehood.

Bibliography

Aquinas, Thomas, *Summa Theologiae*, trans. T. Gilby and others (New York, Image Books, 1969).

———*On the Truth of the Catholic Church: Summa Contra Gentiles*, trans, Anton C. Pegis (Garden City, New York, Image Books, 1955).

Aristotle, *Nicomachean Ethics,* Lesley Brown ed. David Ross trans. (Oxford, Oxford World's Classics, 2009).

Augustine, *The City of God,* trans. John Healey, edited R. V. G. Tasker, Two volumes (London, J. M. Dent & Sons, 1945).

———*The Enchiridion on Faith, Hope and Love*, trans. J. F. Shaw (Chicago, Henry Regnery, 1961).

Baschera, Luca, 'Peter Martyr Vermigli on Free Will: The Aristotelian Heritage of Reformed Theology', *Calvin Theological Journal* 12. p. 2 (2007).

Berkeley, George, *A Treatise Concerning Human Knowledge* (1710), in *A New Theory of Vision and Other Wrings* (London, J. M.Dent & Sons Ltd, 1910).

Berkhof, Louis, *Systematic Theology*, 1941 (London, Banner of Truth Trust, 1959).

Bingham, Matthew C., Caughey, Chris, Clark, R. Scott, Gribben, Crawford and Hart, D. G., *On Being Reformed, Debates over a Theological Identity* (London, Palgrave Macmillan, 2018).

Boethius, *The Consolation of Philosophy*, trans. V. E. Watts (Harmondsworth, Middx, Penguin Books, 1969).

Calvin, John, *On the Eternal Predestination of God* (1552), trans. J. K. S. Reid (London, James Clarke and Co., 1961).

———*Sermons on Galatians*, trans. Kathy Childress (Edinburgh, Banner of Truth, 1997).

———*Sermons on Isaiah's Prophecy of the Death and Passion of Christ*, trans. and ed. T. H. L. Parker (London, James Clarke and Co. 1956).

———*The Bondage and Liberation of the Will: A Defence of the Orthodox Doctrine of Human Choice against Pighius*. Ed. A. N. S. Lane, trans, G. I. Davies (Grand Rapids, Baker, 1996).

———*The Institutes of the Christian Religion* (1559), trans. Willliam Beveridge (various editions).

Crisp, Oliver, *Jonathan Edwards on God and Creation* (New York, OUP, 2012).

Cross, Richard, *Duns Scotus on God* (Aldershot, Ashgate, 2005).

Descartes, René, *Descartes' Conversation with Burman,* Translated with Introduction and Commentary by John Cottingham (Oxford, Clarendon Press, 1976).

Dolezal, James E., 'God Without Parts: Simplicity and the Metaphysics of Divine Absoluteness' (Ph.D thesis, Westminster Theological Seminary, 2011).

———*God without Parts: Divine Simplicity and the Metaphysics of God's Absoluteness* (Eugene, Or., Pickwick Publications, 2011).

Duncan, John, *Colloquia Peripatetica*, Collected by William Knight, Sixth Edition (Edinburgh, Oliphant, Anderson & Ferrier, 1907).

Edwards, Jonathan, *Freedom of the Will*, edited by Paul Ramsey, Volume 1 of *The Works of Jonathan Edwards*, New Haven, Conn. Yale University Press, 1957–2008 (*WJE 1*).

———*Miscellanies, Nos, 501-832*, New Haven, Conn, Yale University Press, 2000 (*WJE* 18).

———*The Religious Affections,* New Haven, Conn. Yale University Press, 1959 *(WJE 2)*.

Falcon, Andrea, 'Aristotle on Causality', *The Stanford Encyclopedia of Philosophy* (Spring 2015 Edition), Edward N. Zalta (ed.).

Fennema, Scott, 'George Berkeley and Jonathan Edwards on Idealism: Considering an Old Question in Light of New Evidence' (*Intellectual History Review*, 2017).

Fesko, J.V. *The Theology of the Westminster Standards* (Wheaton, Ill. Crossway, 2014).

Gilson, Etienne, *The Christian Philosophy of St. Thomas Aquinas* (New York, Random House, 1956).

Goudriaan, Aza, 'Descartes, Cartesianism and Theology', *The Oxford Handbook of Early Modern Theology 1600–1680*, edited by Ulrich L. Lehrer, Richard A. Muller, and A. G. Roeber (Oxford University Press, 2015).

———*Reformed Orthodoxy and Philosophy, 1625–1750* (Leiden, Brill, 2006).

Graybill, Gregory B., *Evangelical Free Will, Philipp Melanchthon's Doctrinal Journey on the Origins of Faith* (Oxford, Oxford University Press, 2010).

Hamilton, S. Mark, *A Treatise on Jonathan Edwards Continuous Creation and Christology* (JE Society Press, 2017).

Helm, Paul, 'A Different Kind of Calvinism? Edwardsianism Compared with Older Forms of Reformed Thought' in *After Jonathan Edwards*, eds. Oliver D. Crisp and Douglas A. Sweeney (New York, Oxford University Press, 2012).

———*Calvin at the Centre* (Oxford, Oxford University Press, 2010).

———'Calvin, the "Two Issues", and the Structure of the *Institutes.*' *Calvin Theological Journal*, p. 42 (2007), pp. 341-348.

———'Francis Turretin and Jonathan Edwards on Compatibilism' (*Journal of Reformed Theology*, 2018).

———*Human Nature from Calvin to Edwards* (Grand Rapids, Reformed Heritage Books, 2018).

———'Jonathan Edwards and the Parting of the Ways', *Jonathan Edwards Studies,* 2014.

———'Necessity, Contingency and the Freedom of God', *Journal of Reformed Theology*, 2014.

———'*Reformed Thought on Freedom*: Some Further Thoughts', *Journal of Reformed Theology*, 2010.

———'Synchronic Contingency in Reformed Scholasticism. A Note of Caution' (*Nederlands Theologisch Tijdschrift*, p. 57. 3, July 2003, pp. 207-222). This issue of the journal also contains a response by A. J. Beck and A. Vos, 'Conceptual Patterns related to Reformed Scholasticism' (pp. 223-233), and my reply, 'Synchronic Contingency Again'.

———'The "Openness" in Compatibilism', in *Philosophical Essays Against Open Theism,* ed. Benjamin H. Arbour (London, Routledge, 2019).

———'Turretin and Edwards Once More', *Jonathan Edwards Studies*, 2014.

———'Turretin and Edwards Once More', *Jonathan Edwards Studies*, Vol. 4 No/2, 2014.

Hobbes, Thomas, *Human Nature: or The Fundamental Elements of Policie* (1650).

Kane, Robert, *Contemporary Introduction to Free Will* (Oxford: Oxford University Press, 2005).

Kim, Hyun Kwan, 'The Doctrine of Free Choice' in *A New Divinity*, edd. Mark Jones and Michael G, Haykin (Gottingen, Vandenhoeck & Ruprecht, 2018).

Kretzmann, Norman, 'Ockham and the Creation of the Beginningless World' (*Franciscan Studies,* Vol. 45, Annual XXIII, 1985).

———*The Metaphysics of Creation* (Oxford, Clarendon Press, 1999).

———*The Metaphysics of Theism* (Oxford, Clarendon Press, 1997).

Leftow, Brian, 'Aquinas, Divine Simplicity and Divine Freedom' in *Metaphysics and God: Essays in Honor of Eleonore Stump*, ed. Kevin Timpe (New York and London: Routledge, 2009).

Lucas, J. R. *The Future* (Oxford, Basil Blackwell, 1989).

Luther, Martin, *The Bondage of the Will* (1525), trans. J. I. Packer and O. R. Johnston (London, James Clarke & Co, Ltd, 1957).

Maccovius, Johannes (1588–1644*). On Theological and Philosophical Distinctions and Rules*, trans. Willem J. van Asselt, Michael D. Bell, Gert van den Brink, Rein Ferwerda (Apeldoorn, Holland, Instituut voor Reformatieonderzoek, Apeldoorn, Holland, 2009).

Muller, Richard, *Calvin and the Reformed Tradition, On the Work of Christ, and the Order of Salvation* (Grand Rapids, Baker, 2012).

———*Divine Will and Human Choice* (Grand Rapids, Mich. Baker, 2017).

———'Jonathan Edwards and Francis Turretin on Necessity, Contingency and Freedom of Will, in Response to Paul Helm' (*Jonathan Edwards Studies*, 2014).

———'Jonathan Edwards and the Absence of Free Choice: A Parting of Ways in the Reformed Tradition' (*Jonathan Edwards Studies*, 2011).

———'Neither Libertarian nor Compatibilist: A Reply to Paul Helm' (*Journal of Reformed Theology* 13 (2019), pp. 267-86.

———'Not Scotist: Understandings of Being, Univocity, and Analogy in Early-Modern Reformed Thought' (*Reformation and Renaissance Review,* 2012).

———'The "Reception of Calvin" in Later Reformed Theology: Concluding Thoughts' (*Church History and Religious Culture,* 2011).

Muller, Richard A., and Ward, Rowland S., *Ad fontes Argumentorum:* The Sources of Reformed Theology in the 17th C, Inaugural Lecture, University of Utrecht, 1999.' Reprinted in *After Calvin* (New York, Oxford University Press, 2003).

———*Dictionary of Latin and Greek Theological Terms* (Grand Rapids, Baker, 1985).

———'Grace, Election and Contingent Choice: Arminius's Gambit and the Reformed Response', in *The Grace of God, The Bondage of the Will*, 2 vols. Eds. Thomas Schreiner and Bruce A. Ware (Grand Rapids, Mich., Baker, 1995).

————*Post-Reformation Reformed Dogmatics*, Second Edition (Grand Rapids, Mich, Baker, 2003).

————*Scripture and Worship* (Phillipsburg, NJ, P&R Publishing, 2007).

Norton, John, *The Orthodox Evangelist* (London, John Macok, for Ludwick Lloyd, 1657).

O'Daly, Gerard, 'Predestination and Freedom in Augustine's Ethics', *The Philosophy in Christianity*, Ed. G. Vesey (C.U.P. 1989).

Owen, John, *Works,* ed. W.H. Goold (Edinburgh, Banner of Truth Trust, 1965).

Pemble, William*, Vindiciae Gratiae, A Plea for Grace, More Especially Grace and Faith,* in *The Workes of that Late Learned Minister of God's Holy Word, Mr William Pemble* (Oxford, Henry Hall, 1659).

Preciado, Michael, *A Reformed View of Freedom: The Compatibility of Guidance Control and Reformed Theology* (Eugene, Or., Pickwick Publications, 2019).

Prior, A. N., *Papers on Time and Tense* (Oxford: Clarendon Press, 1968).

Rogers, Katherin, *Anselm on Freedom* (Oxford, Oxford University Press, 2008).

————'Augustine's Compatibilism' (*Religious Studies*, 2004).

Salles, Ricardo, *The Stoics on Determinism and Compatibilism* (Aldershot, Ashgate, 2005).

Scotus, John Duns, *Contingency and Freedom, Lectura* I. p. 39, trans. A. Vos Jaczn, H. Veldhuis, A. H. Looman-Graaskamp, E. Dekker, and N. W. den Bok (Dordrecht, Kluwer Publishing Co., 1994), The New Synthese Historical Library, Vol. 42.

Skinner, Quentin, 'Meaning and Understanding in the History of Ideas' (*History and Theory*, 1969).

Strawson, Galen, *Selves: An Essay in Revisionary Metaphysics* (Oxford, Oxford University Press, 2011).

Stump, Eleonore, 'Aquinas's Account of Freedom; Intellect and Will', *The Monist*, 1997.

Twisse, William, *The Riches of God's Love unto the Vessels of Mercy, Consistent with His Absolute Hatred or Reprobation of the Vessells of Wrath*, Two Volumes (Oxford, Th. Robinson, 1653).

Van Asselt, Willem, Bac, J. Martin and te Velde, Roelf T., *Reformed Thought on Freedom, The Concept of Free Choice in Early Modern Reformed Theology* (Grand Rapids, Mich. Baker, 2010).

Van Asselt, Willem, *Introduction to Reformed Scholasticism*, trans. Albert Gootjes (Grand Rapids, Reformation Heritage Books, 2009).

Van Mastricht, Petrus, *Theoretical-Practical Theology*, trans. Todd M. Rester, ed. Joel R. Beeke (Grand Rapids, Mich., Reformation Heritage Books, 2019).

Vermigi, Peter Martyr, The Peter Martyr Library, Vol. 8 (Kirksville, Miss. 2003), *Predestination and Justification*, ed. Frank A. James III.

Vos, Antonie, 'Always on Time: The Immutability of God', in *Understanding the Attributes of God*, eds., Gijsbert van den Brink and Marcel Sarot (Peter Lang, Frankfurt 1999) eds.

Vos, Antonie, 'Paul Helm on Medieval Scholasticism' (*Journal of Reformed Theology*, 2014).

———'Scholasticism and Reformation' in *Reformation and Scholasticism*, eds., Willem J. Van Asselt and Eef Dekker (Grand Rapids, Mich., Baker, 2001).

———'The Systematic Place of Reformed Scholasticism: Reflections Concerning the Reception of Calvin's Thought', *Church History and Religious Culture* (2011).

———*The Theology of John Duns Scotus* (Edinburgh: Edinburgh University Press, 2006).

Wootton, David, ed., *Divine Right and Democracy: An Anthology of Political Writing in Stuart England* (London, Penguin Books, 1986).

Scripture Index

Subject Index

ISBN 978-1-5271-0391-7

Clash of Visions

Populism and Elitism in New Testament Theology

Robert W. Yarbrough

Each year thousands die for the Jesus they read about in the Bible. At the same time scholars worldwide reject central truths of the Book. Here is an analysis of two contrasting approaches to biblical interpretation: one which has encouraged many to abandon the Christian heritage, the other which has informed the largest numeric increase of professing Christians in world history in recent generations and which is projected to continue.

This is a book that every Christian student should read before studying at a non–evangelical institution. Even those at Bible–believing institutions (including seminaries) will benefit, since they will likely be reading books by 'elitists' and may at some point study under them in graduate school. I found the book riveting and had a hard time putting it down. The two appendices about the life–pilgrimage of two 'populist' theologians are worth the price of the book.

G. K. Beale
Professor of New Testament and Biblical Theology, Westminster Theological Seminary, Philadelphia, Pennsylvania

Christian Focus Publications

Our mission statement —

STAYING FAITHFUL

In dependence upon God we seek to impact the world through literature faithful to His infallible Word, the Bible. Our aim is to ensure that the Lord Jesus Christ is presented as the only hope to obtain forgiveness of sin, live a useful life and look forward to heaven with Him.

Our books are published in four imprints:

CHRISTIAN
FOCUS

Popular works including biographies, commentaries, basic doctrine and Christian living.

CHRISTIAN
HERITAGE

Books representing some of the best material from the rich heritage of the church.

MENTOR

CF4•K

Books written at a level suitable for Bible College and seminary students, pastors, and other serious readers. The imprint includes commentaries, doctrinal studies, examination of current issues and church history.

Children's books for quality Bible teaching and for all age groups: Sunday school curriculum, puzzle and activity books; personal and family devotional titles, biographies and inspirational stories — because you are never too young to know Jesus!

Christian Focus Publications Ltd,
Geanies House, Fearn, Ross-shire,
IV20 1TW, Scotland, United Kingdom.
www.christianfocus.com
blog.christianfocus.com